Interest Groups
and Political Change
in Israel

SUNY Series in Israeli Studies
Russell Stone, Editor

Interest Groups
and Political Change in Israel

Marcia Drezon-Tepler

State University of New York Press

Published by
State University of New York Press, Albany

Printed in the United States of America

For information, address State University of New York
Press, State University Plaza, Albany, N.Y., 12246

Library of Congress Cataloging-in-Publication Data

Drezon-Tepler, Marcia, 1948–
    Interest groups and political change in Israel / Marcia Drezon-
Tepler.
        p.   cm. – (SUNY series in Israeli studies)
    Based on the author's thesis (doctoral – Columbia University)
    Bibliography: p.
    Includes index.
    ISBN 0-7914-0207-X. – ISBN 0-7914-0208–8 (pbk.)
    1. Pressure groups – Israel.   2. Israel – Politics and government.
3. Hit 'ahdut ha-ta' aśiyanim be-Yiśra 'el – Political activity.
4. Industrialists – Israel – Societies, etc. – Political activity.
5. Iḥud ha-ḳevutsot veha-ḳibutsim (Israel) – Political activity.
6. Kibbutzim – Societies, etc. – Political activity.   7. Gush emunim
(Israel)   I. Title.   II. Series.
JQ1825.P359D74   1990
322.4'3'095694 – dc20   89–4581
                                                                            CIP

10 9 8 7 6 5 4 3 2 1

Contents

Part V. Conclusion

Acknowledgments

While studying three different interest groups was a demanding, sometimes daunting, task, it also afforded me the invaluable opportunity to experience a broad spectrum of Israeli society and to understand the culture's subtleties and even idiosyncracies. Agriculturalists, industrialists, politicians, military officials, religious observers, secularists, idealists, and pragmatists all were delightful to meet and yielded distinct perspectives on Israel's past and present.

This book began as a doctoral dissertation at Columbia University. The research period was necessarily intense, but the work was eased financially, academically, and spiritually by several foundations and individuals who merit mention here. A grant under the Fulbright-Hays Doctoral Dissertation Research Abroad Program not only sustained the project monetarily, but the term "Fulbright Scholar" was the "open sesame" to many a balky door. A sum from the Memorial Foundation for Jewish Culture permitted an extended research period.

The interviewees listed in the bibliography actually formed the essence of the work, and I am immensely grateful to them all for designating unusually long segments of time from their pressurized schedules, often under inconvenient circumstances. Several individuals and groups, however, showed special interest in the topic and made an extra effort to help. Yechiel Kadishai of Prime Minister Menachem Begin's office in a grandfatherly way guided me through an interview with the gracious Prime Minister and ran interference for me with more reluctant government officials. At the Manufacturers' Association, Chezy Klapka volunteered to serve as my "man" in the organization, all the personnel extended themselves beyond any call of duty, and the Association not only opened its archives to me but provided me with a comfortable private office in which to peruse them.

On the homefront, thanks are owed to Professor Mark Kesselman, an astute political scientist and caring mentor close to the project from the proposal stage, who constantly prodded me to move to higher intellectual and theoretical planes, and to Professor J. C. Hurewitz, who with his wisdom and encyclopedic knowledge of Israel and the Middle East put the theory in a down to earth perspective. Any errors, of course, are solely my responsibility.

On the closest domestic front, thanks to my husband Itzhak are virtually inexpressible. His sensitivity and sacrifice for scholarship and for my aspirations bordered on saintliness. Intimately involved with all facets of the work, he not only illuminated some very baffling aspects of Israeli behavior but illuminated my soul through several trying times. His practical outlook provided a needed foil to my penchant for perfection, and he became a self-appointed project director without whom a finished product may never have appeared.

Hugs and thanks also must go to my baby son Ephraim who not too gladly sacrificed from his 110 percent of mom's attention. To my husband and son, to my father and late mother, I dedicate this book.

Chapter 1

A Theoretical Framework

A typical response of an Israeli to a proposed study of interest group development in Israel is, "But how can you study interest groups? There aren't any." Indeed, the comment reflects the conventional wisdom about Israel that ideological political parties have permeated the system, subordinating interest groups and shaping all other institutions. A view prevails that the electorate has been unimportant in decision-making and that associations of citizens have felt powerless. Parties seemed to exercise such pervasive influence that one observer remarked, "Israel can be regarded as an example, *par excellence*, of the *Etat partitaire* or *Parteinstaat*."[1]

Observers have commented and focused their analyses almost exclusively upon Israel's many parties, for these parties were intricately involved in establishing and developing the state. The few political analysts who paid any attention to interest groups understood the groups as playing secondary roles and holding positions subordinate to parties. All the parties were believed to operate similarly. Moreover, observers expected that the multi-party arrangement would continue because rather than coalescing into broad governing and opposition entities, most parties sought to preserve some political benefits by participating in coalition governments. Therefore, it seemed inconceivable to citizens and observers alike that individuals or groups could rise to challenge the parties or would consider mounting a challenge desirable.

This static conception of party-group relations in Israel requires reevaluation. Indeed, changes may be discerned, especially in interest group development, but also in the realm of parties. Groups have exerted influence upon parties, several autonomous groups have arisen, cause groups have grown, and several parties have coalesced. Stirrings of change started during the first decade of Israel's indepen-

1

dence. A closer look reveals that not all parties had identical attributes or behaved uniformly.

Later literature on Israeli politics has not dealt with these new occurrences, particularly the rise of interest groups, in any substantial way. Even recent analyses emphasize parties. Concentrating on the development and behavior of interest groups and dealing systematically with many of the changes in Israel's political system, this book fills a void in the study of Israel's politics. Before proceeding, a definition of interest groups as used in this study is required. Interest groups may be defined as organized groups of persons sharing particular concerns and impacting upon the political process by requiring policymakers to respond to their demands in some way. I refer to citizens' groups which make demands upon government, and not to institutional groups such as the military or civil service bureaucracy whose members are organized together to perform functions in society other than interest expression. While focusing on interest groups, I want to explore the extent to which the view of Israel's politics as dominated by ideology and party is accurate, to what extent that system prevailed or may have changed through time, and if it changed, how and why. This is a study in political change that focuses on the relationship between interest groups and parties in Israel and the effect of these groups and parties upon the decision-making process.

With its emphasis on groups, systems, and change, this study significantly advances political science interest group theory. Although interest groups as a valuable and valid research area has progressed since David B. Truman prodded political scientists to transcend the notion of interest groups as aberrations, "pathological features," or undesirable phenomena on the political scene, many of the interest group studies have been descriptive and static.[2] Much of the literature has only generally described traits and operating tactics of interest groups, treating them as isolated entities. Many studies have dealt with specific groups or with groups in one setting or political system. If systemic variables are included, usually the analysis is unidirectional, observing the system's effect upon group behavior. Under the assumption that "where the power is, there the pressure will be applied,"[3] interest group theorists usually first look at a system's structure for guidance in determining the tactics groups are likely to adopt and the targets and action arenas that they are likely to impinge upon.[4]

Nothing is "wrong" with such analyses, for it would be absurd to deny that institutions and structure influence interest group behavior. However, these studies do not take the next step and examine any impact of interest group activity upon the form and operations of the structures themselves or any changes in institutions, groups, or the system as a whole resulting from the interplay among the system's components. These deficiencies may have occurred because researchers, in examining long established systems, were inclined to treat structural features as "givens" and overlooked possibilities of change.

Samuel H. Beer in *British Politics in the Collectivist Age* attempts to break the static approach to interest group research.[5] Distinguishing several "types of politics" in Britain, he studies continuities and change in the whole system and its components over time with due attention to political culture. Beer's work has been a useful guide in determining variables to include and relationships to observe for studying groups within a systemic context in Israel. Unlike Beer, I concentrate upon the groups and, though focusing on Israel, hope to move beyond Beer to explain how in general groups arise, the role of groups in a political system, and how groups interact with the system and may contribute to system change.

Three Models for Decision-Making

In order to specify and classify any changes, it is necessary to establish a starting point and further guideposts, in other words, to draw up an analytical framework. The political science literature provides three models for groups and parties in decision-making and conflict resolution within democracies that seem appropriate guideposts for the Israeli case. Israel's politics, especially in the country's early years, bears remarkable resemblance to a strong party model. As mentioned, certain changes have taken place, and therefore, the strong party model may no longer aptly describe the country's politics. Developments seem to have brought Israel closer to a pluralist pattern or corporatist arrangement.

One purpose of this book is to analyze the degree to which Israel's politics has conformed to each one of the models—strong party, pluralist, and corporatist—and how change may have occurred from one model to another. Each model presents a different relationship between parties and groups, and I propose to analyze any change through a study of the interest group portion, inquiring primarily about the extent to which the interest group configuration in Israel has conformed to each one of the models. Nevertheless, I treat interest groups as one part of a system and therefore engage in several levels of analysis. I examine the interest group subsystem itself to determine how groups form and express and—when successful—obtain their interests. I also observe interest groups as they interrelate with each other and with other institutions of the political system, especially the parties but also the legislature, executive, and bureaucracy. Interest groups may affect the operations of other institutions in the system, possibly effecting or hastening change in them or in the system as a whole. At the same time, interest groups maneuver within the existing political system, and any changes in the overall system or parts thereof affect the behavior of interest groups. Interest groups may be both a sign and source of change.

Change in this study refers to change in the process of decision-making and to change in the power relationships among the participants in the process. Change does not refer to an alteration in a law or program. Those alterations, however, and the ability of interest groups to obtain them, are included within the analysis of the interest group subsystem. Such changes in processes and relationships may not result from direct demands by interest groups; change may be indirect, incremental, and unintended. In determining how interest groups may effect change, I shall draw attention to types of demands groups may make. Demands may be very particularistic, for or against a certain policy or portion thereof; demands may, in fact, be more systemic, for alteration of the mechanism by which demands are processed; or, they may be particularistic but have consequences, perhaps unintended and unforeseen, for system change. This somewhat abstract discussion of groups, demands, and system change will become clearer as the models are specified.

To construct the analytical framework, I shall first describe the three models generally and then focus specifically on the interest group component. According to the strong party model, the party in power and its leaders are responsible for major decisions, for "governing." To use this model for understanding Israel, the party should be understood as an ideological party, one that has a specific program for governing. In order to have and hold this governing power, the party organizes participation, aggregates interests, and serves as the link between social forces and the government.[6] The party does not allow social and economic forces to overwhelm it with material or with participatory demands but rather anticipates the pressure and contains it by taking the initiative and organizing groups within the party. Groups may not directly or continually be involved in specific decisions, however; they may be mobilized solely for elections. In this model, leeway and initiative in actual decision-making is left to the top leadership echelon.

Whereas a strong party model highlights the role of parties in organizing participation and setting policy, a pluralist model accents the role of groups. Here it is helpful to bear in mind that no model attributes all relevant political activity to any one part or institution of the political system. Rather, the emphasis and relationships vary from one model to another.

The pluralist view of politics is one of myriad, usually independent, groups, continually active, exerting influence, using various methods, and calling upon diverse resources, in various arenas. In a pluralist system, groups of pragmatic individuals unite to press issues but are willing to compromise and discuss points in question. Decisions result from the "constant negotiations" that are necessary among the competing groups.[7] Decisions are possible with a minimum of violent conflict, and no single group can monopolize power, because individuals belong to, or identify with, several groups that have varying degrees of importance to them, because not all groups are interested in the same or all issues, and similarly, because not all issues generate the same division among groups. Possibilities for conflict are further reduced because every group has some means of influence and therefore will not be completely frustrated. Moreover, pluralist theory assumes that on any given issue, the constituent groups will participate and compete. Though groups may be unequal in potential influence, the inequalities are not cumulative, and every group probably can achieve some aims, some time, somewhere. No single group comprises a majority, and therefore, the several minority groups realize advantages in compromising. Striking a bargain, adhering to the process, and avoiding conflict are valued almost as highly as winning itself.

Government mediates among the groups and aids in striking that bargain. Government is not only a mediator, however, and political leaders and officials may contribute their own ideas and preferences to shape policy. In addition, government leaders retain greater leeway on issues that are less important to groups.

A pluralist system provides groups with several decision-making arenas where groups can build coalitions and promote their viewpoints to affect policy. These several sites prevent groups from despairing or feeling ineffective because a group that loses in one arena can try again in another. Paradoxically, while many arenas with varied powers and power bases expand opportunities for group influence, they simultaneously increase the difficulty for groups to achieve their aims. Groups may have to struggle in more than one forum and become sophisticated in designing tactics to meet the peculiar requirements of several institutions.

Pluralist theory distinguishes between the functions of groups and parties. Parties essentially mobilize for elections, and groups promote particular policies. Parties in a pluralist model are not ideologically distinct from one another. Nor, in contrast to the strong party model, are they highly disciplined, centrally organized, or hierarchical. Parties are conglomerates of individuals and groups. In order to compose majorities for winning elections, parties formulate programs to attract as many groups as possible, in other words, to "catch-all" groups. Groups form a separate subsystem of the polity, independent of the party subsystem. In a strong party model, parties organize groups; in the pluralist model, parties become another arena where groups attempt to forge coalitions and exercise influence.

The party-group relationship is voluntary, not compulsory. Parties attempt to attract votes from groups but may not seek to formally attach organized groups to the party apparatus. Groups form on their own initiative and need not affiliate with a particular party in order to press demands and achieve favorable results. In fact, groups may simultaneously attempt to influence more than one party. In the party-group relationship, autonomous groups freely choose whether to extend their support.

The corporatist model, like the pluralist model, accents the role of groups, but it rests upon a different set of assumptions.[8] According to corporatist theory, decisions are too important to be left to the uncertainty of group participation and the vagaries of competition among groups. Rather, interest groups which control important resources and are highly organized are considered powerful and crucial to effective policy-making. Certain issue areas, though not the entire political universe, are dominated by such organized groups which frequently make opposing claims. Compared to the many, free floating groups of pluralism, under the corporatist model, a given interest or side to an issue usually forms one well-articulated structure or group. The group, therefore, is recognized by government as possessing a quasi-legal monopoly of authority to represent the interest. Decisions result from reconciliation among these groups rather than from conflict and competition.

Government's role is to encourage and ensure group involvement in aspects of policy-making and implementation. "Government" in the corporatist model refers to the executive or bureaucracy. The corporatist model does not delineate the roles of the parties and the legislature, nor the relationship between parties and groups. Government resolves or avoids conflict in vital areas by delegating responsibility for a solution to the representative interest organizations. The groups hold face-to-face negotiating sessions where they set policy and, in some instances, plan and accept responsibility for administering programs. Government may confine itself to mediating among the groups or to approving the negotiated agreement. Or, government may participate in the process as a director to contour the final outcome or as an equal partner to press for specific provisions. The negotiated deals are accepted by the participants as binding and become public or government policy.

It should be noted that corporatist theory is at an embryonic stage, and therefore, the model presented here is incomplete. As with most theories, corporatist theory is being developed from a combination of empirical observation and thought. Corporatist patterns have most frequently been observed on labor issues and related economic policies in developed, industrialized democratic nations. The labor and employer/business segments of the economy form large interest organizations. Representatives of these organizations and government comprise an economic policy board and cooperatively formulate policies on labor, wages, prices, taxes, and so forth. The extent of legislative approval needed, the amount of government authority delegated to the board, and the scope of the board's decisions have varied from one setting to another.

It is important not to confuse developing corporatist theory with the authoritarian fascist version. In authoritarian corporatism, the state organized the economic sectors and strictly regulated economic policies for those associations. In contrast, liberal corporatism is marked by a high degree of collaboration among autonomous groups, and the resulting arrangements are accepted by the state. The power granted to groups in the corporatist model, where groups actually are surrogate governments, distinguishes corporatism from pluralism. Pluralism envisions groups outside the arenas impinging upon them whereas corporatist theory brings the groups within the decision-making circle.

Implicit in the foregoing discussion of the three frameworks has been the element of political culture, integrally part of each model. Political culture is a society's values and attitudes toward politics. As more elaborately explained in the next chapter, it bears a special significance for Israel's politics, and therefore, the variable calls for special highlighting.

Israel's political culture, especially in the early years, was markedly ideological. Immigrants came with distinct ideas for shaping Israel's society. Though, of course, not every segment of the population held their values with equal intensity, those who did hold them dominated the scene. Politics became a matter of grand principle, and winning was considered important. Such an ideological milieu usually is compatible with the strong party model. Strong parties with complex structures develop to promote a principle, and in so doing, subordinate specific interests and groups to the organization and its broad vision.

The pluralist model usually is understood as accompanied by a pragmatic political culture, or a least one that is ideologically homogeneous, where the stakes of winning or losing are not high. Politics is regarded as a game, an arena for competition but one where playing by the rules and preserving the game itself are as important as winning. The corporatist model also is characterized by a pragmatic culture, but attitudes are more cooperative than competitive. In view of the added element of political culture, this inquiry may be restated as, to what extent Israel's political system was characterized by an ideological/strong party model and to what extent that model has changed to one that is pragmatic/pluralist or pragmatic/corporatist.

From a group's perspective, which model informs the political system makes a crucial difference. For a group, the significance of these models lies in the scope of claims that is possible for a group to make, the amount of power accruing to the group, and the effort a group need exert in order to obtain any aim.

The strong party model probably offers the broadest scope for claims because a party in office seeks to enact a broad program. A group in this model has less autonomy and probably less power than in the other two patterns, as the party would seek to maintain control over group activity, but the route for achieving an aim is more streamlined than in the other models. A group may suggest an entire program and need only convince the party leadership of the necessity for its idea. Nevertheless, succeeding in convincing the leadership may be a formidable task. As a prerequisite, the group may be required to invest great effort in the party organization.

In the pluralist model, the scope of claims is more limited, and achieving aims is more complicated. Because every group vies with every other one, and because approval must be sought in several arenas, each of which may make amendments, comprehensive or procedural reform is not impossible but much less probable. Therefore, any single group in the pluralist model has autonomy but may encounter difficulty in exercising power. To obtain its aims, a group must exert an effort upon the several arenas. Therefore, achieving an aim is time-consuming.

In the corporatist model, a group has autonomy and power as the legal representative of a specific economic or social sector. However, while comprehensive reform may be possible to arrange among the groups, claims still may be limited, and achieving them depends upon the balance of power, negotiating skill, and willingness to compromise and innovate among the groups themselves.

The Interest Group Subsystem

To focus upon and compare groups among the models, I have created an analytical framework for interest groups, identifying the following characteristics for examining an interest group subsystem: the number and type of groups or tendency to form groups; the degree of politicization of groups by parties; the aims and degree of ideological expression; the targets emphasized; the tactics; and ultimate organizational structure. These characteristics and their combination are different in each model. They are summarized in Table I.

In the ideological/strong party model, interest groups are expected to organize and behave as follows: the number and type of interest groups are limited and the tendency to form groups is low; interest groups are not autonomous of political parties and are highly politicized; interest groups often are economic/occupational with particularistic aims but express demands using terms of party ideologies rather than using terms specific to the interest; few groups that attempt some autonomy represent ideologies incompatible with the prevailing ideology; interest groups aim at the leadership of the affiliated party or use the leaders to reach ministers or bureaucrats; bargaining with the party leadership is the main tactic that interest groups use; interest groups may become small political parties.

In a system that is pragmatic and pluralist, interest groups are assumed to organize and behave as follows: many and varied groups exist and the tendency to form groups is high; interest groups are autonomous of political parties, and their leadership is committed to the group, not to a party; interest groups may vary in aims and express demands in particularistic or ideological terms depending upon the nature of the interest; interest groups aim at various targets including more than one party, members of the legislature, ministers, and bureaucrats; interest groups adopt various tactics including threatening to switch their members' votes to another party; interest groups remain as groups rather than become parties.

Although the corporatist pattern is less developed, groups may be expected to behave as follows: there is a tendency to form groups but interests are concentrated into a limited number of large groups; interest groups may or may not be affiliated with a party; interest groups usually have aims related to economic issues; interest groups interrelate with other groups, ministers, and bureaucrats; negotiating is the main tactic. Interest groups in Israel will be examined to determine the extent to which they conformed to any one of these sets of specifications.

Besides identifying the pattern of government and interest group activity that has prevailed in Israel, this study inquires whether any change has occurred from one model to another. For purposes of that analysis, the three models have been presented as discrete entities with change, encompassing institutions and culture, expected to occur from one whole model to another. Nevertheless, the models do not form a progressive scale, and change may occur in any direction. Several reasons may be postulated to explain the system's evolution: (1) The political culture may change. A new population structure may occur as a result of immigration or new births. These persons may not have had the same experiences or hold the same expectations of a political system as their predecessors. Alternatively, the original population, pragmatists or idealists, may modify their political world view as a result of their daily experiences. (2) A party may expand, becoming amorphous and less ideological. As a result, it may lose its ability to reconcile group conflicts and formulate policy. Groups may be "squeezed out" of the party. Groups may then articulate policy and press demands upon the parties and other institutions from the outside. (3) A party may become rigid or stagnate. It may be unaccommodating to new and even to old groups. As a result, groups may become autonomous and seek other avenues for influencing decisions.

Examination of the specific groups in Israel, in addition to determining the extent to which each model has existed, will reveal: (1) whether, in fact, the models existed singly or may have overlapped; (2) whether the expectation of change en toto proved correct or if different elements changed at varying rates; and (3) whether change occurred, in which direction, why (whether one of the foregoing postulates proved true), and how. The Israeli case may show that aspects of the different models may coexist or that the models require refinement. The study, therefore, should enrich our knowledge not only about Israel specifically but about each pattern of government, the role of groups in each pattern, and the effect of groups upon system change.

Table I
Framework for Interest Group Development

Group Characteristics	Ideological/Strong Party	Pragmatic/Pluralist	Pragmatic/Corporatist
Number and Type of Groups or Tendency to Form Groups	Groups limited in number and type (often economic/occupational). Tendency to form groups low. Organizing a group not usually first line of action to achieve satisfaction of demands. Usually seek party patronage.	Many groups and various types. High tendency to form. Persons concerned with an issue form groups.	High tendency to form; interests concentrated into limited number of large groups.
Autonomy/Politicization	Most groups not autonomous; organized groups linked to a party; interests may be divided among parties. Organized groups highly politicized, penetrated by parties, possibly established by parties.	Autonomous, external to parties; may be linked more to one party but potentially subject to change; groups organized on grass roots level and not penetrated by parties.	May or may not be affiliated.
Aims/Ideological Expression	Groups with particularistic aims but express demands in terms of prevailing party ideologies. Group that attempts some autonomy usually incompatible with prevailing ideology.	Groups have particularistic or broader aims and express them in terms depending upon the interest.	Aims usually related to economic issues and, though usually particularistic, may be broad.
Targets	Leadership of affiliated party; ministers, bureaucrats, legislators through the party.	Legislature including individuals and committees across parties; several parties, candidates, bureaucrats.	Interrelate with groups, ministers, bureaucrats.
Tactics	Mainly bargaining with party leadership.	Varied: power of vote, petition campaigns, information dissemination, media appeals, private influence including consultation and negotiation, public protest, strikes.	Mainly negotiating.
Ultimate Organizational Structure	May become a political party.	Remain as interest groups.	

Groups in Israel

To obtain a comprehensive view of groups in Israel for studying system change, I selected a sample representing different types of groups, different times, and different positions vis-à-vis the party system and ideological spectrum. The groups selected have represented significant sectors of Israeli society, and therefore, they may not be easily dismissed as marginal to the system and insignificant. Before specifying these cases, in order to understand the selection, an overview of groups in Israel is in order.

In Israel's early years, when parties were based upon ideologies, groups formed around material concerns. Economic or occupational groups were most pronounced. The most usual groups were labor unions, professional unions or associations, farmers' federations, and various business and manufacturing associations. These economic and occupational groups meshed with the political system, as most groups affiliated with parties, although some remained autonomous. In some instances, an "interest" was fragmented; several groups were concerned with one issue area or "interest," and each group affiliated with a different party. For example, each party might have an agricultural group aligned with it. To act as a cohesive interest group, the various associations tended to form an umbrella organization or act jointly on specific concerns.

With the development of the state and unavoidable testing of the various ideologies against everyday, sometimes harsh, reality, several ideologies underwent modification or revealed themselves as inadequate. As ideological intensity lessened or changed on the party plane, ideological and idea or policy oriented groups emerged, thereby filling the gap. In addition to the existing economic groups, which continued functioning and even broadened their aims, new groups arose around a plethora of issues – environmental issues, child care concerns, housing problems, ethnic concerns, as well as around questions of nationalism and foreign policy. These groups often were not only politically independent but more aggressive, actually impinging upon parties and institutions.

To illustrate these developments, groups from both time periods were selected. From the early phase, two economic groups, representing different sectors and holding different positions toward parties, were chosen. The Manufacturers' Association of Israel is an organization of private industrialists and has maintained independence from the parties, although its ideals could be considered close to the Right. The *Ihud ha-Kvutzot ve-ha-Kibbutzim*, the Union of Kvutzot and Kibbutzim (a *kvutzah* is smaller than a *kibbutz*), is a federation of collective settlements representing primarily agricultural concerns and has been associated with a party of the Left. The Ihud's selection serves an additional purpose. It represents an interest area that has been fragmented among various groups and parties; besides the Ihud, there are other collective agricultural federations, each affiliated with a different party, as well as cooperative and private agricultural groups. Following the Ihud's movements, how in certain instances the Ihud cooperated with other associations and at other times kept a distance, should enlighten our understanding of interest group formation, behavior, and development. To exemplify groups of the later period, a policy-oriented group was selected. *Gush Emunim* (Bloc of the Faithful) formed around the issue of settling Jews on the West Bank. Gush Emunim extended its concerns to related foreign policy questions. It illustrates a non-aligned, more politically aggressive group. Concentrating on these specific cases, I use them as spotlights for illuminating the development of an interest group subsystem and other aspects of the political process. Before embarking upon such an analysis, further preparation of the political and economic context in Israel and explanation of the system's development are needed.

Part I

The Setting

Chapter 2

Politics and the Economy

The Political Culture

It is impossible to understand how Israel's political system formed and has operated without first understanding its political culture, especially its ideological quality. Ideological attachments, which originated in the pre-state period, have influenced all aspects of the political system – the parties, including their internal organization, the nature of group relations, and the scope of bargaining and decision-making. In order to preserve ideological integrity while making decisions, political actors have adopted behavioral traits that have continued to affect decision-making long after some of the specific ideologies have lost their relevance. I will first sketch the different outlooks and then point out the far-reaching consequences for the country's politics.

Various groups that immigrated into Palestine early in the twentieth century held different views of the type of society they sought to shape. Religiously motivated persons envisioned a state based upon Jewish law. Those from countries with developing socialist movements came with visions of a Marxist socialist state or a social democracy. Still others visualized an agrarian or an industrial economy, in either case directed by the state. Some favored an economy based upon private enterprise. Foreign policy opened up another political gap. At times even before reaching Palestine, proponents of a particular set of views created their own political party. When the state came into being, these parties remained in force. Each party expected to shape the state to fit its special ideology, oblivious to already existing social and political structures. The expectations of many of the party stalwarts exceeded their experience in compromising and governing. When faced with that necessity, each group

17

developed its own response to the challenge, although not necessarily rising to it.

Although Leonard Fein does not discern the complete significance of ideological politics, he colorfully conveys the nature of an ideological culture for readers who have not lived in one, as he remarks,

> The tacit requirement that all political debate be phrased ideologically necessarily affects the substance of the debate, limits what can be said on either side, invests discussion of simple policy problems with emotion appropriate only to more fundamental questions. The White Knight and the Black Knight tilt, in full regalia, in defense of Virtue, where the real issue is an increment to the cost of living allowance provided government clerks. Gog and Magog meet in cataclysmic battle over a decision by the Minister of Agriculture to change the government subsidies for various breeds of tomato. But the very fact that the discussion draws from the vocabulary of political philosophy rather than the lexicon of political bargaining changes the substance of what gets discussed, and thereby changes also the substance of the final compromise.[1]

Ideology affects not only the content of debate and compromise that concern Fein but whether any debate and compromise will occur at all. Certain issues are too sensitive and are therefore avoided. In some cases this avoidance may occur in less than obvious ways. As Fein recognizes, one often is amazed that in a country where vital issues demand discussion, debate centers on picayune details or irrelevant personal qualities of those engaged in the debate. However, it is not, as Fein interprets, that ideology transforms minor matters into major causes, but rather by obsessing over a minor matter, the participants in the debate avoid dealing with a more difficult major issue. It is not that a discussion on a cost of living increment for government clerks becomes a battle of right versus wrong, but rather by debating a small cost of living increment, the participants avoid turning to the larger question of equality and distribution of resources.

A slight variation on this ideological usage also results in issue avoidance or at least foreclosure or diversion of discussion. Sometimes a minor issue is raised to the ideological level signalling that it is a matter of "principle" that cannot be touched. Although debate occurs, and on the surface the system seems to encourage discussion, there is little real meaningful exchange of views. Debate is held not so much to resolve a problem but rather to ensure one's view is presented. People talk past each other, not to each other. Positions are stated, not discussed.

Yet, for all the ideological intensity and dysfunctional ramifications, decision-making does occur. Observers therefore have concluded that, despite all the sound and fury, the system works and has not become immobilized. Fein explains that decision-making following an ideological battle is a source of cynicism toward politics in Israel because "the citizen must conclude that the accusations and counteraccusations, the solemn commitments and dire warnings, were merely so much rhetoric, never meant to be taken seriously, or that the political leaders have sold their principles for a mess of pottage."[2] What has not been perceived is that the accusations were on the whole meant to be taken seriously and principles were not sold for pottage. Rather, a deal was struck in order to preserve those principles. Pragmatism is not valued for its own sake as a non-violent way of resolving conflict as in the United States, for example, and compromise does not signify ideological decline and political development. Rather, only the trappings of pragmatism exist, which the participants force themselves to accept. The system appears pragmatic and functional, but actually, it is severely limited. Mainly issues that lend themselves to resolution by back-room bargaining can be handled most effectively. Macro-level issues that require calm discussion on their merits and may entail long term planning are problematic for decision-makers.

A corollary of such bargaining is another behavioral trait important for understanding the country's political development – the fostering of dependency. If one – whether group, party, or individual – cannot persuade another of a position by rational argument, then one seeks to assure adherence to a cause by other means. Concomitantly, if one cannot identify with another ideology but needs something practical from the bearers of that ideology, one tries to ensure present and future needs by striking a bargain in the form of, "I'll do for you; you'll be *obligated* to do for me." To assure that needs are continually met, one must constantly be at work to create new bonds and strengthen old ones. Parties, groups, and individuals survive by sacrificing their independence and striving to maximize another's dependence. Webs are created from which it becomes increasingly difficult to break free. Extricating oneself risks breaking some of those bonds which could have profound effects upon one's life. Those who dare to be independent are perceived as threats to all those who are dependent, and the term "independent" is used to refer disparagingly to someone who attempts to live without accepting favors or incurring obligations.

Avoiding issues, posturing rather than discussing, emphasizing picayune details and personal qualities, bargaining rather than reasoned policy-making, and fostering dependency have so conditioned the atmosphere that political and non-political relations are automatically conducted according to these precepts without reference to or perhaps even recognition of the underlying ideological differences.

The Political Institutions: Pre-State Precedents

When Israel declared its independence on May 14, 1948, establishing workable governing institutions to cope with the ideological diversity was not a problem that suddenly arose. The Jewish Community in Palestine, known as the Yishuv, and the worldwide Jewish community participating in the World Zionist Organization had developed governing bodies and decision-making procedures.

The Zionist Organization, which first convened in Switzerland in 1897, was an international voluntary framework for Jews seeking to establish a Jewish state. To enable non-Zionist Jews to support Jewish settlement and social welfare efforts in Palestine and participate in administering those enterprises, the Zionist Organization established a Jewish Agency for Palestine in 1929 to include Zionist and non-Zionist representatives. (Labeled non-Zionists, there were those who favored a Jewish community in Palestine but not the establishment of a Jewish political entity.) Except that it lacked sovereignty, the Jewish Agency otherwise functioned as a national government, comprising various departments similar to ministries. Concurrently, the Yishuv developed organs to administer and supervise the community's internal, immediate needs.

All three governing systems—World Zionist Organization, Jewish Agency, and Yishuv—were similarly structured, with broadly based elected assemblies in turn electing smaller bodies from their own membership. In this way, the Executives of each became the most powerful bodies. Each system's base assembly, even that of the worldwide Zionist Organization, held elections according to proportional representation of parties without reference to geographical constituencies. Party considerations in the pre-state period were so significant that a transitional government that was to assume power upon termination of the British mandate was negotiated among the parties and members of the Jewish Agency and the Yishuv National Executive. Thus, a pyramidal structure, proportional representation of parties, and party influence set the pattern for governing arrangements in the state period, whether of parties, unions, settlement federations, or citizens' groups.

Establishment of the state did not entail dissolution of the Zionist Organization or of the Jewish Agency. According to a new arrangement made for the Jewish Agency in September 1948, it would finance and promote immigration, conduct public relations for Israel around the world, and supervise new settlement in Israel. Nevertheless, bureaucratic overlap between the Jewish Agency and state ministries has occurred. State take-over of Agency functions or modes for consolidation and cooperation continue to be developed.

The Parties

The multi-party hallmark of the pre-state era continued to dominate the state period, influencing the form and activities of all other political elements. Many of these parties were ideologically narrow and highly exclusionary; members who disagreed would leave and form another party. By Israel's independence many parties had repeatedly married and divorced, on grounds of ideological incompatibility, and even disappeared. A detailed survey therefore would be irrelevant for this study, but the main entities extant during the early years of Israel's independence and active thereafter require review.

These parties may be broadly categorized as Left, Right, territorial maximalist, and religious. Most of the parties originated in Europe and maintained organizations worldwide and within Palestine. Most, too, were not merely doctrine espousing propaganda machines but were comprehensive organizations, providing a framework for the daily life of members. They established agricultural villages, labor organizations, and other institutions and provided a variety of services to members.

Starting left of center and moving leftward, the party spectrum was divided among Mapai, Ahdut ha-'Avodah, and Mapam, with Mapam at one time sympathetic to the Soviet Union. There also was a small Communist segment. The Right was composed of the General Zionists, the Progressives, and Herut. All of the Right parties advocated minimum government control of the economy, private enterprise, and individual initiative. To Herut, more important than economics was the issue of national security and the state's boundaries; Herut supported a maximalist policy. In addition to the left-right division there was a religious sector which wanted to establish religious tenets as the basis of the state. This sector also was composed of several parties, differing in emphasis on labor issues, specific religious matters, and the very existence of the state. The National Religious Party (NRP) that exists today was established in 1956, a merger of two parties. While the religious parties have exerted pressure on individual religious issues, prompting some observers to compare them to pressure groups, their ultimate objective has been to establish a religious state, thus making them comprehensive, ideological entities similar to the other occupants of the political space.

The Political Institutions: The State

The party and ideological diversity account in large part for the rather fluid governmental framework adopted at independence. Although a Constituent Assembly was elected in January 1949, a written, formal constitution was not adopted mainly to avoid divisive, ideological disputes. Passing the Transition Law of February 16, 1949, the Assembly transformed itself into a parliament (called Kneset). Instead of adopting a written constitution, the Kneset passed a resolution on June 13, 1950, enabling the later formulation of laws delineating structures and functions of government, termed Basic or Fundamental Laws, that eventually would comprise a formal constitution. Except for certain provisions, these laws require only a simple majority for amendment. Israel's government operates according to ordinary laws passed by the legislature as needed. At least theoretically, therefore, Israel's system does not present extraordinary structural obstacles to groups seeking change.

As established by the transitional legislature, and then by subsequent elected legislatures, Israel is a parliamentary democratic republic with a ceremonial President and with a Prime Minister and Cabinet nominally deriving power from the legislature. The Kneset is a 120 member unicameral body elected for four years. All citizens over eighteen years are enfranchised. Carrying over the system used during the pre-state period, the country forms a single constituency, and party lists compete and are seated according to proportional representation.

Since no party ever has received a majority, Cabinets have all been coalitions. After elections, usually the head of the plurality winning party receives the mantle from the President to form a Cabinet (called the Government).[3] The party head usually becomes Prime Minister. The coalition forming party seeks to embrace several smaller parties, although not necessarily those closest to it in electoral gains, which will provide it with a majority in the Kneset. Until 1977, Mapai formed every coalition, taking as partners other socialist parties, the Progressive Party, and religious parties. Except for the early 1950s and a period of a National Unity Government established on the eve of the 1967 war, the General Zionists (later Liberals) did not participate in the Government. Likewise, except for that National Unity Government, Herut never sat in the Cabinet.

The size of the Cabinet is not fixed, nor are the jurisdictions of the ministries. The parties appoint their allotted members to the Cabinet, and ministries and posts within them may be combined, separated, or added to accommodate party demands. Ministers need not be Kneset members, although any deputy ministers – where appointed – must be. The Prime Minister is *primus inter pares*, and unless a party breaches collective responsibility, does not have the right to dismiss ministers or replace those that resign. Of course, there are informal variations, and a forceful personality may compel at least his own party to comply with his judgments. Thus, groups seeking to influence the Government must keep current about changing power relationships and be flexible about rebuilding personal, party, and bureaucratic ties.

Although an ideological, multi-party system may have been expected to produce unstable coalitions subordinate to a fractious legislature, in a remarkable turnabout in Israel, relatively cohesive Cabinets have controlled the legislative branch. This stability has been due to devices invented by David Ben Gurion, widely regarded as Israel's leader during the pre-state era and Prime Minister for thirteen of Israel's first fifteen years as a state. Ben Gurion laid down rules for Cabinet decisions to be made by majority vote (at least four) and collective responsibility for all Cabinet decisions. He devised a system where prospective coalition partners draw up a document, called Basic Principles, agreeing in advance on legislation to be proposed, positions to be taken on issues important to them, and the distribution of offices among them. The parties agree to abide by these principles and to enforce Cabinet decisions by exerting party discipline upon their respective Kneset members. An individual or party offender could be forced to resign by the Cabinet. In exceptional instances, on especially intractable or intense issues of conscience, the Basic Principles may explicitly permit coalition parties to abstain on votes, exempt parties from imposing discipline, or allow members to vote freely. Since coalition parties command a majority in the Kneset, party discipline thus ensures Kneset approval of Cabinet initiated proposals. Almost all laws are initiated by the Cabinet, since to succeed, legislation requires prior agreement among the coalition parties. And since the party forming the coalition maintains a majority in the Cabinet, it can be assured its policies will be enacted or implemented. Ben Gurion's ingenious pre-screening arrangement and Cabinet operating procedures cope with ideological politics by enabling distinct parties to agree to disagree and preserve their important principles as well as a piece of the patronage pie. Both the procedure of drawing up a post-election agreement and collective responsibility have been enacted into law.

Stable coalition government is not without consequences. The Basic Principles set limits for decision-making. Matters considered too sensitive for inclusion in the Basic Principles may never reach the Government's agenda. Nevertheless, the procedure does leave room for some policy initiatives. An issue not included within, or contrary to, the Basic Principles might be raised. Moreover, leeway for action is left to ministers. The Cabinet and its members possess delegated responsibility from the Kneset. Laws often are not detailed, and the Cabinet and each minister in his domain can issue regulations with the force of law to implement legislation. To an extent, ministers may use their power to design programs and institute policies without receiving explicit approval from the Kneset or Government. They may bypass party offices and partisan disputes. As will be developed in this study, there is scope in the system for interest groups to operate.

While generally a rubber stamp for the Government, the Kneset has functions and informal power in the system, providing a worthwhile target for interest groups. Formally, the Kneset is the country's legislative authority. The Kneset approves the Cabinet and can bring down the Government by a vote of no-confidence. A Cabinet resignation does not automatically trigger new elections; only the Kneset can dissolve itself and call new elections.

The Kneset operates according to procedures set by law and custom, guided in many respects by party considerations. Debate time is allotted, and committee seats are allocated, according to proportional representation. The Kneset conducts a question period at the beginning of its sessions where ministers and other officials may be requested to appear, thereby holding officials accountable to it. The Kneset can hold a plenary discussion on any subject, and its committees may examine any subject within their purview and call for witnesses and records.

Although usually private members' bills are not enacted and Government initiated legislation is assured passage in the Kneset, the Kneset can play a role in modifying a bill. To legislate, the Kneset holds three readings. The first reading is held to decide whether to refer a bill to the appropriate committee. Most bills are referred, although the Kneset has the power to reject a bill or return it to the Government. At a closed committee session, the proposal is closely reviewed. A ministry representative participates, and the committee is empowered to call private experts or Government officials to advise, testify, or answer questions. The committee may propose amendments by majority vote. A second reading, conducted paragraph by paragraph, is held when the bill emerges from committee. At the third reading, the Kneset votes on the entire revised bill, and party discipline is enforced, which, of course, ensures enactment.

In many respects, the Kneset offers openings for group influence. A group may prevail upon an individual member to call for a general debate, to present its view in the debate, call for a committee inquiry into a subject, or to introduce a private bill. The Kneset's role on Government proposed legislation, however, offers the greatest opportunity for successful group influence. Groups may convince coalition party members to exert pressure to prevent a bill from being introduced, although this is a delicate and rare maneuver. More usual, groups may seek to testify or provide experts to testify at committee sessions in order to obtain amendments.

Since Israel does not have a written constitution or set of laws of privileged character, there is no power of judicial review. Hence, the court system, an avenue often open to group appeals in other settings, is constricted in Israel. Nevertheless, that arena is not completely closed. Actions of officials and their regulations are subject to judgment. These may be found to be inconsistent with laws upon which they rest, unnecessary for implementing those laws, or exceeding the authority granted in the law. Citizens' groups have not hesitated to avail themselves of this judicial authority, appealing for relief from regulations and officials' actions or requesting Government compliance with regulations issued. Most appeals have pertained to economic matters.

The Economy

Upon the establishment of the state, Israel, small, poor in natural resources, and surrounded by hostile states, faced formidable tasks of economic development. During the first three and a half years of the state's existence, 684,000 immigrants arrived, more than doubling the population of Palestine of May 1948. The practical necessities of providing for the increasing population, overcoming the country's resource limitations, preparing for defense and accommodating the various ideologies referred to previously have guided the structure and developmental priorities of the economy and have generated interest group formation.

Like the political system, Israel's economic structure originated during the pre-state period and derived from the different economic and social ideas and resources of the immigrants. Long considered a primary expression of Zionism, agriculture always was emphasized. Early immigrants founded collective agricultural villages, kibbutzim, and also established *moshavim*, cooperative agricultural villages where people hold land and live privately but conduct certain activities, such as purchasing and marketing, as a group. In contrast to agriculture, manufacturing was of secondary importance to leaders of the Zionist Organization and also ran into opposition from the mandatory authority which was reluctant to encourage competition with British industry.

Israel's economy has been divided into government, cooperative, and private sectors, which became formally organized during the pre-state period. Several leftist political parties established the Histadrut in 1920 initially to organize labor, including the agricultural laborer "pioneers." Concomitantly, private sector industry and construction formed an organization, and other associations arose in various branches of the private economy.

After the state was established, government greatly increased its role.[4] Government acquired this prominent role partly because a central authority was deemed necessary to allocate scarce resources, provide for impoverished immigrants, and handle the transfer of foreign aid and partly because ruling coalitions were predominantly socialist, generally favoring state directed economies. The government has owned and operated the railroads and post, telegraph, telephone and broadcasting services; has conducted public works projects; has progressively taken control of education from the parties; and has provided social welfare services. The government also owns more than half the shares in public corporations which produce for defense and develop various natural resources. The government has thereby become a large employer, counting teachers, social workers, technicians, and engineers among its employees besides the "regular" civil service. For many years the sole importer and distributor of raw materials and recipient and controller of foreign capital, the government further expanded its power. By controlling prices and offering subsidies, tax concessions, export incentives, and bank loans and guarantees, the government can influence the direction of the economy. Government therefore became the address for requests and demands for aid from all branches of the economy, often in competition with each other.

Israel's cooperative sector is unique in the annals of Western social democracies. These systems usually have substituted nationalized enterprises for the labor-controlled production envisioned in socialist ideology. While one might claim that Israel's cooperative sector is not actually labor owned and directed, several enterprises, notably agricultural, are, and the cooperative sector certainly falls somewhere in between private ownership and state-run production. The overseer of the cooperative sector is the Histadrut. Begun as a labor organization, the Histadrut became extensively involved in economic activities. Though several of its functions were taken over by the state, under Histadrut aegis are agricultural cooperatives and enterprises in industry, construction, public works, banking, insurance, marketing, supply, transport, and retail activities. In several enterprises, such as the national shipping line and airline, the Histadrut is a partner with the Jewish Agency or the government. The Histadrut also runs a health service and directs the workers' pension fund. Thus, the Histadrut has the anomalous distinction of not only representing labor but also serving as a large employer. Despite its ramified reach, the Histadrut is not a monolithic monster, as its various enterprises and their directors often have been at odds with each other and against the central Histadrut leadership. As elections to Histadrut directing bodies are conducted by party list, Mapai has been able to be the controlling factor.[5]

It is estimated that a little more than half of the GNP is generated by the private sector, which has a hold in industry, agriculture, construction, and services. In certain branches, the private sector contribution is estimated at an even higher level. Considering ownership, it is estimated that today enterprises in various branches are 70–90 percent in private hands with the estimate for private sector ownership overall at 70 percent. In industry, figures for 1967 estimate that the private sector owned 90 percent of the enterprises, employed 75 percent of industrial workers, and accounted for 70 percent of total industrial output. More recent data have the private sector accounting for over 70 percent of the country's industrial output and at least 72 percent of industrial personnel. In recent years, the number of private enterprises has been increasing but not their proportion in output and employment as the public and Histadrut sectors own larger firms and have augmented their share of industrial activities. In addition, the kibbutz movements have entered industries other than those that are food related, which has further altered the proportions among the sectors. Further complicating the picture, sometimes the three sectors together own shares in enterprises.[6]

These different forms of ownership cut across economic branches of production, which have consisted of a large service sector, industry and mining, agriculture, and construction. The overall aim of Israel's economic policy has been to provide for basic domestic consumption, including defense needs, while increasing the country's competitiveness and integration on the world market by expanding its exports and reducing its import bill. To meet these objectives, development within each branch and each area's relative contribution to the GNP have varied. Thus, for example, while agriculture has consistently received attention and often priority over other economic branches, industry also received encouragement, starting slowly in the mid-fifties when more investment capital was available.

The economic sectors and branches and their subdivisions were potential candidates for interest group formation as they understood that development decisions held life or death consequences for them. A matrix of criss-crossing alliances as well as rivalries theoretically was possible, as different groups would seek input into decisions and react to decisions already taken in order to express their concerns, protect their livelihoods, and, in some cases, protect their principles. Indeed, the political and economic systems gave rise to interest groups. Which groups formed, how they operated within the political and economic milieu, and how they in turn affected the political system becomes the topic of this study. Highlighting the main interactions will aid in understanding this study's specific cases.

Chapter 3

The System in Operation

Views have diverged about how to describe Israel's political system and development: (1) whether the party system was a pure multi-party system or rather was a dominant party type and whether the system was evolving into a looser, two-party arrangement, (2) similarly, whether groups felt compelled to seek party patrons in a multi-party system, related primarily to a dominant party, or were more free-wheeling, (3) whether ideological distinctions prevailed or became less intense, and (4) whether the country was ruled by an oligarchy that became even smaller.[1] The different interpretations may be reconciled if they are understood as characterizing different parts of the political system and periods of Israel's political development. The main developments are traced here, providing a backdrop against which the specific cases may be observed.

Early Years of Independence: The Multi-Party Period

Indeed, during the early period, a multi-party system prevailed. From 1952–1955, the Mapai-led Government included representatives of the General Zionist, Progressive, and religious parties. Many institutions, such as the Histadrut, were directed by executive boards composed of party representatives, actually "mini-coalition governments." In the Government and these institutions, however, Mapai held many powerful posts. The Kneset was a weak body. The single constituency electoral arrangement with parties presenting country-wide lists did not provide for individual representation or grass-roots group input, and the citizen's political world view was that of party activity and party loyalty.

The bureaucracy was subordinate to the parties which directed the ministries, and different ministries became preserves of specific parties. Distributing scarce resources, the bureaucracy accrued great power. Despite party control over Government offices, ministers frequently called upon groups to fill positions, primarily because they needed experienced persons in public service but also because they sought a means of controlling groups.

Including group representatives in the bureaucracy was possible because interest groups were economic or occupational. The party-based ideological atmosphere actually precluded idea groups from forming by coopting their potential realm. Instead, it fostered economic, functional groups that could be dealt with by bargaining.

Although parties predominated, party-group relations were not uniform on the Left and Right. A picture of party core surrounded by groups is most appropriate for parties of the Left, and among these, Mapai was the most aggressive in accumulating groups and establishing formal organizational ties. On the Right, party-group relations were much more tenuous and tentative. Parties of the Right were not as aggressive in attracting clients, partly because their ideology esteemed individual initiative and independence. Some groups, therefore, which might have been expected to identify with the Right did not formally align themselves with those parties. Whereas on the Left, groups affiliated with parties for ideological reasons, on the Right ideology actually engendered group autonomy. Since many group members as individuals held allegiance to different parties, the groups as entities remained autonomous in order to prevent politicization and disintegration. Contrary to the image of almost compulsory party-client relationships, certain groups chose autonomy.

Applying any model to party-group relations risks being too rigid, especially in the very first years of independence. Israel was a small country with a small population at an early stage of state building. Transcending party boundaries and differences was a sense of solidarity among those persons who had shared in leading the country to statehood. These leaders often wore several "hats" in party, groups, and governing institutions. Conflicts of interest did not worry them or anyone very much. Personal relations became an important factor or tactic for all groups seeking access to decision-makers. Groups which were not affiliated with any party were led by persons who played a role similar to that of a party boss. When negotiating for their group, they went directly to Government ministers with whom they were on good personal terms, often stemming from joint efforts during the pre-state period or during the struggle for independence. On many issues, groups affiliated with parties designated emissaries who were personally acquainted with Government ministers. Especially within Mapai, distinctions between leaders of groups, party, and governing bodies were not so finely drawn. In fact, the entire period irrespective of party could be termed the era of personal politics.

Besides exploiting personal connections, groups pressured the parties since party control over the ministries made that channel worthwhile and necessary. In some instances, particularly those involving unaffiliated groups, parties compelled groups to work through them.

Groups also attempted to bypass the party apparatus and deal directly with ministers. Unaffiliated groups were especially prescient in spotting that decision-making would settle in the Government. They also determined that a ministry important to them might not be held by a party which they favored. Therefore, they attempted to establish a non-partisan relationship to ministries relevant to their concerns. (For the Manufacturers' Association relevant ministries were Commerce and Industry and Finance and for the Ihud pertinent ministries were Agriculture, Finance, and Housing.)

Since most decision-making power resided with Government ministers, groups tended to neglect, although not completely, the Kneset as a target. It is interesting to note, however, the role of individual Kneset members. Kneset members concurrently belonged to groups and the legislature, advising groups on matters before that body. On the Left, the relationship between group and legislator became formalized with certain groups entitled to a specific number of representatives on a party list. The legislator from the Right acted individually without formal party involvement.

Independent groups pioneered with new tactics. They began to approach Kneset committees and were conscious about achieving publicity in the media. Later, these tactics would be adopted by other groups.

Groups making demands upon Government usually engender some Government response in trying to regulate, reconcile, and resolve rivalries. Israel's Government often made use of what I call committee politics. To resolve issues that involved competing claims among groups, economic sectors, or various parties, the Government might establish a committee which included persons considered "experts" on the subject as well as ministers, politicians, or group representatives. Such a committee would accept testimony or position papers from interest groups. Often a committee's report became official policy.

Expanding upon the committee concept, Mapai Government

ministers experimented with what could be called a corporatist approach, first among groups affiliated with the Left. Forums for thrashing out issues among rival interest groups were established. Government ministers frequently cooperated with the forums by submitting proposed legislation or programs to them for comment or by requiring that demands be presented through the forums. One such body for agricultural groups, called the Agricultural Center, was established within the Histadrut. Settlement movements of the Left (and the religious sector) were represented there via the political parties with which each was affiliated.

The Two Phases of Dominant Party Politics: Consolidation (1955–1959) and Confusion (1960–1967)

As General Zionist Party participation in the Government ended in 1955, the period of dominant party politics began.[2] Although the small Progressive Party retained one seat in the coalition formed after elections that year, it seemed that the Right would not meaningfully participate in the Government for a long time and that Mapai domination would continue. Groups and institutions began gearing their policies and activities to Mapai's position.

Mapai consolidated its power by penetrating and controlling "functional and occupational organizations." It operated through its members within groups who electorally competed against other political parties and won control of those groups. Mapai hoped "the welding influence of common party loyalty and aspirations would facilitate smooth and efficient policy-making."[3] However, Mapai leaders did not provide an ideological basis for such devotion to develop. Mapai encompassed groups not strongly committed to its socialist principles, but Mapai did not modify its credo to match its expanding and varied make-up. Rather, it bound groups to it physically by entitling group representatives to hold Kneset seats and by distributing benefits. This dichotomy between an aggregative structure without appropriate ideological underpinnings eventually would impede Mapai's progress.

Moreover, the Government was continually composed of the same Mapai leaders. An oligarchy became responsible for major decisions despite the party's widespread network. This power imbalance was another source of Mapai's malaise.

Mapai's leadership was increasingly rife with disputes, among contemporaries as well as between generations, creating a turbulent atmosphere within which groups had to operate. Younger party members expressed dissatisfaction as early as 1956. Mapai's Youth Faction attacked institutions and ideas such as the Histadrut, the civil service, and the country's pioneering ethos, that were integrally part of Mapai's socialist outlook.[4] Their struggle may be considered as an attempt to reconcile Mapai ideology and practice by modifying its socialist-pioneering doctrine. The Youth Faction challenge set a precedent for publicly addressing ideological issues.

Mapai lost prestige in the early sixties as the resurrection of the Lavon Affair, originally arising over a security mishap in 1954 and interpreted by many as a personal power struggle, led Prime Minister Ben Gurion to resign, followed by elections in 1961. Personal and power disputes continued after the elections, with ministers publicly criticizing each other. The decline in party discipline and collective Government responsibility created systemic openings which interest groups could exploit.

These disputes continued beyond 1965. Ironically, at the same time, Mapai was negotiating a union with Ahdut ha-'Avodah, a party to its left. In 1965, Mapai and Ahdut ha-'Avodah joined to form the Alignment, not a complete union as each party component maintained some autonomy. A faction under Ben Gurion then split from Mapai and formed a new party, Rafi. Rafi continually criticized then Prime Minister Levi Eshkol, specifically for his management of defense matters. This marks a turning point for the Left, for defense policy, which previously had enjoyed considerable consensus or at least had been above partisan attacks, now became a target of criticism. Thus, despite the step toward unity in the form of the new Alignment, the Left was in disarray.

While the Left went from coherence to confusion, the Right, in contrast, moved from disorder to reconstruction.[5] Activists of the Right-wing parties made efforts to increase their support. The General Zionists, who lost support in 1955, were not prepared forever to accept a minor role and attempted to become more flexible. The Herut Party also began to broaden its appeal as early as 1951 by proposing welfare measures. Herut's 1959 platform challenged labor's role in the economy and called for social services.[6] Rather than compete with Mapai in amalgamating and controlling organized groups, the Right maintained a looser relationship with affiliated groups, and Herut in particular appealed to unorganized elements of the population.

Consolidation on the Right to become a viable opposition began in earnest in the early sixties. In 1961, the General Zionists and Progressives formed the Liberal Party, while Herut again gained second place in elections called that year.[7] Herut's 1965 platform altered its stance on foreign policy and included planks on various social welfare issues. In 1965, the Liberal Party and Herut formed the Gahal bloc, which, like on the Left, was not a complete union. (The former Progressives did not consent to this alliance and formed the Independent Liberal Party.) Gahal decided to contest the elections in the Histadrut that year, emerging second with 15.2 percent of the vote.[8] While advocating private sector interests, the Right also sought support among lower economic groups and workers. Thus, the Right was attempting to become a true "catch-all" party, its policy influenced by various organized and unorganized interests. Gahal's entry into the National Unity Government on the eve of the 1967 war heightened the public's perception of Gahal as a constructive, potential governing force.

The National Unity Government accelerated the personalization of Israeli politics. (Personalization of politics differs from personal politics heretofore discussed. Whereas personal politics refers to close relationships among members of an active elite arising from previous shared experiences, personalization of politics means the popularity of a particular individual among the electorate without reference to party lines.) Pressure, for example, mounted on Prime Minister Eshkol to relinquish the defense portfolio to Moshe Dayan, then of Rafi.

Despite the challenges on Left and Right, Mapai remained the political keystone during this period, and groups, whether party aligned or not, usually started their maneuvers with reference to Mapai preferences. However, groups did not focus upon Mapai party offices or officials but rather upon Government ministers who held portfolios which affected the groups' concerns. This occurred because the Government bureaucracy increasingly controlled programs previously conducted by other bodies such as the parties, the Histadrut, and the Jewish Agency, a process known in Israel as statism. The Government became a distinct entity, further removed from party dictates, as Government ministers planned, struggled with one another, and decided upon policy. Moreover, the Government provided a target for groups unaffiliated with the dominant party. And even dominant party groups, which at times sought to increase their leverage by cooperating with others, also preferred a Government forum.

Mapai's desire to preserve its dominance as well as to maintain a working relationship with independent groups affected the kinds and scope of issues that groups addressed as well as the targets and tactics of such address. Behavioral traits conditioned by the ideological political culture (what I term the ideological dimension: avoiding issues, posturing rather than discussing, emphasizing details and personal qualities, bargaining, and fostering dependency) now arose. Many issues, therefore, were avoided. Mapai's historical promulgation of a socialist ideology, increasingly interpreted as meeting trade union demands, precluded addressing issues that appeared to challenge them.

Moreover, in order to govern, Mapai had to deal with constituent groups that did not ideologically identify with the party and also with groups outside the party which represented important economic sectors. Mapai ministers managed the resulting dilemmas by bargaining with groups to distribute benefits, thereby fostering dependency on the party and Government. This bargaining arrangement permitted only matters limited in scope to be raised, such as those concerning benefit distribution or a program modification, and discouraged comprehensive planning or change. Groups trimmed their aims accordingly and conformed to the bargaining pattern.

Occasionally, the Mapai party served as a forum where deals were brokered, especially when the contending sides could be confined to Mapai—between Mapai ministers, between Mapai affiliated groups, or between a Mapai minister and a Mapai group. However, a party official or committee did not make the final decision. Rather, the party provided a table where the disputants could negotiate with each other.

As the Kneset and its committees could modify proposed legislation, and as it was just those limited alterations that interest groups could hope to obtain, the Kneset increased as an important address. A little noted custom developed where the Kneset Economic Committee was controlled by the main opposition party. Although a Kneset Finance Committee, controlled by the governing party and therefore more powerful, also existed, it is significant that specific room was made in the legislature for expressing varied views. Kneset committees also began taking testimony from groups when considering legislation.[9] Groups took advantage of these channels and occasions for expression.

Personal and party relations continued to be relevant, but over time, political struggles rendered these connections more strained, especially on the Left, while economic sophistication reduced their necessity. By 1966, relations between Government and groups became more formalized as groups sought to insulate economic affairs from politics, institutionalize group roles in policy-making, and preserve group cohesion. Formality also increased, and an interest group subsystem began to coalesce, as groups, whether affiliated or not, formed broad organizations with other groups within their respective interest spheres. A dichotomy developed between political party activity and interest group activity.

While the Government continued a central role in decision-making, by the mid-sixties, some subtle changes could be discerned in Government-group-party relations. Government officials distinguished themselves from party officials, and the role of Government became institutionalized and separate from the role of party. As a consequence of the personal and political infighting on the Left, group activity on the Left became differentiated from party affairs. Undeterred by the political turmoil occurring on the Left, independent groups spearheaded change in the system by testing new tactics and targets, raising formerly taboo subjects, and suggesting new modes of policy-making. And independent groups began to gain a more legitimate place in decision-making as one of the sides with which the Government bargained. Their role, however, was not yet a really effective one such as characterizes groups in the British system. Nevertheless, all groups expressed themselves in terms of specific interests and began to perceive the possibility of distinguishing interest activity from the political party arena.

Maintaining a Shaky Status-Quo, 1967-1973

Following the 1967 war, much of the population expected major changes in the country's governmental structure and outlook as well as in its territorial make-up. But to the disappointment of many, a Government uncertain of future territorial boundaries undertook no noteworthy initiatives, neither on the domestic political and economic fronts nor in foreign affairs.

Offering a moderate platform for the 1969 elections and participating in the grand coalition, the Right continued to present a general appeal. Not wanting to lose its traditional nationalistic support, however, it contributed money to a new group which advocated retaining the administered territories. Thus, the Right attempted to project a new image without relinquishing the old.

Concentrating on organization rather than ideas, the Left tried to realign its component parts, both parties and groups. The Labor Party was established in January 1968 as a merger (but not a completely integrated structure) of Mapai, Rafi, and Ahdut ha-'Avodah. In 1969 Mapam allied with the party forming a larger, but still loose entity, again called the Alignment. The Left still did not develop a new creed consonant with the times. Nor did it forthrightly proclaim itself a "catch-all" type party. Thus, the Left's mergers did not enhance its leadership capabilities and only confirmed the status quo ante.

The National Unity Government remained in place through the 1969 elections (in which the Labor Alignment gained 56 seats and Gahal 26) until the middle of 1970. It was in the interest of both developing party blocs to maintain the status quo of a grand coalition—the dominant Left so it could maintain power and the Right so it could build up its image as a responsible party with governing potential. Nevertheless, Gahal left the coalition in August 1970 when the Government voted to accept an American proposal for a limited ceasefire with Egypt and indirect peace negotiations with Israel's Arab neighbors.[10]

While parties were busy maintaining the status quo, groups were pressing for systemic changes consonant with the great geographical and even psychological transformation that the country experienced after the 1967 war. Existing groups expanded their level of concerns and expanded their arenas for action. Groups affiliated with the dominant party began reexamining that relationship and questioning long-standing instruments for interest articulation and decision-making. The groups' new tactics all had the effect of creating centrifugal access points for influencing policy that challenged Government and party control.

Kneset members cooperated in furthering group appeals. Kneset members who considered themselves representatives of group interests formed caucuses across party lines. In addition, Kneset members lobbied ministers, becoming ombudsmen for their group constituents. In this way, the Kneset continued developing distinctive institutional practices.

During this period, a new phenomenon occurred in the nature of groups. Idea groups or groups concerned with a policy objective began to appear, and these groups were independent of political parties. The atmosphere for challenging established policy that I noted had begun before the 1967 war prepared the way for these later groups which raised issues previously considered appropriate only for parties. One such group was the Black Panthers, which primarily called for social change and incidentally took a stand on foreign policy as well. This group, however, was too extremist and too poor in suitable leaders to be taken seriously by the established political system. Some of the issues it raised, however, were discussed within the Government. Foreign policy and security also became issues around which new interest groups could form. After the 1967 war but before the war of

1973, persons promoting settlement on the West Bank formed groups and asked Prime Minister Golda Meir to approve their settlement plans. These groups proved more adept at organizing than the Black Panthers and foreshadowed the proliferation of independent, policy interest groups. Thus, within the status quo that set in after the 1967 war, any impetus for change in process or policy originated with interest groups, not with the parties or the Government.

Aftershock, Realignments, Reassessments, and Agitations, 1973–1977

Israel was in a state of shock after the 1973 war. The Left was returned to office in the December elections, but forming a stable Government required several months.

Superficially, it seemed that a strong, two-party system was emerging. Simultaneous with party mergers, however, was a loosening of old party alignments that was significantly different from past patterns. In the past, when factions split from parties, they normally established a small minor party but remained on the same side of the political spectrum as the party from which they had departed. Now, the State List that had split from the Labor Party actually joined the Right bloc. Able to attract former Left partisans, the Right now sought to consolidate its "catch-all" character to become a party of individuals with diverse general views banded together for electoral purposes. Gahal aligned with the State List and with another small party in 1973 to form the Likud bloc (not a completely integrated unit). The Right continued to make a wide appeal, vying for the workers' vote in the Histadrut. And it addressed the broad electorate without forging direct organizational ties to either old or new interest groups. Its strategy seemed to succeed, for in the 1973 elections Likud received 39 seats (to the Alignment's 51), a significant increase for the Right.

The Left, despite a façade of unity, was wracked with disputes among its leaders, even within its supposedly "new leadership," represented by Yitzhak Rabin whose Government replaced Meir's in June 1974. The rifts between Prime Minister Rabin and Defense Minister Shimon Peres seemed to violate the mores of collective responsibility and diminished the Prime Minister's authority.[11] Although the Labor Party established new organs for discussion and decision-making, the party's representatives did not consider themselves bound by party decisions. In fact, Rabin spoke bitterly about there being no such concept as "party unity."[12] In addition, the old party machine was allowed to deteriorate.

With the Left restructuring and searching for a coherent policy and the Right developing a general appeal, the period after the 1973 war was a time of insecurity for many interest groups. Compounding the problem of weak Government was the fact that Pinhas Sapir, a skilled minister-broker, was not a member of the Rabin Government and died in 1975.

One group was seemingly unaffected by the governmental weakness and political realignments. On the contrary, Gush Emunim, among the new genre of idea groups, was able to use this situation to its advantage in a curious combination of ideology and practical politics. Cultivating and exploiting the primordial ideological current ever beneath the surface of Israeli society, Gush Emunim resurrected the pre-state issue of the country's boundaries and emphasized the religious nature of the state. Moreover, this group observed and drew lessons from the developing political system, designing sophisticated new techniques for manipulating the system as it evolved. Gush Emunim founders established an autonomous, agitational interest group with anchorage in several parties. Comprehending and reacting to the developing centrifugal trends of the political system, Gush Emunim varied its tactics and impinged upon many targets including individual ministers, Kneset members, and supporters in various parties.

In an attempt to overcome its weakness, to achieve a broad consensus for its policies, and probably to avoid establishing a grand coalition, the Government again resorted to committee politics. The Government established a Committee for Planning the Economy for 1974 which included group members without regard to party affiliation. However, full group partnership did not materialize, and Government ministers often presented the committee with a fait accompli after bargaining singly with groups elsewhere.

Change and Continuity, 1977–1980s

By 1977 the atmosphere was set for change. The two major party blocs had each become more ideologically diffuse but as a result of different processes with different consequences. On the Left, diffusion gave an impression of incoherence whereas on the Right it signalled moderation and apparent broadening of appeal.

In preparation for the 1977 elections, a new party formed which represented a significant break from past party formations. The Democratic Movement for Change was established primarily on the issue of electoral reform. The DMC succeeded in drawing enough votes from Labor to make it possible for the Likud to form a Government. (The Likud received 43 seats, the Alignment 32, and the DMC received 15.) A coalition with the religious parties was formed in June 1977, and the DMC joined in October.

The new post-election Prime Minister Menachem Begin made several appointments that reinforced the importance of an individual's merit, personality, and personal power over party affiliation as criteria for attaining office. The appointment of Dayan of the Labor opposition as Minister for Foreign Affairs was one illustration of this development. Dayan's appointment demonstrated Likud's flexibility and pointed up the state of flux within all parties on various issues. His dramatic defection also showed that party ties and loyalty were becoming less important for aspiring politicians. Similarly, incorporating Ariel Sharon into the coalition as Minister of Agriculture vindicated Sharon's strategy of having formed his own party for the elections and reinforced the impression that individuals were increasing in power over party machines. Significant realignments across traditional party boundaries might be expected in the future.

Likud's increased openness to ideas and individuals, which had been an advantage in election campaigns, became a liability for it in Government. This Government, like Labor, was plagued by ministers acting independently and making contradictory statements. Its individually strong ministers had no history of working together, and the Likud itself was not well structured for directing a Government. Moreover, the Likud permitted many opposition appointees to remain in place, even some in important ambassadorial posts.[13] The Likud did this because for years, the Left had pinned the title "fascist" on the Likud, and the Likud was sensitive to the fearful expectations of a "revolution" that existed after the election. At times, the holdovers impeded smooth policy implementation. As a result, the Government appeared indecisive and fraught with dissension.

Increasing individualism also manifested itself in the legislature. The Kneset became an action arena for individual members irrespective of their party's positions and concerns.

The Left did not use its time out of office to begin restructuring itself. Individuals of the Left, however, attempted to establish or attract groups in order to bolster their standing within the party. Their efforts further marked the influence and power of individual personalities in all parties. All these independent initiatives and the party volatility across the political spectrum signalled system change, for they augmented potential access points and opportunities available for interest group pressure and expression.

The Right's accession to office in 1977 did not substitute one party and set of groups for another. Rather, the Right regarded the party and party-in-Government as responsible for governing for the whole society. Therefore, the Likud sought to maintain its appeal to as many diverse groupings, organized and unorganized, within the electorate as possible, juggling any competing claims made by them. Decision-making was considered the purview of Government ministers, who were not strictly accountable to party structures. Accordingly, decisions were made in a piecemeal manner, similar to the pattern followed by Mapai/Labor. Groups took on the role the Right ascribed to them and did not rush to make a political realignment.

By the 1981 elections, Labor had not revitalized itself. While the Alignment regained some places from the DMC's dissolution, the Likud tied with it at 46 seats, receiving the presidential nod to form a Government. Though the second Likud Government encompassed a controversial war in Lebanon that led to Prime Minister Begin's retirement, and encountered a severe economic crisis with triple-digit inflation, the electorate evidently still did not consider Labor the country's redeemer. In 1984, election results again were close; the Alignment received 44 seats and Likud 41. This split spawned a unique National Unity Government with rotating heads. Labor (minus Mapam which withdrew from the Alignment over the issue), Likud, and several religious and smaller parties formed a Government with Labor's Peres as Prime Minister and Likud's Yitzhak Shamir as alternate Prime Minister and Foreign Minister until October 1986 when they would switch places.

In such tentative times, groups were active. One Ihud member, in fact, noted that opposition to the Likud had moved from the Labor Party to groups demonstrating in the street.[14] Indeed, during the term of the 1984 National Unity Government, the kibbutz groups and Manufacturers' Association pursued public action, while ironically, Gush Emunim became more subdued. Initially confused, groups eventually targeted the most powerful minister sympathetic to a particular cause. When called upon, particularly during Peres's tenure as Prime Minister, groups cooperated with each other and with the ministers to formulate and implement policy, thus demonstrating once again how interest groups fill in systemic gaps.

Political Change in Israel: Some Preliminary Observations

By the 1980s, Israel's political system had undergone a gradual evolution, and the process was continuing. Various institutions had carved out spheres of activity. Party blocs of Left and Right had become looser, though for different reasons and therefore with different implications for possible future development.

The Right may be considered a real "catch-all" party, whereas this term would be a misnomer for the Left. The Left encompassed many elements yet failed to modify its ideology to suit its components. Nor did it candidly eschew its socialist ideology and present itself as a comprehensive catch-all type organization. Rather, the Left, particularly Mapai, permitted a few persons to conduct its affairs. The oligarchy preserved principle by bargaining with diverse elements of the party and polity on pieces of policy and minor positions. Such an incoherent process of governing can last only a limited time before pressure mounts for sharing power and more comprehensive policy-making. When leadership was expanded, it was too late. The "new" leadership was not properly trained as a cooperative team, one reason that both party unity and collective responsibility declined.

At the other end of the political spectrum, the Right consciously diversified its interests from a party based upon a single principle to a more comprehensive type. It became a "catch-all" party of individuals desiring to hold Government office. When in power after 1977, however, the Right also suffered from a lack of collective responsibility and party unity, partly because it was composed of individuals with little background in cooperative teamwork.

Several additional reasons account for the decline in collective responsibility and party unity within both Left and Right party blocs. Channels to political power were limited. Economic and intellectual elites as potential political elites did not develop and were not cultivated. The Left's ideology, that disparages wealth as a basis for power, and a general Israeli societal esteem for amateurism and spontaneity as supposedly expressing equality and democracy effectively discouraged these channels from opening. Party politics, therefore, became a main route to power for Right and Left. Power positions to which persons could aspire also were limited. Both limited channels and positions led to great rivalries and jealousy. Once in office, as evidenced by the Lavon-Ben Gurion rivalry, the Peres-Rabin feud, and similar feuds on the Right, ministers sought to maximize their authority and prevent others from developing political appeal. The Left's ideology which suppresses acknowledgment of personal ambition exacerbated the effects of this factor on the Left as the frustration of those who had to pretend they were not personally ambitious often exploded.

While centrifugal developments in the system might be applauded as the assertion of autonomy from party control, these developments run the risk of relegating politics to the realm of the ridiculous. Politics has become associated with personal power plays, antics, and petty party rivalries rather than with competing positions on issues. He "dabbles" in politics is an oft-heard description of persons involved in political party affairs.

Paralleling these developments in the party system and the societal culture, interest groups attempted to "fill in the gaps," sometimes spurring change in procedure, structure, and culture and sometimes serving as counterweights to changes that occurred. When ideology was more intense among parties, groups were functional. When parties became less ideologically intense or divided on ideological issues, more ideologically oriented interest groups emerged.

This overview has shown Israel's political development from a multi-party phase to one that may be described as dominant party. Accompanying this movement was a change from a broad oligarchy or ruling elite to one that was smaller, composed primarily of Mapai's leaders. These developments concomitantly stimulated centrifugal forces in reaction. Ideology became less intense or salient on the party plane, and parties attempted to expand. This expansion provided grounds for observers to postulate that the system was headed toward a looser, two-party arrangement. Thus, the various views of Israel's political history presented at the beginning of this chapter may be understood as reflecting the development of different parts and phases of the system. I now turn to examine the evolution of Israel's interest groups more precisely, exploring their role in system change.

Part II

The Manufacturers' Association

Chapter 4

The Early Years:
Alternatives to Politicization

Organized and operational even before the state was created, the Manufacturers' Association may be considered the new nation's first independent interest group, forming a prototype for later groups choosing an independent path. The group formulated its aims and its mode of action in response to a fragmented and politicized economic environment. The Manufacturers' Association provided an element of rationality, attempting to insulate the private sector of the economy from party influences. It regarded itself as representing industrial interests in general, private industrial interests in particular, as well as general private capital and employers' interests. Emphasis on the particularistic and general aspects of these concerns varied in different periods, but throughout all periods, the Manufacturers' Association tried to create a unified industrial interest regardless of sectoral origin. In pursuing these aims, the Association at times challenged prevailing socialist ideology and Government preferred policies and impinged upon the decision-making process. Tracing this group's aims over time and how it pursued them should enhance our understanding of group behavior, its impact upon developing political and economic systems, and its influence upon the decision-making process itself.

The Manufacturers' Association disproves the frequent contention that all interest groups in Israel are party created and controlled. Impelled by Histadrut-led strikes in the building sector, manufacturers, craftsmen, and building contractors organized an association in 1921 with two main aims, to represent employers and to promote private industrial interests. As part of its activity the group protested what manufacturers perceived as discriminatory economic policies

47

pursued by the mandatory government in favor of Britain. The nascent group encountered organizational and identity problems: one of its early leaders emigrated, and the three component elements found they had few common interests to sustain a single organization.[1] Therefore, the group split and reorganized in 1925 composed only of industrialists. Soon after, the organization withstood an attempt to politicize it. Its third chairman, Dr. Walter Moses, elected in 1927, tried and failed to win support for Zev Jabotinsky, the Revisionist[2] leader, who had included a plank favoring manufacturing in his political program.

With the election of Aryeh Shenkar, a textile manufacturer from Moscow, as chairman in 1931, the organization became more stable, and subsequent attempts at politicization were rebuffed. Shenkar shepherded the organization through the transition from mandate to sovereignty and continued as its leader until his death in 1959. He is credited with the Association's achieving a recognized position in Israel's political-economic system, and he is considered the father of the organization.

Maneuvering in the Multi-Party Maze

With the establishment of the state the Manufacturers' Association continued its dual aims: providing a counterweight to the labor organization and pressing for policies favorable to private industrial development. It pursued these aims free from party control or formal affiliation, thus disproving the characterization of the General Zionist Party as a federation of various interest groups that included the Manufacturers' Association.[3] Indeed, the General Zionists contained many members of the Manufacturers' Association, but the Association was not formally affiliated and did not, for example, as an organization send delegations to party conferences. Nor were all members of the Manufacturers' Association General Zionists; members of the Manufacturers' Association belonged to various parties of the Right. These individuals did not form party factions within the group, and the Association did not develop a structure similar to that of the Histadrut, organized on a party basis and directed by a Mapai/Labor dominated coalition executive. Moreover, the party known as the most all embracing, Mapai, never entered the picture of the Manufacturers' Association.

The Manufacturers' Association was structured strictly for industrial considerations. It was a voluntary organization open to any owner of an enterprise that produced a product for the marketplace and that employed at least six persons (later amended several times). The membership, organized into industrial divisions, constituted a body called the General Assembly which convened annually.

The governing structure of the Association consisted of a President, a Presidium, and an Executive Committee, all elected biannually. The Executive Committee comprised over sixty members, part elected by the General Assembly, part by the industrial divisions, and part coopted by the Executive Committee itself. The Executive Committee elected the Presidium which comprised about fourteen members. The President of the Association was elected by the General Assembly. To work on public issues of concern to industrialists as well as on internal organizational matters, the Presidium and Executive Committee established committees and departments, manned by manufacturers and hired staff. In addition, hired staff filled the administrative positions of General Director and Secretary.

Although the Association prevented political penetration of its organization and avoided formal affiliation with any party, it could not altogether escape the party-permeated environment. Compelled to work within it, the Manufacturers' Association maneuvered among the various partisan forces. Because many Government functions were divided among parties and because many institutions and governing boards were organized on a proportional party representation basis, the Manufacturers' Association necessarily directed many of its efforts to the party that occupied positions relevant to its concerns. Moreover, many members of the group were sympathetic to parties of the Right. During the early state period, therefore, a tenuous tie existed between the Manufacturers' Association and the General Zionist Party, especially when this party participated in the governing coalition, but the flow of influence always went from group to party, and the Association constantly strove to inure itself from the vicissitudes of party activity.

A Bureaucratic Link

Always careful not to link its fate to the party sphere, the Association started protecting itself by positioning its people in the bureaucracy. Meeting in October 1951, when the General Zionists were not in the Government, the Manufacturers' Association Presidium discussed whether one of its members should accept an appointment directing the department of textiles and leather within the Ministry of Commerce and Industry. A dichotomy between interest activity and party activity emerged from the discussion. Although Presidium members desired General Zionist participation in the Government, they did not propose postponing their concerns until the party received a portfolio. Hence, they rejected the argument of one member who opposed aiding a Government that excluded General Zionists. Shenkar argued that manufacturers must occupy key positions in the administration to ensure allocation of raw materials to private industry. The group's consensus followed the reasoning of Moshe Weisglass, a metals industrialist, that Governments come and go, and the Manufacturers' Association must preserve the economy regardless of the party in power. They approved the appointment of textiles manufacturer Avraham Klir as director, taking courage from one member who remarked that it would not be the first time the Manufacturers' Association had acted against the wishes of the General Zionists.[4]

When the General Zionist Party later entered the coalition but was unable to fulfill the Association's expectations and demands, the already tenuous tie became even weaker. The Association proceeded to establish access points that could become permanent regardless of coalition composition. Several instances that occurred before and during General Zionist participation in Government illustrate the growing self-sufficiency of the Manufacturers' Association.

Attempting to alleviate a grave economic situation marked by commodity shortages and high inflation, the Government, sans General Zionists, announced the country's first currency devaluation in February 1952, the New Economic Policy (NEP). As an undesirable inflationary side effect, the measure increased the value of equipment and inventory. To prevent the inflationary impact and to preclude owners from deriving a windfall profit, the Government imposed a surtax on the difference in value of inventory before and after devaluation as well as a surtax on equipment retroactive to 1949 and demanded immediate payment of the inventory surtax.

Announcement of the New Economic Policy coincided with the Manufacturers' Association's annual meeting. Concerned about the resultant increased cost of replacing equipment and obtaining credit to finance new purchases, the Manufacturers' Association charged the President to do everything possible to obtain a policy change and scheduled a special evaluatory session in May. President Shenkar, accompanied by Presidium member Weisglass, met with the Ministers of Commerce and Industry, Communication, and Agriculture about the NEP generated problems – surtax, prices, and replacing equipment. Shenkar did not request any party members to intervene with the Government or to raise the issue in the Kneset. Included in these meetings, however,was Klir, the Association's "man" in the bureaucracy.

The Manufacturers' Association compromised by opposing only immediate payment and not demanding complete cancellation. A manufacturers' committee and Minister of Commerce and Industry Dov Yosef eventually agreed to defer part of the tax. In special cases where manufacturers could not pay, the President of the Association was empowered to recommend relief in the payments. Attributing the Government's concession on the immediate payment demand to the Association's efforts, Weisglass defended the Association and the agreement reached, arguing that "the Manufacturers' Association represents the interests of industry and not political strength. The representatives do their best to preserve the prestige of the Manufacturers' Association.... An agreement that is less satisfactory is better than no agreement!"[5]

In this instance, the Manufacturers' Association did not near its aim, notwithstanding having a representative in the bureaucracy. However, it did not fare much better when the General Zionists sat in the Government. Ironically, in order to keep the General Zionists in the coalition, the Manufacturers' Association sacrificed some demands.

Tenuous Party Ties

In January 1953, the Government proposed a property tax in the form of an obligatory loan. Recently recovered from the inventory surtax struggle, the Manufacturers' Association opposed the new tax, pleading inability to pay. With the General Zionists holding the portfolio of Commerce and Industry, the Association turned to them, expecting them to prevent enactment. Shenkar met with Minister of Commerce and Industry Peretz Bernstein to explain the manufacturers' position, and explanatory material was submitted to the party's economic department as well. Bernstein explained that the coalition agreement with Mapai had provided for a property tax and that opposing it could split the coalition, an outcome, he contended, the manufacturers would not favor. He defended the General Zionists' efforts to amend the proposal.

Nevertheless, the Association did not immediately acquiesce, and many criticized the General Zionists. Shenkar seemed the most conciliatory or perhaps the most resigned, suggesting that they accept the tax in order to preserve the coalition but oppose setting an amount to be collected. More optimistic about future General Zionist support, another member also favored helping the Government by agreeing to the tax. Others, however, urged continued opposition and suggested sending a delegation to the Kneset Finance Committee. Weisglass was particularly perturbed that the party had not consulted the Association. To express its dissatisfaction, the Presidium dispatched a delegation to the Minister of Commerce and Industry.[6]

When passage of the tax seemed certain, Presidium members differed about trying to influence the law's final form by supplying information to a General Zionist Party committee. The Presidium was limited in possible courses of action because the organization's Executive Committee had decided against cooperating with that party. While some members favored submitting information because they perceived that the party was working to improve payment terms, strong voices also were raised against any cooperation. Members expressed dismay at industry's disadvantageous position within the General Zionist Party, contending that the party had transferred the tax burden from merchants and orchard growers to industrialists. Deciding to continue its opposition, the Presidium appointed a team to meet with the General Zionist ministers and with an official of the Progressive Party as well. Simultaneously, however, it prepared a delegation to the Kneset Finance Committee, a move which signified it accepted the tax in principle but wanted to negotiate the best terms. Indeed, the Presidium and Executive Committee eventually commented on the contents of the law. Manufacturers noted the irony that industry's political efficacy had declined when General Zionists participated in the coalition. Considering his own efforts more effective than the party's, Shenkar doubted if the tax would have been passed without the General Zionists because he believed he had impressed the previous Mapai minister with the manufacturers' opposition.[7]

Diversifying Tactics

The Association's tactics started to acquire a discernible pattern. Though the Association attempted to establish and enhance access points to the General Zionist Party, it was not impelled by any special party affinity but rather compelled to adapt to the party's Government position and the party's imposed method of conducting ministry business. Manufacturers often tried to avoid party offices, addressing ministers directly and positioning group members in the bureaucracy. Meeting with General Zionist ministers, an Association delegation tried convincing them to consult with the Manufacturers' Association.

The delegation complained that the party favored the interests of commerce over industry, singling out the director-general, who, they contended, obliged manufacturers to import raw materials through commercial channels. Attempting to establish a direct presence in the ministry rather than in the party, they demanded a special director-general for industry within the ministry and proposed placing three Presidium members within the ministry's director-general's office. Responding, Yosef Sapir, then the Minister of Communication and a powerful party personage, expressed the party's willingness to seek a mode of cooperation between the ministry and the Association.

The delegation's report to the Presidium prompted a political discussion. Viewing the General Zionist Party as the only vehicle that could represent their interests vis-à-vis the Finance Ministry, which was controlled by Mapai, several Association members counselled strengthening the group's position within the party, perhaps by developing closer ties to the craftsmen. They considered the Mapai controlled Finance Ministry more obstructive to industrial interests than the General Zionists and believed a personnel change might improve the Ministry of Commerce and Industry. Others, however, including General Zionist members, advised approaching even ministers of other parties who worked on economic affairs.

The Manufacturers' Association continued warily on the General Zionist course. Eventually, Shenkar obtained a promise from the General Zionists to appoint a committee of Presidium members to advise General Zionist ministers. Eventually, too, the party appointed an individual acceptable to the Manufacturers' Association as director-general of the Ministry of Commerce and Industry and upgraded the status of the director of the industrial section.

Although the General Zionists agreed to these arrangements and provided a channel through which the Manufacturers' Association could bring its demands, this clearly was only one channel and one which the Manufacturers' Association had to cultivate and could by no means take for granted. With few legal restrictions on "conflicts of interest," the Manufacturers' Association was aided in access especially to the General Zionists by Shimon Bejarano, a cigarette manufacturer, who simultaneously sat on the Association's Presidium as an industrialist and in the Kneset as a General Zionist representative. How, when, and why the Manufacturers' Association pursued varied means to press its demands is further illustrated by the linkage of loans issue.

The Finance Minister in 1954 proposed linking Government loans made from the development budget to some monetary index (dollar rate or cost of living) in order to protect Government funds from the effects of inflation. Afraid that linkage would be adopted by all creditors, not only the Government, the Manufacturers' Association marshalled its forces to oppose linkage in any form on any loan. The Finance Minister was the target. Manufacturers' Association President Shenkar and an Association delegation met directly with the Finance Minister to discuss the issue and press their opposition. Concurrently, the Association took its case directly to the public, holding a press conference to explain its view on linkage.

From the meetings with the Finance Minister, Shenkar perceived the possibility of negotiating to exempt loans for operating capital from the linkage provision. He and others urged immediately undertaking these negotiations to at least partially resolve the matter on an administrative level before the issue could be proposed as a law in the Kneset where "it will go from economic lines to political lines."[8] Before embarking upon this course, MK Bejarano advised waiting until the General Zionists expressed opposition to linkage. General Zionist support, however, was not understood to be automatically assured, for one member proposed meeting with the General Zionists only on condition that they supported the Association's position. Though Shenkar, always the realistic compromiser, and others preferred to start negotiating with the Finance Minister, they deferred to Bejarano who undertook to arrange a General Zionist meeting. Bejarano, accompanied by other Association members, requested the General Zionist ministers to raise the issue in the Government. The target still was the Finance Minister, but now he would be pressured not only directly and through public opinion, but also via a Government coalition partner.

The Government decided not to link short-term development budget loans for operating capital. For investment loans from the development budget, the Finance Minister agreed to establish a committee to recommend proposals for ensuring the value of returned monies. A borrower not agreeing to the committee's arrangement would be permitted time to return outstanding loans without linkage. Shenkar, accompanied by a Manufacturers' Association delegation, met again with the Finance Minister and his aides to assure these arrangements. Something went awry, however, because the Bank Leumi, a commercial bank, insisted that a borrower initially choose a form of linkage. Shenkar then suggested that Bejarano raise the Bank Leumi matter in the Kneset Finance Committee. Shenkar was convinced that General Zionist MKs would support the Manufacturers' Association and create an opposition that could succeed. He also suggested that Bejarano take up the issue with the General Zionist ministers. Bejarano agreed to these suggestions and also obtained a seat on the committee, called the Lehman Committee, to resolve the linkage issue.

Bejarano reported on the committee's progress to the Presidium. The committee's proceedings, however, were considered secret, and his Presidium report accordingly was termed a "consultation" without a formal vote and decision taken.[9] Thus, through Bejarano and the General Zionists, the Manufacturers' Association had privileged and increased access to Government sponsored deliberations. The committee eventually recommended limited linkage arrangements.

Although still concerned that the linkage concept would spread, the Manufacturers' Association accepted the committee's report. On a particularly difficult issue, the Manufacturers' Association had employed various tactics and pursued varied courses of action, including the party route. In each course the Manufacturers' Association had to press its view and could not rely upon automatic agreement from any quarter. The Kneset member was especially helpful, not as lawmaker per se, but rather as a self-appointed liaison between group and party and as a spokesperson in parliamentary debates. The Kneset itself was regarded as a forum of last resort where little of substance could be addressed.

In none of the examples of Manufacturers' Association activity could the Association rely upon General Zionist support or direct the party's line. One might argue that it hardly could expect such an influential position when it had eschewed formal alignment. Despite that cost, the Manufacturers' Association deemed limiting its political identification worthwhile for two reasons. It realized that in a multiparty or dominant party system, close identification with any single party, especially one likely to be in the opposition or perhaps not hold a relevant portfolio, would not reap any practical benefit. Presciently, the Association anticipated the polity's development from a multiparty to dominant party system, and positioned itself accordingly. When the General Zionists in the coalition proved impotent on industrial issues, the Association's resolve to forego a formal political tie was reinforced. The second reason was internal. Association members belonged to different parties (or to none), and although those parties were all of the Right, ideological intensity was such that in order not to fracture the group, the Manufacturers' Association prudently avoided a tie with any one party. An unwritten agreement evolved among members of the Association not to involve party matters in its internal operations and deliberations. In this respect, the

Manufacturers' Association's political independence did not signify political strength but rather was a defensive tactic, preventing group disintegration and actually reflecting the passionate political atmosphere. A pragmatic atmosphere where interest groups could freely swing support to political parties did not exist. By limiting political party identification and building nonpolitical, bureaucratic ties, the Manufacturers' Association attempted to strengthen its bargaining position on issues, but was precluded from employing the ultimate weapon of an interest group, the promise of the group's collective support in the form of votes and money.

In lieu of a party path, the Manufacturers' Association fended for itself in negotiations. As in the various tax and loan incidents, the Manufacturers' Association addressed Government ministers of all parties and pioneered in media appeals which Association leaders considered invaluable in creating an "atmosphere" for change.[10] The Association also soon learned what level of change the system would tolerate, modifying its aspirations accordingly. It therefore softened its stand on issues that appeared to challenge the prevailing ideology or status quo in power arrangements, such as overall tax reform, and focused instead on obtaining more contained amendments. While developing a certain sophistication in action, it relied heavily upon the personal intervention of its President. A constant refrain running through all matters was, 'We'll leave this to Shenkar."

Personal Politics:
Easing the Transition from Multi-Party to Dominant Party Phases

Transcending political party as well as bureaucratic boundaries was the personal political tie which the Manufacturers' Association employed to the fullest extent possible during the early years of independence and the dominant party phase. By personal politics I mean the phenomenon where powerful personalities shape policies by interacting informally with each other in a "clubby" type of network. Individuals rather than particular offices or institutions are important for formulating policy. The effectiveness of these individuals is not necessarily limited by the formal titles of their office, and they may hold more than one formal place in the Government or state institutions. Part of this relationship involves the practice of granting favors to each other or to adherents of each other's group.

Early Government leaders acted in such a manner. Typical of this type was Pinhas Sapir, Minister of Commerce and Industry beginning in 1956 and later Finance Minister, who, according to one manufacturer, "gave a big push to industry" without being "systematic." "He was a simple man...[with an] individual way of operating. Someone would go to him and say he needed something."[11] The Manufacturers' Association easily adjusted to this personal style because in addition to aiming for some systemic change, it represented individual manufacturers before ministers and bureaucrats. Through Shenkar, the Manufacturers' Association gained access to this network and was able to express its particular and systemic interests, but especially and more successfully, the particular ones. Instead of acting through a political party as broker, the longtime president of the Association adopted that role himself, negotiating directly with ministers and developing close personal ties with them.

Shenkar's good working relationship with members of the state's first Governments stemmed from his relationship with them during the pre-state period. Although Shenkar had devoted himself to developing the manufacturers' organization and private industry in Palestine/Israel, his support of the private sector did not preclude him from cooperating with officials of the Jewish Agency to help establish a Jewish state even though their ideology differed. His aid won him respect from Jewish Agency members who later became ministers in the Government of Israel. In 1936, for example, when the Jewish Agency desperately needed to mobilize capital, it appealed to Shenkar, who raised a large sum of money. The working relationship thus established carried over into the state period. As noted in the property tax agreement, Government ministers delegated considerable power to Shenkar, allowing him to recommend tax exemptions.

Shenkar relished the role of private industry's representative and jealously guarded his right to meet with Government ministers to the exclusion of other Association leaders. In fact, if other Association officials met with a minister, they kept the meeting a secret from Shenkar![12] Shenkar's high Government contacts enabled him to grant favors to manufacturers either in respect to their personal lives or to their businesses. A limited patron-client relationship existed between the Association's leader and many members, similar to the relationship that often exists between a political party boss and his supporters. The Association's ability to manage its own patronage and obtain favors further obviated the need for structural ties to the General Zionist Party.

Shenkar's personal politics aided the Manufacturers' Association from the early years of independence well into the dominant party period, overshadowing any General Zionist Party efforts. Achievements on such a fundamental issue as tax reform were attributed to the personal dealings of Shenkar with a Mapai-led Government. Since 1949, the Manufacturers' Association had objected to aspects of the income tax law. Among the demands, manufacturers called for revising the method for calculating depreciation of equipment, including, since the devaluation of 1952, a demand to revaluate equipment compatible with the different exchange rate; limiting the company tax rate; lowering the tax rate on profits designated for reinvestment; limiting the maximum tax rate to 50 percent of income subject to tax; reducing the maximum marginal tax rate to 60 percent; and unifying a company tax on profits and an income tax on dividends.

The General Zionists in Government did not make an exceptional effort to achieve tax reform. A tax committee was established at the end of 1954 under General Zionist Deputy Minister of Commerce and Industry, Zalman Suzayev, but when he appeared at an Association Presidium meeting, he claimed that certain issues were not within his committee's jurisdiction. He also was criticized for not having an Association representative on the committee. No significant measures resulted from this committee, and the issue was not addressed again until late 1956, after the General Zionists had left the Government. The Mapai Minister of Commerce and Industry appeared before the Association's Presidium and Executive Committee and promised that recommendations on depreciation, including the matter of revaluating equipment, would be forthcoming by April.[13]

The Manufacturers' Association did not await the Government's fulfillment of its promise but sought input into the process. By January 1957, the Government had appointed a committee, and the Kneset had tax proposals before it. The Manufacturers' Association appeared before the Government committee and at a Kneset Finance Committee session held with Finance Ministry officials present. The Association also submitted a memo to the chairman of the Kneset Finance Committee and to officials in the Finance Ministry.

Association pressure for tax reform intensified in April after the Kneset decided to extend the defense loan. First, Shenkar met with the Ministers of Finance and Commerce and Industry. Then a delegation from the Association met several times with those ministers and with officials of the Finance Ministry. Demands for reform were limited to depreciation and revaluating equipment.

As matters seemed to drag, Shenkar met with the Finance Minister and obtained his agreement to permit revaluating equipment for calculating depreciation. Hailing the agreement as an unprecedented success, the Association attributed it entirely to Shenkar's personal intervention, as one member proclaimed in amazement and gratitude, "In a personal meeting with the minister, the President succeeded in reaching a great financial achievement."[14] Indulging in a bit of self-praise, the President himself thanked Association members for their effort but said that the many meetings had not produced real results.[15] The Manufacturers' Association had scored a victory, one reached without a political party as broker and regarded as an achievement of personal politics.

Although personal politics marked the early period, it was not inevitable that it develop to the wide extent it did. Shenkar's methods and the Association's choice of tactics and targets certainly prolonged the phenomenon. The Association's activities exemplify how an interest group impinging upon the political system can help shape its processes.

According to manufacturers who observed the early period, although personal politics was important and Government ministers played a central policy-making role, the legislature was not powerless, and the potential existed for it to become stronger. The Kneset Finance Committee, for example, had power to approve measures proposed by the Finance Ministry or Government, and manufacturers considered it worthwhile to explain their views to committee members. Articles in *Ha-Ta'asiyyah*, the Association's periodical, including one by a former Kneset member, urged the Manufacturers' Association to make better use of the Kneset.[16] These articles would confirm there were manufacturers who perceived the usefulness of approaching the legislature and that the Association previously had not fully exploited that channel. The Association's restraint stemmed from Shenkar's preference for dealing directly with ministers.[17] To some extent, therefore, a personal trait of Shenkar caused the Manufacturers' Association to minimize its lobbying of Kneset members and to concentrate on influencing Cabinet ministers. The Manufacturers' Association, therefore, is an example of an interest group that not only reacted to power points in the system but under the influence of a strong leader actually helped create those power points. Had Shenkar emphasized the Kneset as well, his actions may have strengthened Kneset members. Instead, he directed his efforts mainly to the ministers, thereby enhancing their role in the system.

Of course, influence and power flow in two directions. Shenkar's method coincided with a mode the Government ministers found convenient. When the politically powerful personages of Pinhas Sapir and Eshkol (both from Mapai) came to occupy the Ministries of Commerce and Industry and Finance, the "club" was complete. Sapir especially was a powerful person in his party and in the Government, and it was comfortable for him to act as a power broker. As a result of these personalities in the Government and the party, the Kneset may have remained a weak institution in any case. There is little doubt, however, that the activities of interest groups such as the Manufacturers' Association contributed to the Kneset's weakness.

Chapter 5

Dominant Party Politics

Bargaining on Small Steps for Change

Closer examination of the illustrative issues reveals other characteristics of group politics that became more distinct within the dominant party phase. Bargaining through personal politics was a main tactic but one that could be employed successfully only on issues that did not involve comprehensive change. Here the Manufacturers' Association could succeed by presenting itself as a limited interest group with which the Government could negotiate and balance against other interest groups in the society. On the tax issue, for example, the Manufacturers' Association originally composed a lengthy list of desired changes in the tax system, some of which, such as the 50 percent tax limitation and the limitation on company tax, would have entailed considerable revamping of the tax structure and philosophy behind it. The Association attained only one aim, however, and that one was limited in scope. Revaluation of equipment was the extent of its victory. That issue appeared as very specific to industry, and the party in power could close such a deal without altering its principles on the distribution of wealth in the country. It also was a sufficiently narrow issue to be handled by two political "bosses." It may not be argued that the Manufacturers' Association produced a long list only as a strategy for obtaining its real desired change because, subsequent to its success, it continued to press for additional amendments.

The dominant party's socialist ideology subtly affected how the Manufacturers' Association perceived itself and presented its interests. It is relatively rare to find references to the private sector of industry even in unpublished minutes. Rather, the Manufacturers' Association presented itself as the defender of the industrial segment of the economy in general. This was not a mere ploy, but the Association actually inculcated this view. The Association understood that in order to succeed it had to narrow its aspirations for economic or social reform but not to the extreme of pressing for the "selfish" interests of private capital. Hence, it could openly promote industry but not the aspect of private gain or motivation. Therefore, when the Manufacturers' Association requested an appearance before the Kneset Finance Committee in March 1961 to oppose a proposed property tax (for industrialists, this meant an inventory tax on equipment, not only a tax on land), it sought a time slot separate from other economic organizations because the Association wanted to emphasize its opposition as industrialists, not as property owners. The strategy was to argue against any injury to industrial profitability.[1]

The stance emphasizing industry was also necessary to counter the then prevailing expression of Zionism as agricultural development. The Manufacturers' Association had to educate the Government and the public to the importance of industry. Once this was accomplished, the Manufacturers' Association hoped the private sector naturally would obtain its due share. Eventually, the Manufacturers' Association gained an ally within the dominant Mapai party sympathetic to industry, and its stress on industrial development in general rather than private capital or private industry enabled it to establish a common line on this point with Mapai and Government.

The nature of the developing cooperative arrangement was most obvious on the cost of living allowance (COLA) issue. To understand the analysis that here follows, it is necessary to understand the COLA system in Israel. Inflation has been a chronic problem, and to compensate labor, there developed the practice of negotiating cost of living allowances in addition to wage agreements. These adjustments were negotiated between the Histadrut and the Manufacturers' Association and were followed by other sectors of the economy. In the early years of the state, such agreements were negotiated rather frequently based upon the rise in the cost of living measured by a detailed point index. The correspondence between the rise in the index and a payment was considered rather automatic.

Although the Government controlled most aspects of the economy, it refused responsibility for negotiating COLA agreements, acting only as a broker, sometimes an influential one, between the Histadrut and the Manufacturers' Association. The Government declined direct responsibility for this area mainly because the Left feared that this could entail measures that would alienate a large part of its constituency. By abdicating its authority, the Government gambled on the Association's ability to obtain an agreement at least equal to one the Government might have concluded. Although acting as labor negotiator might be expected to enhance the Association's power, the Association actually was in a weak position because it was not the country's largest employer and almost always was under pressure to concede.

Although the Manufacturers' Association considered the COLA system inflationary and obstructive to rational fiscal planning and cost control, it usually acquiesced in the arrangement because (1) manufacturers considered a COLA preferable to renegotiating complicated wage agreements, (2) to a certain extent employers favored compensating labor for inflation, and (3) most importantly, the Government usually allowed the COLA payment to be considered when setting prices. From time to time, however, disputes arose not only over the amount of COLA to be paid, but over the value of the system itself, the method of calculation, and responsibility for its negotiation.

Efforts to alter the COLA system became especially intense in 1956 when the index unexpectedly rose soon after the Manufacturers' Association and Histadrut had signed a wage agreement. As the July payment neared, the Presidium met to plan its strategy both on this particular payment and the COLA issue generally. Discussion of both aspects became very interrelated. Although some voices called for completely cancelling COLA, or at least pressing the Government to accept negotiating responsibility, most began to recognize the impossibility and even undesirability of those objectives and suggested instead pressing for two changes originally proposed by the Association in 1953 – calculating COLA semiannually instead of quarterly, and paying when the index change equalled a certain percentage of salary instead of paying for each small increment in the points. Regarding the July payment specifically, opinions varied about paying and signing an agreement. One member envisioned a novel new catalytic role for the Government, suggesting that the Government convene a meeting of all employers to determine a policy for the July COLA payment. Considering this suggestion to be unrealistic, another member explained that a workers' Government would not organize employers. Others supported contacting other organizations that comprised employers without Government participation.

An Association delegation met with the ministers, testing some of the suggestions for Government cooperation. The delegation argued that the Manufacturers' Association was not formally or morally obligated to sign an agreement, could not bear the burden of a payment following the wage increase, and could not be the only organization responsible for such agreements. Manufacturers blamed the

Government's tax policies for having caused the cost of living increase. The delegation perceived the ministers to be in a quandary about how to respond and annoyed about the Association's accusation on taxes. Finance Minister Eshkol explained that although he understood the situation, the Government could become involved only when labor unrest compelled it to enter the dispute.

At this meeting Shenkar injected the issue of credit for industry, thereby hinting at the possibility of some quid pro quo arrangement on COLA. The Minister of Commerce and Industry replied that he was working on the credit matter which was irrelevant to their present discussion. It is interesting that Shenkar raised this issue at all because at an earlier Presidium meeting he had defended the Government's efforts on credit and opposed linking the two matters. Raising the issue indicated the Association's sharpened skill in bargaining.

The Presidium met to discuss the delegation's impressions and to decide on a course of action. Having heard the ministers in effect declare themselves powerless in the face of labor pressure, no one any longer recommended urging the Government to accept sole responsibility for COLA agreements. Manufacturers finally realized they were compelled to accept the negotiating role. In fact, voices now were raised not to allow the matter to leave their hands, and they began considering strategies for strengthening the Association's position, such as forming a more comprehensive organization of employers that would include even cooperative enterprises.[2] The President's moderate opinion of not calling for abolishing the COLA system prevailed, and the meeting ended by selecting a team to negotiate with the Histadrut.

Ministers Eshkol and Sapir tacitly supported the Manufacturers' Association's offer on the July payment by not paying Government workers. A Government payment would have undercut the negotiations and would have precipitated payment by other employers without a written agreement. However, the Histadrut hardened its stance, and the ministers lacked sufficient influence on the union. At a Presidium meeting to assess the COLA negotiations, Weisglass understood that, despite the union's apparent unyielding position, there was an atmosphere for change in the method if not relief on this particular payment because several ministers, staff members of Mapai, and the general public considered COLA a tragedy for the economy. The Association agreed with his assessment that in order to effectively mobilize opposition to the COLA method, the Association must not relinquish negotiating responsibility to the Government but retain the role and provide the Government with support. Therefore, manufacturers continued pressing for changes in the method, and they followed classic negotiating procedure: they requested more than was attainable or even desired, demanding abolition of COLA as a dramatic step designed to screen their more limited aims.

As negotiations became more heated, by August 1956, both sides agreed to compromise. They arranged for the July payment but also agreed to continue negotiating on amending the COLA method. At this point, the Mapai party appointed a committee of Government ministers and Histadrut leaders to examine possible changes in the system. The party and Histadrut devised a system that provided for calculating COLA once in six months and paying if the index rose at least 3 percent of salary, both modifications the Manufacturers' Association had earlier suggested. By February 1957, a new COLA arrangement was signed.

While one might argue that change could occur only once the dominant party so decided, the influence of an outside interest group can not be ignored. This COLA agreement must be regarded as an achievement for the Association. Having preceded by years any Government or party suggestions for change, the Manufacturers' Association continually raised the issue, chiseling away at the status quo. Most likely, it was the Association's suggestions that persuaded the ministers and inspired the party committee.

Although in this case, the ministers had not promised the Association their support in advance, in many COLA fights the Government not only supported the Manufacturers' Association when necessary but pre-coordinated their positions. According to Moshe Levi, an industrial equipment producer and director of the Association's labor committee in 1957, Government ministers often would urge the Manufacturers' Association to be steadfast in COLA or wage negotiations and promised Government help. The Manufacturers' Association then would demand that the Government not make a separate agreement with Government workers which could undermine the Association and would also demand that the Government pressure the Histadrut. The Manufacturers' Association would plan to follow the Government's line. This procedure was not always assured, however. Sometimes, according to Levi, after such an auspicious start, the Government ministers would disappear from the talks under pressure from the Histadrut and their party. Thus, the workers' element within the dominant party exerted pressure upon the Government, and the Government had to sustain a balancing act, sometimes supporting the Manufacturers' Association and sometimes unable to provide sufficient backing.[3] Aware of the Government's role, the Manufacturers'

Association adopted a bargaining tactic, at times agreeing to pay COLA if the Government assured certain conditions, e.g., a price increase, sufficient operating capital, a tax moratorium, etc. Indeed, in 1961, the Manufacturers' Association took advantage of its agreement on COLA to complain to the Minister of Commerce and Industry about illogical tax policies (there had been a tax on equipment that year) and the shortage of operating capital.[4] The Manufacturers' Association abandoned attempts at sweeping economic reform, realizing that only certain issues could be addressed and in a piecemeal manner.

Rather than take responsibility for fashioning a comprehensive economic policy, the Government, as broker, negotiated among groups. The Government actually might stress to labor the manufacturers' difficulties as the Minister of Commerce and Industry claimed he did in 1961.[5] On the other hand, the Government might convince the manufacturers to concede on COLA and wage agreements and enable them to do so by providing for sufficient operating capital, by agreeing not to raise certain taxes, or by agreeing to a price increase. The Government then might attempt to curb the inflationary impact of a COLA by taxing the sum. The Government also retained a measure of leverage over manufacturers. Manufacturers sometimes feared that if they refused to absorb COLA, the Government might constrict the flow of operating capital. Although the Government relieved itself of direct responsibility for COLA, it actually enmeshed itself in a complicated web of economic policies. The burden the Government accepted upon itself was highlighted in the COLA argument of 1961. After protracted negotiations, when the Manufacturers' Association temporarily relinquished its aim for a once-a-year payment and agreed to pay COLA in July, which the Government then favored in order to calm labor unrest prior to elections, Sapir promised the Presidium to do everything possible to prevent an index rise even if it meant subsidizing chicken![6]

Although not always receiving the exact COLA agreement or Government support it desired, the Manufacturers' Association realized that Government ministers frequently acted to the extent politically possible, so that Zalman Suzayev, a carton producer and President of the Manufacturers' Association, in 1968 could confirm the essential accuracy of a news report that accused the Government of first "softening up" the labor union before the union sat with the Manufacturers' Association.[7] Thus, the Association perceived the benefit of influencing the Government from the outside while offering its collaboration when expedient. Manufacturers realized they could attain certain goals when Government ministers supported them and pressed their cause within the Mapai party and Government but actually could lose influence by imposing the entire burden upon the Government which would invite greater labor pressure. The reciprocal relationship between the Manufacturers' Association and Government was facilitated especially by the interest that Pinhas Sapir, who from 1955–1974 almost always held the portfolio for commerce and industry or finance or both, assumed in industrial development. In relating Sapir's innovative idea for establishing a financing instrument between Israeli industrialists and American investors, Shenkar could wax euphoric about the Association's close relations with Sapir: "We help him and he helps industry to the extent he is able."[8]

With a minister who championed industrial development, the Manufacturers' Association felt free to stress the more particularistic aspect of industry, the private sector. It endeavored to ensure that private enterprises received a fair share of any benefits allocated to industry in general. The sectoral and bargaining approach the ministers and group had heretofore developed for handling economic and political issues enabled the Manufacturers' Association to succeed not only in its claims on behalf of private industry but in its claim for recognition as that sector's representative. The group already deemed qualified by the Government for directing COLA negotiations was also recognized and strengthened as the general representative of private industry. In 1964, for example, a sum of money was allocated to the Manufacturers' Association for distribution to its members for operating capital loans.

An Override on Partisanship: Committee Politics and Experiments in Limited Corporatism

Although the Manufacturers' Association developed a rather comfortable, reciprocal relationship with the Minister of Commerce and Industry, who served as industry's spokesman in the Government which increasingly became the main arena for decisions, it never wanted to rely completely upon that arrangement, which was inherently tenuous because it depended upon a sympathetic personality. The Manufacturers' Association endeavored to institutionalize the relationship and create a cohesive industrial interest without regard for ownership arrangement and divorced from party politics. It continued to act as an industrial interest group, but by pressing for a more formal, consultative relationship, it sought to affect governmental procedures.

To a certain extent, the Government was receptive to some of these aims, realizing the need to reduce the polemical rhetoric surrounding economic issues. Precedents existed for an apolitical or corporatist approach to decision-making. On a variety of issues, not only industrial, the Government deferred decision-making to committees, sometimes narrowly interministerial but sometimes composed broadly of experts, politicians, and interest group representatives. Even interministerial committees accepted memoranda and heard testimony from groups. Committees usually were established to fairly implement a policy decision, but there were instances of committees recommending basic policy as well. Committee recommendations often were implemented or formed a working basis for a program. In this respect, the committees served as safety valves for ideological politics. Persons of principle could save face by accepting a committee's decision (What do you want from me? The experts said ...). Instances of this abound, such as the already discussed Lehman Committee on linking loans, and encompassed tax policies, credit policies, and even water policies.

Expanding upon the committee concept to apply to comprehensive industrial policy issues and hoping to establish a permanent consultative role for industry and the Manufacturers' Association, Shenkar proposed establishing an industrial advisory council in 1953. Mapai Minister Sapir eventually, although somewhat reluctantly, established an Industrial Council in 1958.

The Council never became the broad and consultative body envisioned by the Association, and its scope and achievements were limited. After the Council's inaugural session, Dr. A. Rafaeli, a pencil manufacturer from Jerusalem, prophetically noted that the Association had believed the Council would examine the burdens on industry, try to find solutions, and bolster the Ministry of Commerce and Industry vis-à-vis other offices, but instead, on the first day, the Council was presented with the issue of reducing protection of local industry by permitting imports.[9] He advised that if they wanted the "forum to do more than just legitimize decisions of the Government," manufacturers must demand that it be the "place where industrial problems are discussed and solved."[10]

Indeed, the consultative nature of the Council soon was called into question. In March 1958, the Government, in need of revenue, had announced new customs on certain raw materials. The measure coincided with discussions on establishing the Industrial Council, and

Shenkar obtained a promise from the Minister of Commerce and Industry that customs would be one of the Council's first topics and that any future imposts would not be imposed without first discussing them in the Council. Nevertheless, the Government announced new customs in September, and the Manufacturers' Association was reduced to fighting in the Council for their abolition or reduction. Portentous for future Council deliberations, in that fight, the Manufacturers' Association was hindered by a cooperative sector representative who explained that as a Mapai party member he understood the Government's need for revenue and therefore he favored a compromise on the amount rather than complete abolition.

The Manufacturers' Association was not entirely free of blame for the Council's course, for the Association was not always united in its position on issues. On the issue of liberalizing imports, for example, the Manufacturers' Association was split and therefore poorly coordinated its policy. The Industrial Council petered out within two years, leaving only an advisory committee on the protection of local products.

The Government's original ambivalence to the Council had never disappeared. The early experiment in corporatism failed, mainly due to the Government's inability to plan comprehensive policy. Although the Manufacturers' Association's uncoordinated approach to several problems may have contributed to the Council's demise and convinced the minister that such a body would not enhance his office, it seems a self-fulfilling prophecy operated. The Government was never fully committed to a comprehensive council, did not develop an economic plan, continued to conduct economic policy in a piecemeal fashion as it had prior to the Council, and on the whole, the Manufacturers' Association merely reacted to the attenuated agenda allowed by the Government.

Further Calls for Corporatism

After Shenkar died in September 1959, the Manufacturers' Association experienced a crisis of purpose. To cope with the shock, the Association closed ranks, altering its internal governing procedures to provide for electing the President on a narrower base, by the Presidium instead of by the General Assembly. His title, appropriately, was changed to Chairman of the Presidium. Nevertheless, the Association had a turnover of three leaders within five years. A declining membership engendered discussion within the organization. Several persons urged upgrading the group's level of concern and activity from the personal "interventionism" Shenkar had pursued. They suggested seeking a recognized formal role from the Government which would agree to enhance their organization by providing certain services only to Manufacturers' Association members or through the Association.[11] Although the Government desired a counterweight to the Histadrut, it never went so far as to formally "incorporate" the Manufacturers' Association. After the abortive Industrial Council experiment, the Manufacturers' Association was relegated back to its place as representing one contained economic sector.

Nevertheless, the Manufacturers' Association did not abandon its efforts to be included in decision-making, at least to be consulted in order to prevent any "surprises," as Yehudah Barnatan, first Association chairman after Shenkar, described the quest.[12] In this period of transition, the Association also experimented with more extreme tactics usually not associated with a businessman's group. The liberalization of imports issue illustrates the group's continual process of defining its aims and tactics.

As previously noted, the body remaining from the Industrial Council was a public advisory committee on protecting local products, and on this committee the Association attempted to maintain more than a rubber stamp role. To understand the following analysis, the import system and the Association's position on tariff liberalization require amplification. At the establishment of the state, import-export activity was tightly regulated under a licensing system, with industry enjoying a high level of protection. The Government sought to institute a tariff system, hoping eventually to lower tariffs in order to make local products internationally competitive and qualified for export. The Manufacturers' Association was divided between those who feared their enterprises would be harmed by competition and those who believed the step necessary despite some possible unfortunate consequences. At the least, the Association wanted to ensure that private industry was not rendered vulnerable while Government and Histadrut industry remained protected. The Association, therefore, allowed those members inclined toward protection to conduct the organization's policy. The entire Association, however, was concerned with procedure and Government relations.

The new import policy was not pressed until spring 1962, when the Government, without consulting with the committee or the Association, published a list of goods on which tariffs would be lowered. Quickly protesting the Government's highhanded manner, the Presidium negotiated with the Ministers of Finance and Commerce and Industry and secured their agreement that all items proposed for tariff reduction would be brought before the public committee for approval. In August the Association again objected to the Government's procedure for selecting products. According to the Association's understanding of the agreement, items considered for tariff reduction were first to be submitted to a trade subcommittee which would then pass recommendations to the advisory committee. The Manufacturers' Association contended that the Government bypassed the trade subcommittee and also did not follow principles established for selecting items. Not achieving satisfaction on the group's procedural suggestions, Association representatives walked out of an advisory committee meeting, a rather bold step for the Association. Gone was Shenkar, the conciliatory mediator. Although later presidents also were mild-mannered, they allowed other, more vocal members to take leading roles, and as a result, those members tested new, more drastic tactics.

A revised procedure and criteria for selecting items were in place by September. The Association was included on a committee to compile a list of items for tariff reduction. Subsequent Government tariff measures continually engendered new rounds of proposals, protests, and boycotts by manufacturers and the creation of reconciliation committees.

The operation of the committee system for industrial protection must receive mixed reviews. The Government realized it could not impose policies without the group's cooperation and acquiescence and therefore established committees to set procedures and resolve disputes. The committees operated rather effectively for limited time periods, although the group continually struggled to meaningfully participate. The Government did not seem to use the committees as effectively as it might have had it submitted proposed tariff reductions to them directly and in advance. Especially because the organization was ambivalent toward protection, policies and processes may have been arranged with less friction. Of course, one might question why the Government should cooperate with a group that would seek to prevent or delay change, but a purpose of the committees was exactly to alleviate that problem, attempting to achieve change via discussion, cooperation, and planning.

As a manufacturers' group, the Association, of course, acted for industrial protection, but via a particularistic issue, it also pressed for opening up the decision-making process. In an administrative system where not all Government measures required parliamentary approval, the committees served as substitute forums where interests and concerns could be expressed, and the Manufacturers' Association was a prime mover in establishing and expanding those procedures.

Undaunted by the limited role of the tariff liberalization committee, the Manufacturers' Association endeavored to further consolidate the industrial interest and the organization's place in policy setting. Actually, the protection issue impressed the Manufacturers' Association with the need for overall, rational, and equitable planning. Recognizing the absurdity and inequity of attempting to lower tariffs on finished goods while for fiscal reasons imposing customs on raw materials and other items, manufacturers realized that tax, tariff, wage, and other policies all required coordination. First floating the idea in 1965, Suzayev, the new head of the Manufacturers' Association, persuaded a reluctant Minister of Commerce and Industry to establish an Industrial Forum composed of representatives of industry from all sectors of the economy—private, cooperative, and state-owned. The first session was held in May 1966 when branch committees were established to develop plans for targeted industries. The Forum was slow in taking off, and when the Government promulgated a New Economic Policy to lift the economy out of recession in 1966, it did not present its position through this body. And to no avail, the Manufacturers' Association suggested that a 1966 order reducing tariff protection be referred to the Forum. With a new Minister of Commerce and Industry, Zev Sharf, taking office in December 1966, Suzayev had to reargue the case. A Forum session was held during the first quarter of 1967, and the branch committees were reactivated for a brief time.

Ironically, the protective tariff issue, which the Manufacturers' Association in 1958 had complained was a relatively narrow issue and one of the few the Government permitted to reach the Industrial Council's agenda, became the focal point on which the Association pressed its "consultation rights" in the Industrial Forum. In September 1968, when the Government, without prior warning, announced a relatively large tariff reduction effective by January 1969, Suzayev considered it an achievement that the Government promised to make no further reductions in 1969 and to bring future tariff matters to the Industrial Forum for discussion. Suzayev's pet project did not progress much further, and in an interview in 1979, his perception was that the Industrial Forum had never been established![13]

These forays into corporatism may be understood as attempts by a group to expand the decision-making process, circumventing and substituting for the political party system. While the Manufacturers' Association did not formally align with a political camp, the group was not oblivious to and unaffected by political developments of the time, and the Forum formed part of that response. The Left's consolidations in 1965 and 1968, although interpreted by political observers as something less than a sign of strength, were noted by several manufacturers with trepidation, as they anticipated "radical changes on the basis of the deep and political strength of the Labor Party."[14]

Not only the political party alignments alarmed the Manufacturers' Association. Manufacturers also feared that within the Government itself the further Left elements were becoming ascendant, as evinced by the Minister of Labor's backing of a package of social welfare legislation in 1965, and that "their" Ministry of Commerce and Industry was unable to protect their interests. To meet this challenge, they established a Coordinating Bureau of Economic Organizations, another Suzayev initiative, thereby following the advice of one member that "in a democracy, where all is organization and pressure groups, [we] must organize."[15] The Coordinating Bureau brought together representatives of private sector groups such as the Farmers' Organization, Center of Builders and Contractors, Organization of Banks, Chambers of Commerce, Organization of General Merchants, and others. The Coordinating Bureau theoretically aspired to unite the private sector of the economy, but it operated effectively primarily on employers' matters, with the Manufacturers' Association acting as a main driving force. By establishing the Coordinating Bureau, the Manufacturers' Association resolved its long time concern that it not be the only group responsible for labor issues.

During Suzayev's term, the Manufacturers' Association also attended to strengthening its own organization. The Association renamed its head as President, instead of Chairman of the Presidium, and broadened the base for his election by transferring that function to the Executive Committee from the Presidium. (In 1972, the base was further widened when the General Assembly was empowered to elect the President.) An office of Vice-President also was instituted, chosen by the Presidium. Thus, internally and through the Coordinating Bureau, the Manufacturers' Association attempted to enhance its position vis-à-vis the Government, while at the same time it attempted to fortify its position within the governmental framework through the Industrial Forum.

These consolidating movements among interest groups coincided with consolidating movements among political parties of the Right. Noting that some of the same persons were active in both realms, it is tempting to attribute a grand political party scheme to these consolidations. However, it seems these activities were parallel and not connected, their coincidental development stemming from individuals active in both spheres. Thus, Suzayev, who in 1953 had been the General Zionist Deputy Minister for Commerce and Industry, continued active in party affairs and was credited with facilitating the alignment in 1965 of the Herut and Liberal parties. Upon heading the Manufacturers' Association, coincidentally also in 1965, he perceived a similar need for consolidation and greater strength in the group's two main areas of concern – industrial interests and employers' interests. He expressed his hope of establishing an organization representing industry from all sectors and an organization of employers, and these were realized with the Industrial Forum and the Coordinating Bureau.[16]

Neither the Forum nor the Bureau was viewed as the start of a new political front, and it would be incorrect to assume that connection between Suzayev's political and group roles. On the whole, the Manufacturers' Association aimed to negotiate, consult, and cooperate with the Government from a position of strength and respect. In fact, Suzayev's conciliatory attitude, especially on the protective tariff issue, brought him into conflict with his own group. At the Association's annual meeting in 1968, the membership did not endorse Suzayev's arrangement with the minister on the tariff issue and voted to demand cancelling the proposed January tariff reduction. At a Presidium discussion about extricating the organization and its President from the embarrassing predicament, one member noted positively that Suzayev was a compromising type, eager to cooperate and loyal to the regime of the day, whatever its composition.[17] Under Suzayev, the Manufacturers' Association sought a cooperative and consultative voice with the Government and sought to strengthen itself in order to merit receiving that position.

Prudent Party Politics

By fostering the development of cooperative councils the Manufacturers' Association did not altogether sever its connections with parties. Indeed, manufacturers at times appealed to, or consulted with, what they called "parties close to us" or "citizens' parties." Nevertheless, they usually were not the initiators in raising an issue to the political party plane and did not consistently call upon one party for support. When an opportunity arose, however, to have a voice on an issue or influence policy through a political party, they did not reject the chance.

The political party route was an additional channel of communication that they endeavored to keep open. Thus, in a report to the Presidium by Manufacturers' Association labor committee chairman Levi on progress in COLA negotiations toward July 1966, "parties close to us" was on a list of several targets to whom the Manufacturers' Association had explained its case in "informal meetings." Other listed targets were the Minister of Labor, Finance Minister, Minister of Commerce and Industry, and members of the Histadrut.[18] Similarly, in 1961, a Manufacturers' Association representative met with a number of "citizens' parties" regarding a draft law in the Kneset on retirement compensation to workers, but the Association also awaited Minister of Commerce and Industry Sapir's return from abroad to contact him. "Look," explained Levi, who was adamant to the point of anger at any suggestion that Association policy was in any way party directed,

> here I want to clarify this further. The Manufacturers' Association or the Coordinating Bureau is composed of persons from different political parties. So, it is clear that at a time we are conducting difficult negotiations with the Histadrut and ... we request help from the Government, ... we speak to all sorts of persons directly or indirectly who are in the Government or the Kneset so they will help us apply pressure on the Government so she will help us.[19]

A discussion of the role of the non-socialist parties and the Manufacturers' Association's connection with them becomes intertwined with the role of the Kneset and Kneset members because the Manufacturers' Association's connections with the non-socialist parties seemed to afford the group the most benefit by facilitating the group's appearances before Kneset committees. The Kneset Economic Committee (distinguished from the Finance Committee) customarily was chaired by one of the opposition parties, providing a platform for expression of varied views, and certain subcommittees of other Kneset committees were headed by non-socialist parties. (I am using the term non-socialist rather than opposition parties here because one such party, the Progressive Party, later called Independent Liberals, usually occupied one seat in Labor coalition Governments.) Although not all Association appearances were arranged or suggested by the non-socialist parties, at times, certain Kneset members of those parties who interested themselves in industrial and economic affairs kept the Manufacturers' Association informed and invited the Association when appropriate. When it deemed a Kneset appearance useful, the Manufacturers' Association accepted these offers.

In its approaches to the Kneset, the Manufacturers' Association did not follow party lines. As Barnatan, Association Chairman of the Presidium 1960–1962, explained,

> The appearance itself was before the entire committee. ... Prior to the appearance there would be discussion with individuals, but I wouldn't say of a particular party. There would be discussion with individuals of the committee in order to influence them to influence the decision of the committee.

When questioned whether the party of a Kneset member affected the Manufacturers' Association's decision to target him, revealingly Barnatan replied,

> I think yes. There are *ezrahiot* [citizens'] parties and socialist parties, and surely, the ezrahiot parties would be more helpful. No, I correct myself. Until the Begin Government, the Labor Party was in power. But in the Labor Party there are persons with different outlooks. There is the Histadrut, and the Histadrut also has industry. So there were many joint interests. We would meet with a Labor Party person or a Histadrut person who had an "open heart."[20]

The Manufacturers' Association thereby developed a true lobbying effort, attempting to build support with anyone who held a common interest across party lines.

The Manufacturers' Association often regarded political parties as occupying a completely separate realm, driven by their own imperatives without intrinsic interest for the group's concerns. When a party's interests incidentally coincided with those of the group, the Association benefited however possible, but the Association did not seek party support nor regard it as reliable. Indicative of the group's attitude, when asked why the Independent Liberals and National Religious Party in the coalition had defended the Association's position on a COLA dispute in 1967, Levi replied that many times parties defended the group's views but "they didn't do it out of concern for the economy but against the Alignment that was in the Government. ... Always there were all sorts of reasons."[21] In fact, ironically, when COLA and wage issues for 1966–1967, the period of recession, reached the political party arena, Finance Minister Sapir contacted the Manufacturers' Association appealing for a compromise in order to prevent Mapam, a party to the left of Mapai, from bringing down the Government.[22] Moreover, the Manufacturers' Association did not act to obtain any one party's support, as Levi emphasized, "I'll say again and again no. ... I only hope that this thing [any implication of party connection] is finished."

While avoiding formal party affiliation and engendering discussion on issues across party lines rather than appealing to a particular party, the Manufacturers' Association did not spurn party initiated offers of support nor reject any contact. Within the General Zionist/ Liberal Party, one party member, Yosef Sapir, took upon himself an interest in economic and industrial matters, and the Manufacturers' Association maintained continual contact with him. When, for example, in November 1969 Sapir promised Association President Mark Moshevitz, who also was active in the Liberal Party, that if he (Sapir) became Minister of Commerce and Industry in the National Unity Government he would create a "brain trust" on industrial matters and would establish a close relationship with the Manufacturers' Association, Presidium members were willing to meet his request to suggest candidates and were especially eager to influence the selection of the ministry's director-general. It must be noted that such a discussion was rather irregular for the Association, and, always fearful of being stigmatized as party aligned, members realized that any recommendations would have to be made "delicately."[23] There is no recorded follow-up discussion. (Yosef Sapir received the appointment, but as the grand coalition broke up less than a year thereafter, there was not much time in which to carry out this plan, and further observations are therefore impossible.) Basically, the Manufacturers' Association accepted any advantage offered but did not as a group help any particular party gain votes or Government portfolios. The Manufacturers' Association thus conducted a prudent political course, keeping all options open in order to promote its interest but not becoming overly, overtly, or officially embroiled with any one political camp.

Chapter 6

A Continuing Spearhead for Change

After 1967: High Hopes for Policy Change

In the euphoria following the June 1967 war and the end of the recession, the Manufacturers' Association, like the rest of the nation, expected, or believed possible, major transformations at least in the country's economic structure and acted to ensure itself a leading role in any new regime that might emerge. The Association presented plans for the whole economy, not just as a strategy for achieving smaller gains but really believing that the wider aims could be achieved.

Perceiving the tax system as the piston driving all other aspects of the economy – investment incentives, labor relations, price controls, and so forth – the Association proposed major tax reform, rather a tax upheaval, not only benefits for business, although they were included. Understanding that comprehensive change could not be achieved by bargaining with ministers or bureaucrats and bewildered about the significance of realignments within the Left and the authority assigned to ministers in the National Unity Government, the manufacturers addressed themselves directly to the Prime Minister, who then was Eshkol, formerly the Finance Minister for many years. Taking this move seriously, they carefully contemplated proposals, concentrating on taxation but commenting on other economic policies as well, and drafted a letter to the head of Government.

Before sending the letter, they conferred with Pinhas Sapir, then the Finance Minister, who attended a Presidium meeting to review the memorandum. Such an advisory session was not the first in Manufacturers' Association history and exemplifies a characteristic relationship between many groups and ministers. Ministers who supported certain policies established connections with groups, advising them on how to present and achieve their aims and arguing on their behalf within the Government.

In their letter, the manufacturers suggested freeing the movement of foreign currency, reducing general income tax, revising tax rates to reduce the steepness at the mid-levels, reducing indirect taxes which they claimed were confusing and discouraging to foreign investors, reducing Government intervention in everyday business operations, and eliminating the sectoral split of the economy into Histadrut, Government, and private sectors.[1] They followed up their written approach by meeting with the Prime Minister and the economic ministers.

After all this energetic activity, the Manufacturers' Association, to its disappointment, was permitted to deal with the Finance Minister only on limited reforms for business. The Government still was not prepared to contemplate comprehensive change or to abandon its piecemeal way of dealing with group demands. Despite its inability to achieve far-reaching reform, the Manufacturers' Association accepted what changes it could obtain and attempted to ensure its voice in the decision-making process by participating in a committee under the Finance Minister to examine several tax amendments relevant to business. Several ameliorations in business taxes were enacted in 1968.

Undeterred by the less than comprehensive change in the tax system, the Manufacturers' Association continued to present ideas for the whole economy, largely at the initiative of Moshevitz (best known as the head of a chocolate and confection company) who revived the tradition of Shenkar in becoming the prime mover of the organization. At the end of 1969, when the Government sought to cover its deficit and workers simultaneously demanded a wage increase, Moshevitz suggested that workers be paid part of the increase in bonds, while manufacturers would promise not to raise prices, and the Government not to increase taxes. This "package deal," as it became known, would supply the Government with revenue, satisfy labor's need to demonstrate it had achieved an increase and yet not immediately exacerbate inflation.

Although some manufacturers believed it was the province of the Government and the political parties to be concerned about the state of the whole economy, Moshevitz argued, "It is a small economy, and we are part of it. If we can arrive at a situation that they will consult with us and that we will have something to tell, I think we don't have to sit and wait."[2] He argued that a tripartite conciliatory agreement was preferable to the past system of wage negotiations, whereby manufacturers awaited the labor union's announced position, the Association reacted, and negotiations led to a cycle of wage and price increases. The time had come, according to Moshevitz, to change the negotiating process from the present pattern where the manufacturers sat with the Histadrut and said, "you will say thus, and I will say thus and in the end we will reach some monkey-business and in public we will yell one at the other and at the end we will make an agreement and compromise."[3]

A later Manufacturers' Association President, Avraham Shavit, a manufacturer of ovens, described a similar arrangement:

> You see, there's a lot of staging, show, and dramatics in negotiation. So, you can sit down with the Secretary-General of the Histadrut, and we know exactly where we are going to and then decide on the level of noise that each one needs. If it's stronger opposition, I'll give it to him. ... And then we call up each other and say it's about the time, so you say tomorrow we are going to meet, and we meet.

Nevertheless, Shavit argued, "It's not betraying or giving your interests away on both sides. I don't want to give that impression. But there is responsibility on both sides. We know what the country can give."[4] This defense notwithstanding, the stylized posturing that preceded wage agreements seemed absurd even to the participants. Policy had become a complicated web, with each side composed of many different elements with different expectations of their respective leaders. It is significant that a group leader initiated the call for cutting that web, perceiving there could be a better way.

Government Disarray, Group Setback and Disappointment

The political disarray, crisis of confidence, and aura of suspicion that enveloped the nation after the surprise October 1973 war naturally affected relations between the Government and groups, as well as relations among groups. Anticipating difficulties, the Government resorted to the committee method for setting policy, establishing a Committee for Planning the Economy for 1974 composed of subcommittees headed by professors, Government ministers, and group representatives. Never vested with authoritative responsibility for devising policy, this committee served only as an additional arena where groups presented demands and vented frustrations, a façade for the ministers' usual backroom bargaining and manipulation. This time, however, those methods backfired, overcome by the distrust of groups toward the Government and each other. Although the Manufacturers' Association continued recommending cooperative efforts and comprehensive reform, it, too, was caught up in the deterioration. Without a strong Government, the dynamic of cooperation between Government and manufacturers' group diminished.

The year 1974 opened with negotiations between the Histadrut and the Manufacturers' Association on a cost of living allowance via a subcommittee under Hayyim Gvati, Minister of Agriculture. Finance Minister Sapir played his usual backstage role of professing non-involvement while prodding the sides to conclude an agreement, which they did on January 24. Sapir had hinted to the Manufacturers' Association to expect developments in the economy and therefore to conclude an agreement before any changes occurred, but no one anticipated the explosion of discontent that followed the Government's announcement on January 29 cancelling certain food subsidies. Sapir had planned these measures outside of the economic committee, presenting it as a fait accompli. However, he misjudged the response of all sides. Sapir had promised labor compensation by a COLA, but labor demanded a larger payment than the minister had planned. The minister also miscalculated the Manufacturers' Association's reaction to his deal, expecting the Association to agree to an additional COLA payment but back him on the lower amount. The Manufacturers' Association, however, opposed subverting the COLA system to compensate for higher taxes or other fluctuations in the economy. It was also outraged that the Government's new policy and labor's COLA demand followed almost immediately upon the signing of a previous COLA agreement, thereby undermining its long fought for system of semiannual COLA negotiations, and was upset at what it perceived as a separate arrangement between Government and labor on the matter. The Manufacturers' Association demanded that the three sides cooperatively work out a comprehensive arrangement on economic problems, but this cooperation never materialized. Expecting to be compensated by a price increase and concerned to keep wage agreements in force, the Manufacturers' Association eventually agreed to pay a COLA, as the Government already had, as an advance against the payment due in July.

Perceiving that the recent turmoil in the economy was tied to the political uncertainty and consequent Government weakness, Association President Moshevitz initially hoped that the replacement of Meir by Rabin as Prime Minister in June 1974 would stabilize the situation. Moshevitz called for concentrating on the economic and social situation rather than party topics. In his first test as economic broker, the new Finance Minister, Yehoshua Rabinovitz, did not prove successful in implementing the Government's proposed policy, and the Manufacturers' Association felt somewhat deceived and disadvantaged among the economic and political forces in the country. The Government in July 1974 proposed a series of anti-inflation measures designed to absorb excess liquidity in the economy, including a tax on COLA payments and a compulsory employers' loan. When the Histadrut objected to the COLA tax, the Government backed down but proceeded with the measure upon employers.

Although the Government usually conducted economic policy in a piecemeal fashion, Government measures to raise revenue and control inflation while reducing some unpopular effects on labor seemed especially ad hoc throughout 1974 and into 1975. In addition to the July measures, in November the Government devalued the currency and again reduced subsidies and in February 1975 imposed another employers' tax. The Manufacturers' Association might have contented itself with ensuring only its piece of the pie by demanding a price increase parallel to the wage and tax rises, but, while not ignoring that aspect, it recognized the overdue need for a more meaningful comprehensive approach. The Government measures, which prompted street demonstrations by discontented citizens, spurred the Manufacturers' Association to seek overall change in the tax and COLA systems.

On COLA, the Manufacturers' Association took the lead in examining the subject, appointing its own internal committee in July 1974, which by August recommended extracting certain items from the measure of the cost of living such as indirect taxes, price increases occurring abroad, and changes in the exchange rate. Following the November Government decisions, labor again requested a compensatory COLA, but by then, even the Histadrut leader expressed a need for a more "up to date cost of living structure."[5] In April 1975 a committee with Government and interest group economists was established, known as the Zusman Committee, to examine COLA issues, including devising a new measure of the cost of living. The committee concluded its work by July, and among its suggestions proposed that the cost of living allowance reflect only 70 percent of the price rise. The committee's suggested principles were applied beginning April 1976.

Although the change dampened conflict over COLA, there was no decline in the volume of noise and almost constant haggling surrounding labor relations which, unusually, were not fully resolved by election time 1977. The Finance Minister, meeting separately with the Histadrut without consulting the Manufacturers' Association, alienated the Association and could not obtain its agreement to a three month "package deal" of a price, tax, and wage freeze. The Manufacturers' Association did not think the short period constituted a real package deal but was only a stopgap measure to survive the elections. Strikes were rampant, and the situation became so severe that the Manufacturers' Association requested a meeting with the Prime Minister. Eventually, the Government agreed separately to a wage increase for public sector employees, and then, the acting Prime Minister arranged a compromise between the Histadrut and Manufacturers' Association which was not finalized until after the elections.

On tax reform, the Manufacturers' Association was also deeply disappointed. In response to the various revenue raising measures that the Government proposed throughout 1974 and 1975, the Manufacturers' Association urged imposing a value added tax (VAT) at a high enough rate that myriad smaller annoying taxes could be eliminated. Following the furor over the Government tax proposals in July 1974, Finance Minister Rabinovitz promised a VAT would be implemented by April 1975 along with other tax reforms. When a VAT finally was worked out and implemented by the summer of 1976, it was imposed at a lower rate than originally considered, insufficient to eliminate certain indirect taxes.

In its attempts to be a spearhead for change, the Manufacturers' Association was not completely successful, neither on specific measures nor on reforming the decision-making process so it would be automatically included. However, the group never abandoned the struggle to suggest and set policy or to be considered the consultative partner to Government. On narrower issues, such as limiting the size of a tax or achieving a price increase, the Association, as in previous periods, still could succeed, acting within the mold to which the Government confined it. The Government continued to feel comfortable setting policy by negotiating with groups, and on this level the Manufacturers' Association achieved a recognized place in the process.

After 1977: A New Government but Whither the Group?

To lay to rest once and for all the notion of any special connection between any political party and the Manufacturers' Association, one need only note that after the Likud victory in the 1977 elections, the Association's reaction was characterized more by uncertainty than by rejoicing, uncertainty as to policy and procedure that the new Government might follow. The Association was cautiously optimistic that the Government could be convinced to conduct a concerted policy supporting industry and entertained again its perennial hopes of becoming Government's "partner" in the effort. Immediately after the elections, in preparation for its annual meeting, the Manufacturers' Association drew up two documents, one dealing with industrial development and another with labor relations. Its strategy was to focus the Government's attention on the balance of payments problem rather than on inflation, and it proposed a series of measures designed to encourage investment and industrial development.[6] Gradually, however, the Manufacturers' Association perceived that its position vis-à-vis the Government would not be much different from that in the past—that of a tolerated, even respected, advisory agency and negotiator on industrial and economic issues, but not a sought-after consultant nor a full partner in economic planning. It would have to continue presenting and pressing its views on many separate issues and on many fronts.

The Association received an inkling of its proposed place from the procedure the Government followed when taking economic steps in July 1977. As Manufacturers' Association President Shavit reported to the Presidium, "There was prior notification as in the past. The behavior of the minister was not different from the behavior of ministers in the past. He did not transmit exact information, but the minister informed [generally] on what he intended to do."[7] Thus, the new Government was not forging any new patterns of activity. The Manufacturers' Association was regarded as sufficiently important to merit communication and information but did not become a full consultative partner to Government or acquire any special status.

The Association did not abandon its aim of involvement in policymaking, however, and in the hope of becoming the Government's partner was ready to sacrifice in areas important to it such as credit. Although the Manufacturers' Association pressed for subsidized credit, when the Government proposed changing credit policies with a view to eventually reducing subsidization, the Manufacturers' Association decided to accept the proposed package, hoping that in the long run it would be considered an important cooperative factor in economic planning and attain other industrial aims.

Although this Government in one startling swoop instituted rather comprehensive liberal economic measures—most notably, removing controls on foreign currency, floating the Israeli pound, reducing import duties and levies, and reducing subsidies and the purchase tax on many products—ironically, their dénouement proved problematic for the Association. The Association objected both to the substance of some of the proposals and to the Government's procedures for relating to the group. As at previous times when currency was devalued, the Government saw no alternative to imposing an inventory tax. Moreover, believing that as a result of floating the pound and freeing the movement of foreign currency, supply and demand would resolve all problems of capital and foreign exchange, the Government eliminated export subsidies and froze credit.

The Manufacturers' Association became increasingly dismayed at the Government's apparent lack of understanding of these problems and the Government's indifference to working out systematic procedures for relating to the group. At a Presidium meeting with Finance Minister Simha Ehrlich, Association President Shavit said that although he understood that prior to the announcement consultation had not been possible, there should have been some contact since that time. The Finance Minister promised some remedies for the credit situation and for problems caused by the inventory tax, but they were insufficient to overcome what manufacturers perceived as a developing disastrous situation in the areas of export and credit.[8] Faced with a Minister of Commerce and Industry who informed them, "I don't intend to sit once a month and ask what topics are bothering you and then go with you to the Finance Minister,"[9] manufacturers were almost in a state of despair. Under the previous Labor Government, the Ministry of Commerce and Industry was their expected channel of communication, recognized as such by the Government and party in power, and that channel under the new Government appeared to be closing.

Dramatizing the manufacturers' dismay, Shavit denounced the Government's proposed budget in December as "non-Zionist."[10] The Government's budget, the minister's attitude, and the apparent lack of Government understanding about the detrimental effects on industry of the economic reform measures all confirmed the Association's perception that this Government was not about to adopt the Manufacturers' Association's ideas for directing the economy nor include it as a full partner in the effort. "There's no one to talk to," Shavit complained to the Presidium, explaining the decline in power of the Ministry of Commerce and Industry and expressing especial concern about the Deputy Minister of Finance, whom he regarded as naively applying grand liberal economic theories blind to the consequences for the country's specific industrial situation. "Someone has to say what is happening here," said Shavit when planning to meet with the Ministers of Finance and Commerce and Industry and the Governor of the Bank of Israel to request action on solving export and credit problems.[11]

Finally realizing that its strategic aim would not be embraced by the Government, the Manufacturers' Association changed tactics, acting on the suggestion of two Presidium members who advised, "We have to see things as when the other Government was in power,"[12] meaning to pressure individuals in the Government and to work piecemeal on achieving items important for the industrial agenda. Reporting on a meeting with the Finance Minister, Shavit repeated his impression of the Government's ineptitude and explained his new tactic:

> I am not sure they know what to do. ... I am simply trying here to go as a small interested party and 'bite off' pieces and gain for industry. ... They threw out all the instruments. It is impossible to speak about reinstating incentives [for export] and not about directed credit [for operating capital]. Come, let us first of all take what is possible and we will see what happens.[13]

Working along these lines, Shavit and the Finance Minister agreed in principle on several items: (1) industry would pay less tax, (2) credit would be released until the end of June, and (3) the method of accounting for inventory would be changed so industry would not show high profits resulting from inflation. Regarding credit, Shavit indeed planned to be particularistic, not only requesting credit for industry but specifically for an increase in the sum to the private sector administered by the Manufacturers' Association.

Shavit's commotion over the budget reached the Prime Minister, who invited him to meet. Reviewing the meeting for the Presidium, Shavit said he had expressed to the Prime Minister his dissatisfaction with the budget as not sufficiently emphasizing the productive sector, but he was not well enough acquainted with the Prime Minister to know if "lightning struck."[14] Not completely abandoning its interest in the direction of the economy and exasperated at not being able to establish a steady relationship with any minister, the Manufacturers' Association continually met with the Prime Minister at the group's initiative, apparently hoping that pressure at the top would affect the ministers and bureaucrats.[15] Manufacturers stressed to the Prime Minister the role of Government in developing an industrial base, the necessity of attracting manpower from services to industry, and the need for investment in research, and voiced concern that the Government's ultra-liberal policies were benefiting competitive import at the expense of local industry.

Although unsuccessful in redirecting Government policy, the Association achieved some of its aims: the amount of credit to the private sector for investment loans in 1978 was increased; by August 1978, the Kneset received a draft law that lowered taxes on companies that reinvested profits and allowed an accounting method for inventory that considered inflation, thereby granting industry further tax relief; tax easements for companies entering the stock market were granted; and certain tax refunds were allowed to exporting enterprises.

Most of these measures were achieved through meeting, discussing, and persuading the Finance Minister. Maintaining these gains, however, was a constant struggle. In 1979, the Finance Minister intended to completely cancel subsidized credit for investment as part of anti-inflationary budget cutting and to lower customs on imports yet again. Subsidized credit was eliminated, although tax relief was renewed. Gains for the Manufacturers' Association, Shavit explained, cannot be tallied like a score card.[16] Gains for industry from the Likud Government were made in different areas from those made under Labor, but on the whole, it was difficult to get from both Governments the kind of concerted emphasis on industry that the Manufacturers' Association wanted.

Party Politics Again

Under this Government, the Manufacturers' Association had to renew its fight against the party stigma. Although Shavit claimed that he, even to a greater extent than some of his predecessors, was "trying to take industry out of the political game," it was he who appealed to Presidium members "close to the parties" to pressure for industry within their respective parties.[17] It should be noted, however, that Presidium members quickly responded that "we never spoke of parties in the Presidium and parties of Presidium members."[18] Although Shavit's statements do not indicate any bond between a particular party and the group nor party control of the group and to the contrary point to an increased sophistication in lobbying, they were a somewhat sharper departure from previous practice.

This more aggressive stance appeared to backfire, creating a negative impression that the Manufacturers' Association had always tried to avoid. Finance Minister Ehrlich accused Shavit of not having criticized the previous Government as much, implying that the Manufacturers' Association was politically motivated and insincere in its aims.[19] The Prime Minister even suspected that Shavit was a Labor partisan.[20] Such observations, though implausible, illustrate how difficult it was for the Manufacturers' Association to project an image of itself as nonpartisan. Projecting such an image was important for the group. If a decision-maker categorizes someone as politically motivated, he may disregard any policy suggestions made by his perceived "opponent," regardless of their merit.

The Manufacturers' Association under both Labor and Likud attempted to prevent industry, even private industry, from becoming a partisan issue. To do that, however, it touched upon the political sphere, but with a measure of understanding of the country's partisan nature. After the elections, Shavit hoped to capitalize upon the fear of kibbutz and Histadrut industries of the new Government to encourage those industries to join the Association, creating an industrial interest.[21] Further pressing its non-partisanship, the Manufacturers' Association lobbied in all appropriate parts of the political spectrum. The Kneset provided a forum for this consensus building.

The Kneset Connection

Perceiving and capitalizing upon the individualistic trend in Israel's politics, and expecting the Likud to be less prone to centrally direct economic policy, the Manufacturers' Association soon after the 1977 elections acted in the Kneset arena, sending forty-five new Kneset members information and inviting them to tour industrial plants. As previously discussed, the Kneset was a longstanding Association target although not always utilized to the extent potentially possible. Perhaps due to the difficulty in establishing a close relationship with a minister in the new Government, but probably due more to a greater sophistication in relating to an increasingly complex political system, a few months later, the Manufacturers' Association established a formal lobbyist in the legislature. Indeed, Kneset members from the coalition parties as well as the opposition were more outspoken on matters favorable and unfavorable to industry, and the Manufacturers' Association monitored events.

Cause and effect in developing political processes are always difficult to pinpoint, but certainly there was an interaction. The Manufacturers' Association made a greater effort upon the Kneset, while the Kneset developed a distinct institutional identity, and Kneset members became more independent of their respective parties. Perhaps sensing from all the Association activity that industry could become an issue on which to make a mark for oneself, Gad Ya'aqobi, a Labor Party Kneset member, established a caucus of Kneset members from several parties interested in industrial issues. In accordance with the Manufacturers' Association's non-party stance, the Association cooperated with this forum, appearing before it and supplying information.

The Manufacturers' Association in the Eighties

The Manufacturers' Association's non-party stance served it well during the eighties, enabling it to relate to the second Likud administration and to the two-headed National Unity Government where several ministers including the Labor Prime Minister dealt with economic affairs.[22] The Manufacturers' Association was a recognized component in consultations and negotiations on economic plans and measures.

Reducing runaway inflation and achieving economic recovery was one reason for forming the National Unity Government, and the Government began acting immediately. Labor Prime Minister Peres played an active part but coordinated with the various economic ministers. This ministerial group frequently met with the Histadrut and the Coordinating Bureau of Economic Organizations, of which the Manufacturers' Association was a major component, and with the Manufacturers' Association itself. In these sessions, the Manufacturers' Association heard explanations of Government policies and raised any problems the Association had encountered.

While the Prime Minister's initiative contained a potential for comprehensive change in policy content and process, as in the past, the Government relied on a piecemeal approach. Besides taking several austerity measures, the Government began negotiating another "package deal," an agreement among labor, employers, and Government to limit wages, prices, and taxes. The process was not smooth or simple. A freeze was not yet feasible, for a COLA agreement was in effect, and prices had just risen. Several complicated schemes were considered. Continuing past committee approaches to economic issues, teams were established to thrash out problems with equal representation for the Government, Histadrut, and the Coordinating Bureau. Despite these cooperative efforts, some muscle-flexing was used to create the necessary balance of forces; Industry and Trade Minister Ariel Sharon announced price control on dozens of products and threatened to permit competitive imports. On the particular price issue, the Manufacturers' Association and the Minister of Industry and Trade agreed on joint action to regulate prices. Two successive package deals eventually were arranged over the period November 1984–July 1985.

The second accord, reached in January 1985, marked a step toward corporatism in Israel. It was not a mere wage-price freeze but was a cooperative Government-group effort to supervise prices. Ministers, Histadrut, and the Manufacturers' Association formed a high level Economic and Social Council to approve requested price increases and any revisions in the arrangement and also established a lower level technical committee. A price increase required approval of all three sides. When introduced, the arrangement was hailed for including groups in economic decision-making.[23] Nevertheless, this council, as its predecessors, never fully achieved its promise to deal with a range of issues and set comprehensive policy. In its limited scope, however, the system set an example for conducting economic policy in a divided political environment.

Over the same period, the Government continually took austerity measures, prodded by the United States which conditioned emergency aid on Israel's efforts at economic improvement. The United States also took a positive step toward Israel's economic betterment, signing a free-trade agreement in the spring of 1985.

Israel's gradual approach was not sufficiently effective. In an eighties example of committee politics, the Government designated Government officials and outside economists to draw up economic plans. Based upon these suggestions, the Government in July 1985 adopted the New Economic Program. Measures significant for industrialists were a wage and price freeze; a devaluation followed by a Government-set exchange rate, ending the floating rate system; and a credit freeze. Understanding the need to control inflation, the Manufacturers' Association agreed to the program and worked with the Government and Histadrut to implement it. The program succeeded in reducing inflation from the three-digit mark to about 16 percent. Despite this enormous achievement, the program left problems in its wake to which the Manufacturers' Association reacted.

For its part in the economic recovery process, the Manufacturers' Association, led by vigorous presidents, contributed to the package deal teams, made economic proposals in press conferences, and met independently with various ministers including the Prime Minister, on an array of industrial and general economic issues and on problems resulting from the Government measures. In some instances it was successful. For example, in 1988 it obtained a fund to aid enterprises temporarily hurt by an unfavorable international trade situation.[24] The Association together with the Finance Ministry and the Ministry of Industry and Trade formed a directorship to distribute the fund. Since the New Economic Program, the Manufacturers' Association has called for policies aimed at economic growth, focusing on export. Exporters have not been able to profit at the established exchange rate, and the Association has called for a devaluation. So far, this problem has not been resolved.

The Association continued courting the Kneset, thus reinforcing the growing stature of that body: it invited Kneset committees to the Association and appeared before them both at the Association's request and in response to invitations. It achieved some amendments and legislation important to industrialists, but also had failures.

The organization also acted aggressively, expanding upon its earlier experiments with public action. When, for example, the Histadrut refused to approve the Association's requested price increases in June 1985, the Manufacturers' Association authorized a production shut-down. Although Ministers Yitzhak Moda'i and Sharon backed the Association and were prepared to circumvent the trilateral system by declaring the products "essential," a compromise was found within the framework. Thus, in the eighties, the Manufacturers' Association confirmed its role as an essential element of the economy.

Conclusion

At the beginning of this book, I portrayed Israelis and Israeli interest groups as feeling powerless in a system permeated by political parties. Yet, in these previous pages, I have traced the activities of the Manufacturers' Association, noting it often received publicity in the Israeli press. This seeming contradiction between perception and reality may be explained by reference to the ideological political culture and its behavioral consequences, what I term the ideological dimension. Where ideology is so intense, one is not permitted to have interests, especially not private interests. Needs are supposed to be high matters of principle, and parties are sufficient to express them. Therefore, denial on a grand scale occurs. Referring to aspects of the ideological dimension will aid in summarizing and understanding the development of the Manufacturers' Association, its interaction with the developing political system, and the limitations on its fulfilling certain aims and achieving procedural change.

The Manufacturers' Association has represented a specific sector of the economy—that of private industry. As such, it had different interests from other elements of the private sector and competed for resources with developing public sector industry as well as agriculture. It also served as the opposite number to the labor union in labor negotiations. In the early period of the state, when many of its rivals were party affiliated, the Manufacturers' Association sought to promote the aims of industry, avoiding party affiliation and minimizing the aspect of private capital. This stance aided the group as the system moved into the dominant party phase.

The Government, which soon was dominated by a party with a vague socialist ideology (but conscious of pressures from parties with more intense ideological identities), attempted to deal with the configuration of groups and parties that confronted it by brokering and bargaining among them. The Manufacturers' Association was one part of this configuration and, particularly in its role as labor negotiator, became very useful to the Government. The group supported the Government by taking a hardline on labor issues which a worker oriented Government could not very well do without seemingly betraying its principles and its constituent groups. As I argued earlier, deal-making is one way to arrive at decisions without assigning a positive value to compromise. One can pretend to oneself that the ideology remains pure.

The Government controlled the economy by negotiating among groups on separate aspects of policy but not in a comprehensive, planned manner. It brokered between labor and the Manufacturers' Association on COLA arrangements. Although the Government controlled prices, it arrived at them by bargaining with groups over the criteria. The Government allocated credit and negotiated on taxes. As in many negotiations in other countries and settings, a complexity of forces existed, called upon by all sides. A group could concede on one matter but expect cooperation or compensation on another. The Manufacturers' Association, for example, might agree to absorb COLA and not request a price increase but expect the Government to supply sufficient operating capital or security for loans for that purpose. The Government also possessed some leverage. Manufacturers often feared that if they would raise prices without Government agreement, the Government might cut-off the supply of operating capital. Sometimes, the Manufacturers' Association would have to obtain the approval or consent from the labor union for a price increase or other benefit to make it easier for a labor supported Government to agree. Once it was established that the private sector would not be eliminated and even had its benefits, groups like the Manufacturers' Association could become part of the bargaining arrangement. The Manufacturers' Association and the private sector were tolerated and recognized, de facto, by a Labor Government.

Accepting its functionally specific role, the Manufacturers' Association could chisel away for change. Certain aims were attainable. I have identified demands made by groups on three levels – (1) very particularistic, for or against a certain policy or portion thereof; (2) more systemic, for alteration of the very system or mechanism by which demands are processed; or (3) particularistic but with consequences, perhaps unforeseen or unintended, for systemic and procedural change. The Manufacturers' Association had aims on all three levels, and the extent to which it could attain them was limited by the ideological political culture. For particularistic demands, change within limits was attainable. The group could achieve benefits for an individual or firm as well as limited aims on industrial or labor issues such as modification of a certain tax or a grant for operating capital. Achieving change in policies where structural interests were at stake such as altering the intervals for calculating COLA, was a more time-consuming and gradual process. To achieve these aims, the Manufacturers' Association played a role as initiator of an idea, continually raising the issue for consideration. Sometimes, it found a receptive minister who was able to overcome his party's supposed principle. Eventually, a change would be attained when circumstances overwhelmed the other side, party and affiliated group. The form of the transition to a changed policy was usually that of a decision by an "impartial committee."

The Manufacturers' Association also pressed directly for procedural change when it suggested establishing a comprehensive industrial and economic board to plan policy. Indirectly, it pressed for procedural change when, for example, it demanded a role in decision-making on import policy. Achieving procedural change, however, was often difficult, especially under a Mapai/Labor Government, owing to a residual ideological factor: when the Government and other groups negotiated with the Manufacturers' Association, the Association was de facto recognized as representing a segment of the economy and therefore due some voice on labor, industrial, and other economic issues. However, this recognition was extended grudgingly or reluctantly; the group was tolerated out of necessity. The Labor Party's ideology would have preferred a minimal private sector, and this ideological predilection, I believe, accounted in part for the ministers' reluctance to relinquish decision-making power to a board that included the private sector as a full partner. To do so would have openly acknowledged that the private sector and group had a role to play and that the ideology was not all inclusive. This remnant of ideology prevented the boards and forums from fully succeeding. Instead, by bargaining among groups, the Government could postpone confronting and redefining its ideological orientation.

The ideological political culture may be discerned as affecting, although to different degrees, the aims, targets, tactics, and even organization of the Manufacturers' Association. As mentioned previously, the Manufacturers' Association made demands on several levels, and the ideological political culture affected its success in achieving them. The political culture also subtly affected how the Manufacturers' Association expressed its aims. In the early period, the group concentrated on a general industrial interest or on the very particular cases of individual industrialists, with little stress on principles of private industry or capital. As the Manufacturers' Association became more confident of its place as a group, even within the dominant party period, it dared to raise more economy-wide issues and suggestions, including some principles of private enterprise and capital.

Adapting to the Government's bargaining style, the Manufacturers' Association identified its targets and shaped its tactics. The group related primarily to the Government ministers who held relevant portfolios. Possessing its own chief bargainer who had good personal relations with the ministers eased the way in the early period. The Association dealt with the Minister of Commerce and Industry and the Finance Minister, and depending upon the particular Minister of Commerce and Industry, manufacturers sometimes coordinated with him in order to influence and convince the Finance Minister.

Although ministers were the primary targets, the Manufacturers' Association did not ignore all others. Not identifying with any one party, the Association kept its options open and did not spurn politicians. However, it dealt with politicians who already were in office, not aiding in campaigns or backing candidates within parties. An interest group subsystem separate from parties was developing, and the Manufacturers' Association played a role in that development. Parties that raised issues to the ideological level would be of no use to the Manufacturers' Association; it kept entirely aloof from such struggles. As for institutions, the group took advantage of any opportunities to exert influence, when possible placing members in the bureaucracy. The Association presented ideas to the Kneset, providing information to the committees and to individuals regardless of party affiliation.

Beyond bargaining with ministers, which was the main emphasis, tactics were diverse, although the eventual aim was to influence the ministers. At select times, the group utilized the power which the system allocated to it in order to pressure the ministers. Thus, the group sometimes withdrew from committees, took a hardline against labor, and threatened not to cooperate with the Government. Part of chiseling away for change involved developing and presenting ideas. The Manufacturers' Association drafted policy papers, disseminating them through the press and to ministers. The Association sought to establish its influence among the public without any party or politician acting as mediator or spokesman. Press relations became an integral part of the group's campaign on an issue or policy. When negotiating on any issue, the group would discuss when to time a press conference and what position to present. The press became an instrument for the group.

Through these efforts, the Manufacturers' Association obtained a recognized role as representative of a contained economic sector meriting explanation and information regarding Government policy. The Manufacturers' Association became accustomed to its role, although it never abandoned attempts to expand its influence on both content and process of policy. One could very well ask, what is there to criticize with such a system? Isn't every group heard somewhere, if not in the legislature or party, then in a certain ministry? Doesn't every group receive some benefit? Perhaps some group for political reasons receives less, but the Government attempts to satisfy everyone with something, and therefore, the system could be considered less conflict prone than some systems with sharper divisions between privileged and unprivileged groups. However, problems occurred in the decision-making process. Decisions during the dominant party period in Israel were not always made on the basis of discussion and cooperative agreement among the affected groups and parties. Rather, Government ministers accepted a tremendous burden upon themselves, engaging in much activity, meeting separately and together with groups to arrange all these agreements and policies. Thus, on the ground, decisions on specific cases could be made, but the ideological tone prevented considering the process of bargaining in a positive light and stymied attempts at comprehensive and coordinated policy planning.

Although the Likud Government did not manifest the exact same ideological behavioral traits as the Labor Party (it did evince some, however, to which I will refer), and although its ideology had become more diffuse and comprehensive, that very all-embracing outlook caused it problems in establishing procedures for dealing with groups. The resultant mode of operating and limitations on policy setting often appeared similar to those under Labor but derived from different causes. Before embarking on a neat explanation of Likud Government-group relations, it must be remembered that the Likud inherited a structure and institutions that it could not quickly change and after being in the opposition for so long, encountered personality problems and governing problems that must be attributed to lack of experience rather than to any esoteric explanation.

It will be recalled that the early ideological outlook of the General Zionist/Liberal Party emphasized the individual, preferring private enterprise to cooperative or state owned enterprise. This liberal ideology undoubtedly was part of the Likud's outlook. The Likud therefore viewed society as a whole, perceiving the economic-political world as composed of individuals and "groupings" (not necessarily organized) making demands upon it (for housing, cheaper goods, etc.). It understood the job of government as responding to these societal demands. Of course, the Likud realized that organized groups existed, inheriting the group configuration remaining from the Labor Party period, but did not regard them in any special way as beneficial to the governmental process, perhaps even impeding it. Organized groups, in the Likud Government's view, took their place beside the more amorphous "groupings," all competing for the Government's attention. The picture is one of a Government besieged by demands.

In accordance with its approach to dealing with the whole society, the Government instituted some macro-level economic policies but did not have an inclusive and coordinated plan for dealing with all the interlocking aspects of the economy. Likud Government members adhered to their diffuse free-market ideology, believing that a broad policy would be sufficient and that planning and filling in the pieces of a program was not necessary. If anyone questioned the workability of the policies, the Likud's response was its own form of avoidance, sometimes dismissing critics as politically motivated and assuring doubters, "not to worry, everything will be all right."

Bypassing organized groups with general policy, the Government opened itself to the clamorings of all. The macro-style policies often alienated organized groups who were more interested in one of the subparts. A more liberal import policy, for example, which theoretically could benefit the individual by lowering prices, alienated agricultural and industrial groups. To deal with the bombardment of demands, Government ministers met with groups, listened, and attempted to satisfy some of each group's wants or explain why it could not comply. On the surface, Government-group relations appeared similar to those during the Labor period, as peripatetic ministers met with various groups, but the ministers did not develop the ability, or see the necessity, of using groups for setting policies. The Government experienced the same difficulty as Labor in planning and setting coordinated policy. What is needed, one manufacturer told me, is an "economic czar."[25] Such statements often are noted with horror by political observers of Israel as indicating an anti-democratic desire for a dictator. The statement may actually represent a desire for coordinated, rational policy-planning—a method of coordinating the clamoring groups, anticipating issues, and rationally and calmly discussing policy. As demonstrated by the Government's piecemeal method of setting economic policy, this procedure has been lacking in Israel.

The Likud Government's attitude toward groups, although not rigidly ideological, affected the Association's aims, tactics, and targets. In reaction to this Government's preference for dealing with policy on the macro-level, the Manufacturers' Association eventually raised more specific concerns, although it did not abandon suggesting alternatives to the macro-level. The Association did not perceive its rival as agriculture or public sector industry but the consumer components of the country's budget. Theoretically, the "private" aspect of its aims was not expected to be a problem under the Likud, but when the Association did not obtain a Government orientation toward industry in general, it resorted to aiming for and accepting benefits to the private sector specifically. Regarding the systemic level of demands, although the Association hoped for a role in policy setting and a place in procedure, it accepted its contained role as under Labor and acted according to a more "traditional" and limited notion of an interest group, engaging in particularistic interest articulation.

Unsure of the new system and if there would be a new system, the Manufacturers' Association acted on many fronts. At first, expecting that the Likud's more "catch-all" character would mean less ministerial or Government control, the group increased its efforts on the legislature. It soon became apparent that a wide-based party need not mean less central control, but possibly even greater Government direction, and therefore, the Manufacturers' Association targeted the ministers, meeting even with the Prime Minister. Actually, meeting with the Prime Minister resulted from uncertainty about the Government's operating procedures and probably exacerbated the Government's embattled outlook. Tactics did not undergo any great changes, as the group discussed with and persuaded ministers, submitted policy papers, and continued communicating with the public via the press.

It often is noted that systems with "catch-all" parties, considered weak parties, engender strong or well-defined interest groups as if such parties require, foster, and encourage interest groups.[26] I do not think it is necessarily the structure or electoral base of the party that engenders this development but the policy-making procedures of Government or party. Actually, here was a party becoming more "catch-all" in both structure and policy but with little regard or use for organized groups because it believed it the province of Government to govern for the whole. Interests or interest groups that felt slighted by this procedure and policies became determined to make their presence felt and to express themselves.

As the National Unity Government of 1984 combined the two main party blocs, the Manufacturers' Association necessarily called upon all its resources that were developed when those parties singly were in control. It both reacted to and prodded the Government on specific measures and process. Whenever this Government or ministers within it invited groups into the decision-making process, the Manufacturers' Association readily responded. It pressed the industrial interest, but, as in the past, expounded on wider economic matters and continually urged the Government to undertake comprehensive structural reform. Simultaneously, the Manufacturers' Association pursued the varied tactics it had refined – dealing individually with ministers, bargaining with the Histadrut both independently and in conjunction with the Government, disseminating ideas and information via the press, and resorting to public action. Still not party aligned, the Manufacturers' Association expanded its efforts in the Kneset across the political spectrum.

In the introduction, I outlined three models of government for dealing with interest groups and demands and for establishing decision-making and conflict resolution processes – strong party, pluralist, and corporatist. I wanted to understand how change occurs from one model to another and the role groups play in system change. Elements of all three models have been present in Israel. In an earlier period, elements of a strong party model applied. Some observers would characterize the early Mapai in that framework, although modified by the existence of Mapai's affiliated groups. By its very existence as an autonomous interest group, the Manufacturers' Association compelled the system to consider and deal with groups, helped soften partisan influences on decision-making, and established the usefulness of an interest group subsystem, thereby instilling pluralist traits into the system. The system currently appears to fit a pluralist model but with an overlay of residual ideological elements. These ideological features impede one function of pluralist government, that of reconciling diverse interests and demands into a coherent policy. While often demanding its own narrow benefits, the Manufacturers' Association has attempted to smooth the functioning of pluralism by continually trying to raise decision-making above partisanship and ideological rhetoric. Moreover, appealing to industry from all economic sectors to join it, the Association attempted to create a non-partisan industrial group in order to merit a policy-making role. In so doing, the group clearly has been an element for prodding system change, always promoting, perhaps unwittingly, a corporatist element of government.

Groups both respond to and prod political institutions and interact with whole systems. In so acting, the Manufacturers' Association advanced interest group frontiers. To pursue its interest under the Likud Government, while still spurning party affiliation, the Manufacturers' Association further developed contact with the opposition in the Kneset. The Association simultaneously continued efforts to expand, inviting Histadrut, kibbutz, and public sector industry to join the organization. It saw an opportunity to forge an industrial interest by exploiting these groups' opposition to the Likud Government's policies. There may indeed evolve a broader, non-party interest group pressing for policies beneficial to industry from whatever Government is in power. Other industrial segments of the economy have been more party linked, and it will be interesting to note how that obstacle is overcome. Examining how a party affiliated interest group, the Ihud kibbutz movement, has behaved and affected the content and process of decision-making may provide a clue.

Part III

Ihud ha-Kvutzot ve-ha-Kibbutzim

Chapter 7

An Interest Group Emerges

If an Ihud person appears bewildered by the suggestion that interest groups exist in Israel, and moreover, that the Ihud is among them, he more than members of other groups reflects the environment under which the kibbutz movement was established. The kibbutz represented a complete social, economic, and political framework; the kibbutz did not consider itself an interest group like a labor union, which primarily pressures for policy demands or economic gain. Nevertheless, the Ihud evolved into such a demand-making entity, and it is just that development that requires analysis. Behaving as an interest group, the Ihud interacted with the party and political systems, contributed to the emergence of an interest group subsystem, and consequently contributed to the development of pluralism and corporatism in Israel.

The Ihud's special lifestyle gave it a complex interest package, combining elements of occupational and idea groups. Its interests included agricultural and eventually industrial matters, related and general economic policies, kibbutz social interests and values (both general values such as equality and pioneering and specific interests such as demands for housing appropriate to kibbutz life), as well as foreign policy. The importance of each component to the Ihud varied in intensity over time. From its very inception, political party activity and political affairs formed part of the Ihud's interest package. Viewing the Mapai party as the exponent of most of its values, the Ihud always closely associated with it, and Mapai's well being as well as the Ihud's place within the party were important concerns.

Political Prelude

The Ihud actually was born of a political rift and developed

103

parallel to Mapai. During the pre-state period, there were three kibbutz federations of the secular Left: Kibbutz ha-Meuhad, Hever ha-Kvutzot (a kvutzah refers to an entity smaller than a kibbutz), and Kibbutz ha-Artzi. The first two were affiliated with Mapai and the last with a party known as ha-Shomer ha-Tza'ir. In 1944, a more Marxist oriented group broke away from Mapai, and in 1948 this group united with ha-Shomer ha-Tza'ir-Kibbutz ha-Artzi to form the party Mapam. This political split rent the Kibbutz ha-Meuhad federation. A vociferous dispute developed about which party would control the kibbutz federation's educational system and its ideological orientation. Individual kibbutzim divided, a split entailing the emotional equivalent of a marriage divorce. Those kibbutzim and parts of kibbutzim that remained loyal to Mapai merged with Hever ha-Kvutzot in 1951, forming a new federation, Ihud ha-Kvutzot ve-ha-Kibbutzim (literally, the union of kvutzot and kibbutzim. Practically, the distinction between kvutzah and kibbutz disappeared.) When in 1954, Ahdut ha-'Avodah split from Mapam, party-kibbutz alignments became more symmetrical: Ihud – Mapai; Kibbutz ha-Meuhad – Ahdut ha-'Avodah; and Kibbutz ha-Artzi – Mapam.

The organizational structure of national institutions in the young state relevant to agricultural and settlement matters practically compelled agricultural groups to maintain some party tie. It is necessary to outline the operation and jurisdiction of each institution in order to understand how groups related to them. Agricultural settlement was one major area affected by the bureaucratic realignment that occurred at the state's creation. In the pre-state period, the Jewish Agency was responsible for settling the land. After the state was established, the Jewish Agency continued supervising new settlements. The Jewish Agency provided start-up funds in the form of low interest, long term loans, and settlements were under Agency supervision for a number of years. When the Jewish Agency decided a settlement was capable of conducting its own affairs, settlers and Agency signed a contract for a final loan to be given over a certain number of years based upon a standard of necessities according to that settlement's population size (livestock per family, water allotment, etc.). Such a settlement then was considered "consolidated" or "established" and no longer under Jewish Agency jurisdiction. The new state's Ministry of Agriculture became responsible for overseeing the activities of these "established" kibbutzim and moshavim.

Besides the Agency and the ministry, a third institution for agricultural affairs, excluding the private sector, existed in the Histadrut. A forum was established, called the Agricultural Center, where all settlement federations of the Left and the religious were represented via their respective parties. The Agricultural Center was a brainstorm of Avraham Hartzfeld, a Mapai member, who envisaged a united and influential agricultural sector. From the Center, the agricultural sector could address Government, party, and Jewish Agency officials, making them aware of agriculture's needs. The Agricultural Center served as liaison between the federations and state institutions, having input into Government program planning and sometimes participating in implementing policies and programs arranged by the Government and Jewish Agency.

Still another forum relevant to the Ihud was an interkibbutz committee, where representatives of various kibbutz federations worked on common problems and coordinated positions before sitting at the Agricultural Center table. Both the Agricultural Center and the interkibbutz committee were not state institutions but similar to round-tables with access to Government bodies.

Appointments to the Agricultural Center, the Jewish Agency, and the Ministry of Agriculture were made by parties. Several parties were represented in these agencies, although Mapai persons predominated. The Ihud was asked by Mapai to fill positions, as other groups were requested by their respective parties when those parties participated in the organ.

Certain distinctions must be made regarding the nature of a group's authority and function vis-à-vis these bodies. The Agricultural Center's purpose was to provide a forum where group representatives could discuss and negotiate common issues, problems, and any conflicts. Each party, therefore, was expected to allow group representation. Nevertheless, the parties attempted to retain some control or oversight on activities, especially Mapai, which placed the head of the Agricultural Center on its Kneset list. The Jewish Agency was a quasi-state, administrative organ but one where groups were called upon to provide personnel. Groups took advantage of the privilege and began to regard it as a right. Certainly in the Agricultural Center and to some extent in the Jewish Agency, the sending group had a degree of authority over its members. The ministry was somewhat more complicated. The party designated the minister, usually someone from one of its affiliated agricultural groups. A combination of the designee's party affiliation and activity, group membership, and expertise were factors in the appointment decision. Other positions within the office were filled by the minister and party, or by another party if part of the coalition agreement, and the same three elements entered the decision on personnel. Until 1955, Ihud persons dominated positions in the Ministry of Agriculture. Despite this, however, neither the minister nor his staff was directly or formally under the orders, authority, or influence of the Ihud.

Ihud representation via Mapai occurred on three levels. The party reserved a number of Kneset seats for the Ihud, and the Ihud in its administrative bodies, often the Secretariat, selected its candidates. There also were Ihud members active and prominent in the party whom the party requested for public service roles that were approved by the Ihud as a formality only. (The cooperative nature of kibbutz life requires that members receive the group's permission to accept outside positions or jobs.) A third category of representation also existed, one where a position by custom was reserved for a group member, but the group was not granted the right to choose the individual.

These distinctions merit attention because they raise the problem of "true" representation and accountability of those representatives. Political studies commonly analyze the background of a state's key actors, and their societal or group origins, and so infer influence about that group. Regarding Israel, political observers often have noted a kibbutz background of leading Government officials and draw conclusions about kibbutz influence. Such an approach may lead to exaggerated conclusions about that influence, and the mode of selection must be examined more closely. Thus, the Ihud could be proud of members who achieved important positions and because of a common bond may have had easier access to those individuals, but the kibbutz group was limited in its ability to hold them accountable. Moreover, representation of the second and third types is not guaranteed. Any broad generalizations about group, particularly kibbutz, influence must be modified by understanding from where an appointment or assignment derived, i.e., group or party.

Nevertheless, jurisdiction and responsibilities of the state bodies were not always so clear cut, and lines of power and authority were blurred as officials, especially in the beginning of the state, sometimes held positions in more than one organ. For a number of years, for example, Eshkol was Finance Minister as well as Head of the Jewish Agency's Agricultural Settlement Department. Such an overlap between two state or national bodies could be considered similar to one person holding two Government portfolios. This arrangement, therefore, may not embody conflict of interest problems but could affect bureaucratic efficiency, either impeding or perhaps improving it. (When Eshkol was asked how he could hold both positions, he reportedly replied, "In the morning the Head of the Settlement Department curses the Finance Minister, and in the evening the Finance

Minister curses the Head of the Settlement Department."][1] However, there also were instances where one person simultaneously sat in a state office and in a group forum. For a short period of time Hayyim Gvati was director-general of the Ministry of Agriculture and the Ihud's representative in the Agricultural Center. Moreover, Ihud members working in state institutions were included on the Ihud's executive bodies, even if they could not always spare time to be active. Gvati insisted upon his ability to separate these roles – that on the Agricultural Center he represented the Ihud, and in the ministry he represented no one – and expressed wonderment at the very question, claiming that "never did they speak about this" (conflict of interest).[2]

1952: Party Coordination
While Limiting Group Politicization

For the first few years of its existence, the Ihud's leaders were concerned about effecting a successful merger between the federation's two component kibbutz groups and concentrated on mobilizing members for work on various internal committees. The Ihud federation formally was structured in a pyramid, and as in most such structures, the small body at the top held the most power. Though the structure was intermittently modified, essentially it included a Conference, composed of representatives of each kibbutz, at the base, and, moving upward, a Council, a Central Committee, and a Secretariat. The federation was headed by a Secretary-General. The Central Committee numbered over 250 members and always seated Ihud members prominent in national positions.

The Secretariat carried out the daily operations of the Ihud federation and made the important decisions including selecting candidates for Secretary-General and designating members for public service offices. Except for a brief interval, usually there were two secretariats, a Wider Secretariat (about 30–40 members) and a smaller body (about 5–12 members) titled at different times, the Smaller Secretariat or the Active Secretariat. The smaller entity became necessary as the Secretariat was enlarged to include nationally prominent Ihud members and therefore became impractical to convene for daily decisions. To conduct the federation's affairs, the Secretariat established committees, usually headed by a Secretariat member, and assigned kibbutz members to them. While formally reporting to the Secretariat where major issues were debated, the committees worked autonomously to a large extent, discussing and setting policy for the federation and directly supervising the operations of individual kibbutzim.

Until 1955, general political discussion and organizational activity did not occupy a special place on the Ihud's agenda. Ihud leaders made no special efforts to promote their ideas or pursue their demands vis-à-vis Mapai. They assumed that organizing to compete for benefits was unnecessary. They believed that the kibbutz lifestyle was superior and exemplary and that their values and contributions to the state naturally would be esteemed and rewarded by the party. Ihud leaders were ambivalent about their self-image as an interest group vying for tangible benefits. Having inculcated the view that politics must be for values, demanding benefits or acting as what they called "interesantim" seemed demeaning and morally tainted.

Moreover, the cloud of another split constantly hovered over the group, sensitizing it to minority opinions among its members. As the split had most dramatically and traumatically demonstrated, the close interpersonal contact necessary for a communal lifestyle plus a passionate political atmosphere necessitated that most members share the same party persuasion. After the split, the Ihud still was not absolutely homogeneous. The federation included settlements affiliated with a political party on the Right as well as various individuals who voted for parties other than Mapai. Although these elements were a very small minority, the Ihud felt compelled to seek an arrangement permitting individuals some freedom for political activity while minimizing the influence of political differences on daily life. As with the Manufacturers' Association, fear of divisive politicization was the initial and primary impetus for the form of its party relationship.

The mode of the group's party connection became a constant concern for the Ihud leadership. Though Peter Y. Medding emphasizes that the Ihud was not formally and structurally linked to Mapai, his observation is correct only insofar as the Ihud was not an organized faction within the party.[3] Unlike the Manufacturers' Association, the Ihud did not declare a moratorium on political discussion and activity, and Mapai party matters, including the possibility of establishing a more formal structural link, gradually occupied a larger proportion of Ihud deliberations and activities. The Ihud sought a way that would allow it to contribute to Mapai and benefit from any Mapai gains but keep potentially divisive, ideological, personal, and other political feuds from intruding upon Ihud premises and affecting the Ihud structure. The particular arrangement varied, depending upon the nature and intensity of the dispute of the day and the Ihud's judgment of the matter's importance balanced against other interests.

A group's relationship to a party may be understood as comprising certain rights and responsibilities. The party may demand that the group adopt a certain policy line and contribute manpower and money to the party machine. In return, the party may guarantee to the group representation in the party and in state institutions, distribution of tangible benefits, or promise the party's adoption of a policy favored by the group.

In its relationship to Mapai, the Ihud sought to be the controlling factor and to maximize its influence on the party, maintaining autonomy and upholding freedom of action on party directives, tasks made difficult by its self-imposed structural restraints. Matters involving Ihud influence on the party were conducted by an Ihud central administrative body, and on the Ihud Secretariat sat an active party member considered to be the group's party representative. Regarding its "rights" vis-à-vis the party, such as representation, the Ihud sought, first of all, to preserve its claim to representation on even the highest party bodies and state governing institutions, and then to maintain more than formal authority over its delegates and over policy implementation. The Ihud leadership, for example, sought to select, approve, and direct members it allowed into public service.

Arrangements for party activity and influence within the Ihud, however, formally were distanced in separate structures. To fulfill its responsibilities for party activity, the Ihud permitted the party to establish branches in kibbutzim. Members who wished to engage in politics individually could join those branches, and each branch chose its party representative, known as a branch secretary. Party organizational work thereby was contained so that any internal party disputes would not fragment the group. The Ihud endeavored both to maintain itself as an interest group and to engage in Mapai work but without becoming part of the party machine subject to party discipline, direction, or cooptation. Moreover, political activity usually was not a criterion for selecting members to work on internal Ihud committees. Politics became a somewhat separate realm of activity, although Ihud central bodies kept abreast of activities and sought to supervise them. According to an Almond and Powell type structural-functionalist classification, the Ihud would represent an interest group with limited autonomy.[4] The lack of a structural tie was a safety shield but did not indicate indifference, either to party organizational matters per se or to policy issues decided within the party.

The Ihud's tangential party position illuminates the varying nature of party-group relationships in different systems and the balance of power between the two entities. In a strong party system, groups are presumed to "put all their eggs in one basket" and to try within the party to wield their influence. In pluralist systems, political theorists note, groups cannot "put all their eggs in one basket" for fear of alienating some group members with different political sensibilities. Moreover, groups in the pluralist model do not back only one party in order to entice parties to compete in meeting group demands and gaining group support.[5] These two postulates of pluralist theory actually seem contradictory, for if groups cannot "put their eggs in one basket," how can they credibly offer the possibility of their support?

While the Ihud's sensitivity for its members' political leanings created difficulties for it to structurally affiliate with one party, it did not otherwise resemble a group in a pluralist model. Rather, the Ihud illustrates a variation in the strong party model that may exist. The element of group cohesion appears to control the group's influence and bargaining ability in both pluralist and strong party systems. Indeed, Truman notes that contrary to his earlier expectations, groups in pluralist systems may align with parties.[6] High group cohesion would enable a group either to align with one party or to bargain among parties with its support. In both systems, weak group cohesion limits a group's ability to extract concessions from a party. Damaging consequences may be even greater in a party controlled system. Where a group is nominally affiliated with a party, "putting its eggs in one basket" by structurally aligning essentially is its leverage on that one party. If the group cannot completely commit itself, the party may take the group for granted without feeling in any way obligated to bestow benefits. Concerned and constrained by group cohesion, the Ihud took that risk.

Nevertheless, a relationship to Mapai was very important to the Ihud because not only did it generally identify with Mapai's brand of socialism but that party served the Ihud as a vehicle to place members in positions of power. Through Mapai, the Ihud sent members to the Kneset with influence on their committee assignments, positioned members in the Ministry of Agriculture including the ministership itself, and supplied members to a number of state institutions. Although not an organized faction, the Ihud sought the same type of influence that operating as a faction perhaps would have more easily and directly afforded.

The Ihud's distancing of political action was not satisfactory to the party because it sent mixed signals to Ihud members and diminished political involvement. Ihud leaders, too, slowly began realizing the Ihud's consequential decline in influence upon the party and its reduced tangible rewards. From time to time, the Ihud discussed amending the situation both by improving the Ihud's party activity as well as strengthening the Ihud's channels for pressing its interests. Early in

1953, for example, after the party Secretariat pointed out deficiencies in branch activity, the Ihud decided to establish a joint committee between the Ihud and party Secretariats to develop recommendations. Regarding its political demands and channel for expressing them, as early as January 1952 the Ihud, seeking to maintain control, debated demanding that Kneset members simultaneously work in the Ihud's Secretariat as many as three days a week.[7] Realization of a serious problem, however, was slow to develop.

Maneuvering through the Maze

In the early period, Israel's party-group permutations presented a confusing picture not only to the outside observer accustomed to analyzing more crystalline cases but often to involved groups as well. Nevertheless, the Ihud managed to "steer the ship through the different streams [settlement groups] and parties,"[8] traveling under the banner that best served its sometimes very particular interests. Though the Ihud ideologically identified with one party (Mapai), it did not believe that allocating administrative positions in national and economic institutions on a party basis was an expeditious management policy. Indeed, one Ihud member was "terrified" that the country would be divided into [party] "tribes."[9]

Rather than vigorously or directly seeking to change the representation pattern, however, the Ihud worked within the framework. Thus, the Ihud acquiesced in party representation on the Agricultural Center, following party advice to sign an agreement with moshavim in 1955 which fixed a ratio for sharing the party's quota of positions in Center committees between kibbutzim and moshavim. Perceptions of differences between kibbutzim and moshavim were very intense at that time, and even today, veteran kibbutz members occasionally express disdain for the more private, what they consider selfish, moshav lifestyle. Some members, therefore, worried that the moshav agreement might impede their relations with other kibbutz groups both in the upcoming coalition Government and especially in the Agricultural Center, where "not only once did the Ihud go with the other streams against the moshavim."[10] Others, however, reasoned as Meir Mandel that "we have a special interest to build Histadrut Agriculture without being dependent on the two other streams. We have to build it by a party line—an agreement of interests with the moshav movement and not by a line of the form of agriculture."[11] A stronger incentive to their signing was the agreement's provisions on land allocation: Out of an allotment of new settlement spots, the moshavim agreed on a ratio with the Ihud. They also agreed to an Ihud-initiated enterprise, not viewed favorably by the other kibbutz federations, permitting the Ihud to reserve and not forfeit land allotted to it which it was not yet prepared with manpower or machinery to utilize. The Ihud established a special company under Jewish Agency supervision to which Ihud settlements could transfer land, and that company would develop the areas using hired labor until the land could be restored to the Ihud.

While the Ihud sought good relations with other kibbutz federations, when the issue first arose of including those groups via their respective parties in the coalition Government within the Ministry of Agriculture, Ihud members were hardly ecstatic. Their immediate reaction was to prevent it or, accepting that some roles must be provided to other parties entering the coalition, at least to ensure that the composition of the ministry staff "would not slip from the [Mapai] party."[12] Specifically, many wanted to press for retaining two critical members, Yosef Efrati and Gvati, deputy minister and director-general, respectively, finding it intolerable that the kibbutz sector spokesman be from another party. Pressure by the Ihud was brought very circumspectly, however, by a petition from the Mapai faction in the Agricultural Center.

When it became evident that Mapai would retain the minister's seat, the question then became whether Ihud persons as opposed to moshav persons, who also entered claims for major posts, would fill ministry positions. Although two Ihud Secretariat members argued against starting a precedent for dividing the ministry into group blocs, the Secretariat dispatched a delegation to press Efrati's claim to the ministership. When the coalition finally was formed, the Ihud retained the ministership in the hands of Kadish Luz; Gvati remained director-general; the moshavim received no top spot; Ahdut ha-'Avodah soon received the deputy minister post; and Efrati shortly was out of the ministry but in the Kneset Finance Committee. The Ihud managed to vary its tactics and alliances, at times acting with other kibbutz federations, at times with moshavim, to attain positions and policies advantageous to it.

1955: From Prime Party Mover to Reluctant Interest Group

The necessity for all these maneuverings prompted discussion of neglected party topics as the 1955 elections approached. Discussions extended beyond the elections and coalition negotiations, and in the process the Ihud experienced an identity crisis. The Ihud embarked upon redefining its relationship to the party—identifying its interests, assessing its true rivals, and deciding upon the best vehicles for achieving its goals. The subject became complicated because the Ihud was reluctant to project itself as an interest group. Moreover, the Ihud feared that stressing tangible interests would require organizing as a party faction, raising the spectre of another split. These anxieties became evident in Ihud deliberations.

In 1955, members began to feel the full detrimental impact of the earlier kibbutz movement split, lamenting that it had significantly decreased their number and influence within the Mapai party, which enabled the moshav sector to benefit. The Ihud perceived itself a competitor to moshavim within the party, ideologically, numerically, and materially and discussed how to remedy the situation. The Ihud complained the party did not properly value kibbutzim, discriminating against it in various ways, such as failing to provide adequate housing. To improve their situation, some suggested strengthening bonds with the rival moshavim, thereby benefiting from the moshav's popularity, but others viewed such cooperation as impossible because of the ideological differences.

Although noting its declining influence upon the party, the Ihud did not act drastically, remaining ambivalent about the extent of responsibility it desired for party affairs. It accepted its obligation to contribute to the party financially for the 1955 elections and eventually decided upon centrally supervising the collection, but only after considering and rejecting one member's suggestion that the party appeal directly to individual kibbutzim.

Mapai's relatively poor showing in 1955 and the necessity of including Mapam and Ahdut ha-'Avodah in the coalition complicated the Ihud's image of its place in the configuration of parties and groups, increasing the urgency of a full assessment. Ideologically, the Ihud still identified with Mapai, but the group sorrowfully noted that the kibbutz-party relationship had changed from a situation where the "kibbutz movement established the form of the party and its values and was called upon to give persons to every organ" to one where "the party calculated what it owed the movement," a subtle status change showing "that in the party the main element is not ideas but interests, a struggle of interests."[13]

Members attributed the change, correctly, to Mapai's growing mass character. Consequently, Mapai as well as other parties were "abandoning settlement interests and running after votes."[14] The Ihud did not criticize Mapai's expansion but regarded it as problematic for the kibbutz group which "still did not find a way to fit in."[15] Reflecting this difficulty, many members continued speaking generally about "moral interests," "guiding the party on the path to socialism," and striving to promote the values of "equality, simplicity of life, and aspiration for a life of work."[16] They objected to what they perceived as Mapai's efforts to make them a "faction like the moshav and trade union."[17] Rather, they viewed the kibbutz as an innovation within socialism and were concerned about maintaining kibbutz life "as an expression of the vision of the party" so that Mapai would not become like socialist parties in other countries which lacked the unique kibbutz element.[18] These value-oriented kibbutz members, however, did not specify how to promote such values. Others reluctantly recognized a direct correlation between the Ihud's more constricted place within the party and its difficulty in obtaining specific benefits such as aid in servicing a growing debt. Practical minded Ihud members, such as Senta Yoseftal, a veteran of Kibbutz Gal'ed who has held a succession of important positions in the kibbutz movement and in state institutions, attempted a synthesis between promoting values and pressing material interests. She urged Ihud members to recognize the reality that they were "interesantim" just like the trade union, and although "we like to forget this, ... it is time we remembered and organized with all those who are like us, and together our words will be heard in the party."[19]

It has become almost axiomatic that socialist-Zionist and kibbutz pioneering ideology has permeated and dominated Israeli society and values.[20] As a corollary, it is believed that kibbutz interests were therefore always favored and that kibbutzim received a disproportionate share of resources. While kibbutz values may have been highly esteemed (and kibbutz members began to doubt even that), their share in resources was by no means guaranteed; kibbutz members had to compete with every other social group. Ideology may have formed part of their argument and facilitated results, but they still had to present a case. The Ihud itself realized this, and to improve its stature, the Ihud debated targeting the Kneset, the party apparatus itself, as well as other state institutions. The Ihud Secretariat began to perceive drawbacks in its political containment policy. The Secretariat believed that allowing members in state and party positions to act autonomously had resulted in a situation where Ihud members did not vigorously defend kibbutz demands. The Ihud had to decide upon the purpose of its party and institutional connections, understanding that "the problem is if we want to represent the party or to insure our interests." According to one prominent member, "the second factor is the important one at the moment."[21]

The Ihud experienced the classical problem of representation and accountability. Should chosen representatives be deemed strictly accountable to their constituency, or should they be authorized to act autonomously according to judgment? And in a party dominated system, is the constituency the party or the group? The Ihud grappled with these problems as it explored various routes to increased influence.

The Ihud had a right to choose Kneset candidates, and the selection process for 1955 occasioned discussion about the nature and effectiveness of its delegation. The Ihud contemplated an enhanced role for its Kneset members and considered requiring them to increase their activity within the Ihud and to become more accountable to the Ihud's authority when performing their public roles. While deeming increased Kneset member involvement in the Ihud's leadership body desirable, some believed it to be an unrealistic goal, given the Kneset workload.[22] Another voice dampened prospects for the Kneset strategy altogether, noting a loyalty dilemma because the "Kneset is a political body of the state, and a member of Kneset acts according to the party platform and not of the Ihud."[23] It was just these overlapping roles that made the Kneset member so pivotal and important since an active Kneset member could coordinate and act as liaison among group, party, and legislature. Strengthening the Ihud's control over Kneset members, however, would have entailed organizing within the party, to which several Ihud members objected. The Ihud Secretariat chose its candidates in 1955, and the issue of Kneset members' responsibility to the group was never explicitly and formally resolved.

Besides the Kneset, the Ihud considered targeting the party apparatus directly. In this vein, Ihud Kneset member Efrati counselled contributing two or three persons to the party apparatus, as did Aryeh Bahir, also a Kneset member, who believed "the chance for success is the connection between our people to the directorship of the party."[24] Vis-à-vis the party, as vis-à-vis the Government, the Ihud encountered the same problem about directing its delegates, as one leader complained, "Members of the Ihud in the party are not like I knew them in this house."[25] The Ihud's fear of factionalism exacerbated the problem in the party because the group believed it could not "tell members of Ihud who work in the party how to behave in the party ... [because it] means organizing a faction."[26] The question remained how they would organize.

The near loss of the Ministry of Agriculture in 1955 soon was followed by the old guard-young generation dispute within Mapai during which Dayan made comments interpreted by many Ihud leaders as hostile to kibbutzim. Both occurrences made the Ihud acutely aware of its declining influence and prestige within the party. The Ihud, therefore, embarked upon a damage control effort on the party front to strengthen its claim to the Ministry of Agriculture and to promote the value of kibbutz life.

Impeded by its fear of factionalism, however, the Ihud approached the party ambivalently and obliquely and never fully marshalled its potential force. The Ihud wanted to influence the party but without committing the federation as a whole and resisted any reciprocal party efforts to direct the Ihud. Yet, the Ihud leadership demanded that the party relate to the Ihud Secretariat as if it were a demarcated body within the party, expressing, for example, dissatisfaction in 1958 when the Ihud Secretariat was not invited to a party meeting where kibbutz related topics were discussed. Nevertheless, the Ihud had not really elicited such structural consideration, as it had sent representatives only as individuals to party bodies. At times, even Ihud members in the party, perceiving themselves indeed as individual unbound delegates, balked at Ihud Secretariat control. In preparation for the 1956 party conference, the Ihud Wider Secretariat decided to compose a list of candidates for the party's Central Committee for whom Ihud delegates to the conference would be expected to vote. When the conference delegates objected, the Secretariat conceded and granted the delegates freedom to decide, with the Secretariat only making suggestions.

The Ihud always attempted to be the factor impinging upon the party and not vice versa. When party leaders suggested establishing a party settlement committee, contending it would provide the Ihud with a channel of communication, the Ihud agreed only reluctantly, fearing the committee would enable the party to impose its will or compel the Ihud to compromise with moshavim.

Aware that somehow it must tighten its grasp on party matters, the Secretariat charged one member in 1956 to oversee party activity within the Ihud. Finding that arrangement inadequate, the Ihud established a public action committee in 1957 and formally appointed a liaison. Nevertheless, the liaison complained in 1958 that he had not yet received authority to convene regular joint meetings between the Ihud Secretariat and party branch coordinators.

While the old guard-young generation dispute raised the Ihud's consciousness about losing power, simultaneously it discouraged it from engaging more directly in party matters for fear of embroiling the Ihud in the personal aspect of the intra-party struggle. When the

Ihud became a self-contained unit, called region, within the party in 1958 (In the case of the Ihud, this unit was not a geographic entity. Hitherto, party branches within kibbutzim were organized with non-kibbutz branches in geographically based party regions), ostensibly the Ihud was endowed with elements of group representation and had an opportunity to wield influence as a group, but the Ihud declined to accept full responsibility for directing political activity. Although several members in the Ihud Secretariat favored a more direct and unambiguous party link, eventually, they decided to establish separate administrative structures for party activity, thereby vitiating any strength vis-à-vis the party that the group could have gained from the new framework.

Disappointed with Mapai's attitude toward it, the Ihud nevertheless did not regard its differences, material or ideological, with the party as severe enough to warrant a break. The Ihud's ideological tie to Mapai had acquired a vague, historical and emotional nature, as members believed that "the party ... gave us a feeling of establishing the State of Israel in our land."[27] Ihud members agreed generally with Mapai's social ideology but thought the party had deviated in implementation, misguided about the kibbutz. Actually, neither group nor party was willing or able to confront and reconcile ideology with an increasingly different reality. Both party and group coped with change by putting ideological concerns in abeyance. By expanding numerically and dealing with several groups, Mapai weakened its professed ideology but did not attempt to articulate any ideological refinement.

Following a very rational electoral imperative, Mapai expanded, becoming a special type of "catch-all" party, a conglomeration of interest groups. Otto Kirchheimer describes a "catch-all 'people's' party" as a party which "has or seeks an almost nationwide potential constituency, its majority composed of individuals whose relation to politics is both tangential and discontinuous."[28] Because the electoral base is so ephemeral, Kirchheimer contends, the party needs interest groups "to provide mass reservoirs of readily accessible voters."[29] Mapai was becoming such a party, but its emphasis was more upon the groups than upon an amorphous, fickle electorate. Adept at balancing groups, Mapai leaders were content not to confront ideological issues, whether the challenge came from a group closer to it such as the Ihud or one further away such as the Manufacturers' Association. As Beer notes, strong parties do not necessarily mean weak pressure groups, and weak parties do not necessarily mean strong pressure groups.[30] I argue that interest group development depends to a large extent upon a party's policy-making procedures. Mapai may be considered strong in the sense that it dominated many positions in governing institutions. Nevertheless, many of its policies were formulated after elections by overseeing bargains among groups. A vote for Mapai basically became a vote for a leadership group to oversee these bargains. Groups formed and related to Mapai in accordance with Mapai's governing procedures. The party thereby signalled to groups that acting particularistically and bargaining were permissible. The kibbutz group sought to be one of the party's bargaining partners.

In accordance with Mapai's preferred ruling pattern and policy focus and in response to the developing society, the kibbutz group began to concentrate on more particularistic concerns. The kibbutz group realized it was a numerical minority within the country and that urban workers would not abandon factories for the collective farm. Realizing the world would not change in its image, the Ihud took a place within it and decided to attain the maximum for itself. As the party's changing attitude toward the kibbutz manifested itself in material terms, the group reacted on those terms, in effect conforming to the more contained role the party preferred for it. Whereas the Manufacturers' Association expanded its concerns from particular to nation-wide, the Ihud narrowed its emphasis. Not completely abandoning ideological issues or Mapai, the Ihud began distinguishing between ideology and material interests, placing priority upon the material and acting in the mode of a functional interest group. As such (and from Mapai's perspective, probably an unanticipated development), the group acted not only within the party but began seeking alignments with similar groups in other parties, contributing to the development of an autonomous interest group subsystem.

Chapter 8

The Ihud in Operation

Personal Politics: Networking

Perceiving an increasing "insider" power-broker nature to Mapai, the Ihud targeted those leaders directly and pressed to enter its members into their club. The Ihud cultivated a double threaded access network to decision-makers. One thread was the Ihud's party tie, and the Ihud relied upon this almost family-like connection to approach decision-makers who were not longstanding kibbutz or Ihud members. The second thread weaved through its members in the Cabinet, the upper reaches of the bureaucracy, and various state institutions. The party in this case was important to the Ihud because its approval was needed for Ihud persons to occupy those positions, and even that allocation needed the approval of the small "insider" party leadership. The Ihud contained and cultivated members of some expertise appropriate for these bodies and therefore desirable to the party. Often the threads intertwined, and an Ihud member was important in both group and party.

The Ihud fully exploited the opportunity to have members working in various institutions. Two members in particular who were strategically placed either within a state or agricultural body were Gvati and Efrati, and one constantly reads that the Ihud called upon them for aid or for their expertise. While Gvati may have believed he could keep his two roles apart, the Ihud did not make such fine distinctions, and, according to one longtime activist, "always tried and try to have our members in official positions very close to the movement. When we need them, we are not ashamed to ask their help."[1] The Ihud counted upon these well-placed members at least to sympathize, and, within limits to assist in reaching the decisive Government figures or, if they themselves were the decision-makers, to make

119

the desired decisions. Although when necessary, the Ihud transcended the party tie and acted in concert with other similar groups, its first attempt to resolve a problem was to activate all of its personnel, both group and party based, as is illustrated in the issue of the conversion of loans.

Lobbying for Loan Conversion: Activating the Network

Before embarking upon an explanation of the network's operation, it is necessary to understand the state's arrangements for financing agricultural development. Although the Jewish Agency followed procedures previously described for establishing and "weaning" settlements, money given as a final loan was often insufficient to cover all a settlement's costs. Especially for settlements disengaged in 1949, the standard was not on par with terms received by earlier settlements. Some financing for disengaged settlements was available from the Ministry of Agriculture which established a loan program to hasten agricultural production for supplying the growing population. However, these loans were given for seven years with interest and covered only about 50 to 70 percent of investments.[2] To cover all costs, therefore, kibbutzim took short term bank loans as well as loans from private individuals at high interest. Ostensibly, such loans were intended for operating capital, but settlements used them also for investment. With inflation high, the loans were tempting, and settlements continually rolled over their debt with additional loans. When in 1954, credit tightened, inflation started to decline, and agricultural profitability also declined, these indebted settlements found themselves in a precarious financial position.

All looked to Government for debt relief, hoping for a program converting short term debts to long term obligations. Although all kibbutz federations complained together, the political situation required that the Ihud lead the lobbying effort and become the spokesman and spearhead for the entire kibbutz sector. The kibbutz sector was fragmented among parties, separated not so much on specific economic issues but on ideological lines. In the early period, politics was so impassioned that "if Brum [Avraham Brum of the Kibbutz ha-Meuhad federation] had come to Gvati, he would not have listened to him. If Brum had come to Eshkol, who then was Finance Minister, he would not have paid attention to him because he was in the opposition, ... the relationships were very bad."[3] These assertions probably are exaggerated, especially considering Gvati's personality and willingness to

meet with groups when requested. Nevertheless, the political atmosphere within and among the three kibbutz federations was indeed
passionate. Political differences prevented the kibbutz federations
from cooperating even on seemingly mundane activities. The Ihud,
for example, utilized only drivers from its own settlements for heavy
hauling![4] In this politically charged atmosphere, it helped if Mapai
ministers of agriculture and finance were first approached by Ihud
delegates with whom they felt a political affinity. The Ihud accepted
the role of lobby leader and activated its network of strategically
placed members and party contacts. The ultimate target was the
Finance Minister, but intermediate targets were Ihud members in the
Ministry of Agriculture. The Ministry of Agriculture was expected to
campaign for agriculture's interests as groups interpreted them.

First demands for relief were voiced early in 1954, when Ihud
member Efrati served as Deputy Minister of Agriculture and Gvati as
the ministry's director-general. Composing a delegation of distinguished Ihud officials to address the Finance Minister, the Ihud
Secretariat was sure to secure a promise from Gvati and Efrati to participate in any meetings. Claiming that these two members were asked
to help not because they held Government positions but rather
because they were senior, experienced Ihud members, Yoseftal
actually revealed the importance of the personal and party network:

> Even if they [Gvati and Efrati] hadn't had these positions, they were
> very well known in the party ... and they were very close to them
> [Eshkol and Sapir, Finance Ministers at different times] and they
> spoke to them as friends, not so much as officials ... [Eshkol and
> Sapir] felt very close to the Ihud, and we spoke to them like you
> would to good friends. Especially Sapir, he was ready every day and
> every hour of the day to see us and to hear our problems, and he
> usually had an answer for this.[5]

The Ihud first strove to place members in important positions,
especially members who had strong personal and party links to other
officials and then could call upon those same members for assistance.

Efrati especially seemed not at all reluctant to press for the settlement constituency, and when in a public pressure effort (rare for the
Ihud), treasurers of settlements from several federations assembled in
Tel Aviv to publicize the operating capital problem, Efrati not only participated but spoke sympathetically on the settlers' behalf in the
presence of the Minister of Agriculture.[6] Although, in an Agricultural
Center committee meeting on the problem, Efrati stressed he was
merely listening in his capacity as a Center member, in an Ihud meet-

ing, he was not so reticent. Efrati blamed the kibbutz financial situation upon Mapai's allegedly less friendly attitude toward the kibbutz than toward the moshav type of settlement.[7] The financial problem affected mainly kibbutzim because they comprised most settlements consolidated in the early fifties which had taken advantage of the ministry's loan program and had then become financially entangled.

Discussion, not decision, also took place in Mapai's economic committee. Minister of Agriculture and Ihud member Luz participated as well as a moshav representative and the Governor of the Bank of Israel. The party served as a forum where potentially affected and perhaps disputing sides to a problem could meet. This meeting was held to prevent conflict between moshavim and kibbutzim, which had different stakes in conversion, and to explore possible solutions with a banking official.

Gvati also was a target for an appeal designed to convince him to press the Finance Minister for a conversion program. This appeal was a quiet, personal one led by Efrayim Avneri, an Ihud member with some financial expertise and a close friend of the director-general. Avneri participated in a committee with representatives from other kibbutz federations, but it was he who "brought up this claim [for conversion] before Gvati in person. We had to pressure the Government ... [and] the pressing force was the Ihud." Certainly, it was helpful that both were "good friends," and "it also helped me that Gvati was a Mapai person and I was a Mapai person."[8] Thus did the Ihud serve as lobby leader for the kibbutz sector as a whole, calling upon both its party and group connections.

In presenting their claim, kibbutz spokesmen found it helpful to insert an ideological element and play upon the Government's guilt feelings. They argued that the kibbutzim had followed state-set goals for the country's economic independence and had miraculously developed agricultural production in a short time to feed the increasing population. They should not now be penalized, they contended, because the Government had not arranged proper financing, which compelled them to take loans at prohibitive terms. Therefore, they argued at the Ministry of Agriculture "that it is your obligation to correct the financial situation."[9]

These arguments also were presented at the Agricultural Center, where all settlement groups joined in pressing for action because the problem was common to all the kibbutz federations and to a lesser extent to the moshavim. As illustrated by the conversion issue, the Agricultural Center served as an instrument of communication that was available for activation by several sources. Groups could use it to present a common front. A Government official who wanted to aid a certain group or economic sector could work through the Agricultural Center to demonstrate that the matter indeed had wide support and to preclude any accusation of favoritism to one particular group. Finally, the Government, or an official thereof, by dealing with the Agricultural Center, could compel the competing interests to pre-sort and rank their demands. In order for a group to gain the Agricultural Center's backing, it had to bargain with other groups represented there and reach a common stand.

Accordingly, through the Agricultural Center, the pressure for conversion was increased. The Ihud was prominent in prodding the Center. Also, Ministry of Agriculture officials Gvati and Efrati advised the groups there on which tactics to pursue in order to elicit sympathy and action from the Finance Minister. On credit and conversion issues, Gvati even drafted Agricultural Center declarations, and Efrati recommended that "public action" be taken.[10]

Such public action was taken in January 1956, when treasurers from the three kibbutz federations and moshavim held a public meeting in Tel Aviv, termed a "treasurers' revolt" by one newspaper.[11] The meeting attracted the attendance of Government ministers, including Finance, and Jewish Agency officials. Officials heard members of the agricultural community explain the problem, including a statement by Efrati, still Deputy Minister of Agriculture, favoring Government participation in finding an acceptable solution.

Although the Ihud preferred quiet diplomacy, when necessary, it was prepared to engage in activities to attract publicity. In fact, Government officials who were part of the Ihud's network sometimes suggested public action – both to increase the pressure on their Government colleagues and to educate the public to the merits of the group and its claims. For the very reason that an official was part of the Ihud network, he felt it necessary to prove his impartiality by demonstrating that demands, although perhaps of this one sector or vocalized by this one group, were widespread and justified. These officials believed that "such public meetings make it easier to answer those demands."[12] Whereas the Manufacturers' Association, which lacked a party tie, became adept at press relations in order to pressure the Government, the Ihud, which possessed a party tie, resorted to public pressure to enhance the position of a Government member conducting its fight. Having a network was helpful for access but did not assure automatic success.

Mapai affiliation also did not assure attainment of all requests, and, in fact, the Mapai tie actually prompted the group to reach outside the party for extra pressure. Within Mapai, the Ihud competed with moshavim, and despite the Ihud's party connections, Mapai did not always support the Ihud's claims over those of the moshavim. To enhance the perception of its cause and intensify the pressure, the Ihud often transcended party bounds and acted jointly with kibbutz federations affiliated with other parties, sometimes at its own initiative and sometimes at the behest of the other groups. As a lobbying interest group, the kibbutz federations presented a united front, with the Ihud taking initiatives on everyone's behalf, though ideological tensions remained keen within their special universe.

Though the Ihud was not afraid to act independently of Mapai control and to cooperate with other kibbutz federations, party affiliation nevertheless influenced its choice of tactics, as was evident in its maneuvers for achieving the loan conversion program. Meeting to discuss how to push the Government finally to institute a conversion program, the Ihud Secretariat considered proposals by other kibbutz federations for further public meetings and drastic measures such as defaulting on loans or declaring a strike in agricultural production.[13] The Ihud eschewed further public activity as inappropriate, not wanting to embarrass Mapai and let other federations "achieve by scandals things that can be achieved by a safer way."[14] However, the Ihud kept such reservations to itself, cunningly using the threat of public activity as a tactic to secure Government action. Once again, they activated the network, but this time with an extra note of urgency and even threatening undertone. They decided to inform their members in the ministry, Luz and Gvati, Minister of Agriculture and director-general, respectively, about the "steps that the treasurers have in mind" and to "inform [Finance Minister] Eshkol about an assembly of treasurers."[15]

Prompted by a crisis in the Ihud fund, the Secretariat convened again about credit matters in April 1956. (Each kibbutz federation operates a fund composed of monies collected from member kibbutzim. These funds lend money to poorer kibbutzim and also guarantee loans issued by banks to settlements.) The fund's directors had overextended loans and guarantees and feared kibbutzim could not meet their obligations. As one of several necessary measures, some believed the proposed Government conversion program would improve the situation by easing debt payment. Therefore, the Ihud wanted conversion to be implemented quickly. Complaining that the Agricultural Center was not exerting sufficient pressure to achieve conversion, Yoseftal urged her colleagues to consider coordinating with other kibbutz federations (whose funds also were endangered). The Ihud designated a delegation to Finance Minister Eshkol and again functioned as a spearhead and activated its network. Composing the delegation to Eshkol were, notably, Minister of Agriculture Luz, the ministry's director-general, Gvati, and Efrati, then a Kneset member, as well as other prominent Ihud personalities, several with party and personal ties to Eshkol.[16]

As a result of all these entreaties and explanatory efforts, by June, the Finance Minister agreed in principle to a conversion program. Then negotiations began in earnest between the Ministries of Agriculture and Finance and the banks to mobilize monies and arrange terms. The settlement groups relied upon the Ministry of Agriculture to serve as their proxy for obtaining a true conversion with long term loans at low interest. The settlement federations had only "second-line" input in these negotiations via the Agricultural Center and Ministry of Agriculture, expressing their opinions when a ministry official reported to the Center on progress in the negotiations. The Finance Minister, concerned to protect the Government, sought to guarantee as small a proportion of the loans as possible and to limit the amount of Government money involved. Sharing the Finance Minister's goals, the Ministry of Agriculture suggested arrangements that would satisfy them but also tried to obtain optimal terms for the settlements. The Ministry of Agriculture thereby played a pivotal role, hearing opinions of the settlement federations, offering the ministry's views, and also directly participating in negotiations.

By August 1956, the two year persuasion process culminated in a conversion program with an initial sum of eight million lira mobilized from various sources, including workers' pension funds. Though not the only source of pressure and not the sole factor for instituting the program, the Ihud had been a prime mover in the application of pressure on the Government. The Ihud varied its tactics according to opportunities available. When necessary, it cooperated with other federations but reserved room for independent initiatives, at times even disappointing its own Agricultural Center delegates who would have preferred greater utilization of that forum. Most members, however, regarded Ihud activity outside the Agricultural Center as an obvious method. "Here is a kibbutz movement of the party," Shlomo Kinerti explained, "and in a natural way, it has connections."[17] The Ihud called upon those connections in the conversion of loans campaign, applying first to its members in the Ministry of Agriculture to enlist their aid in appealing to the Finance Minister, who also was peripherally part of the Ihud's network within the party sphere.

Of Politics and Particular Benefits

Given the Ihud's reliance upon the Ministry of Agriculture, questions naturally arise whether the Ihud had "captured" the ministry, and if so, whether it could or did appeal solely for its own purposes and gained advantage over other groups. Although the Ihud did not relish the role as lobby leader and resented that other kibbutz federations regarded it as the "ice-breaker"[18] for them, it did not seek to deny them benefits, and, Ihud members contend, rarely requested aid only for the Ihud.[19] Ihud members perceived themselves as loyal to the kibbutz movement as a whole, realizing that economic disaster to a kibbutz of any federation would reflect poorly upon and endanger all kibbutzim, possibly, for example, by lowering the kibbutz sector's credit rating. The Ihud, rather, was frustrated by the political split that persisted among kibbutz groups and prevented the kibbutz sector from achieving greater influence. The Ihud would have preferred a united kibbutz movement together with a united labor party. The group regarded the politically divided kibbutz movement as a liability in its campaigns for aid and as responsible for the diminished enthusiasm of Ben Gurion and other politicians toward the kibbutz movement as a whole.[20] Such reasoning as "if I give you, I'll also have to give Kibbutz ha-Meuhad," some Ihud members believed, accounted for Eshkol's reluctance to immediately embrace the loan conversion proposal.

Despite the Ihud leaders' profession to the contrary, however, the Ihud was not always the altruistic advocate for all kibbutz federations. On occasion it sought to obtain exclusive benefits. These few cases of self-promotion vis-à-vis other kibbutz groups, however, underscore the difficulty any group would encounter in privately arranging and exclusively obtaining benefits. Though formal public discussion and approval was not always required for specific Government expenditures, supplying financial aid without being detected was complicated to arrange and politically problematic for the party in power, which, although it might prefer bestowing benefits upon one group, would not want to be caught and embarrassed. This process thus severely limited the Ihud's ability to be self-serving.

Groups were ever vigilant to make certain that a program's benefits were equally distributed or, if a particular program was inappropriate for them, to receive compensation in a different form. Detection of favoritism by some quarter ready to point a finger was always a risk. When, for example, the Ihud in 1957 arranged with the deputy director-general of the Finance Ministry to receive a loan from a fund held in Bank Leumi, the bank's director-general required that loans to other kibbutz groups also be approved.[21] Another instance of benefits sought solely for the Ihud occurred in regard to a cluster of Ihud kibbutzim which were established or expanded because of the kibbutz movement split (known as Rehabilitated Farms). The Jewish Agency refused responsibility for these settlements whose raison d'être was political, claiming that resources already were expended on the persons involved. These settlements, however, were eligible for loans from the Ministry of Agriculture. When these settlements became financially entangled as the others had, the Ihud pressed for their inclusion in the conversion program, tantamount to an extra advantage for the Ihud. Funding eventually was provided, but the Finance Minister sought to channel sums in such a way as to avoid parliamentary approval. Even to arrange this unique channel, he and the Ihud had to run a gauntlet of criticism from other groups – in this case, more from moshavim than from other kibbutz groups. The land holding enterprise has already been mentioned as another Ihud exclusive benefit. On balance, one must conclude that the political system strictly confined and limited the extent to which the Ihud could seek benefits on its own behalf even though it was well connected with the dominant party.

Committee Decision-Making:
Fostering Compromise and Pre-empting Political Conflict

In fact, the Government's unique response to pressure, as demonstrated in allocating the 1956 conversion funds, actually pre-empted accusations of politically inspired favoritism. The sum provided for loan conversion was insufficient to cover all eligible settlements, necessitating distribution decisions. Should funds be spread out, providing a small amount to each eligible settlement, or should funding be concentrated in order to assure rescue of a few? Should the funds be divided equally among the federations, or should settlements be sequenced based upon need regardless of affiliation? Who would designate the specific amounts and the recipient settlements? Should or could political affiliation be a determining factor, and could one group obtain more because of its political connection? To resolve these rather classic budgeting problems, the Government involved the federations directly in the allocation process. A conversion committee was established under the auspices of the Ministry of Agriculture composed of representatives from each major settlement federation, including moshavim, and a Government representative. In addition to this committee, the kibbutz federations, under the Agricultural Center's umbrella, also negotiated with each other to compose a list of kibbutzim for the committee's consideration.

By permitting these inter-federation deliberations, the Government partially delegated decision-making responsibility to avoid embroiling the Government in group conflict and resultant political complications. One might wonder whether the most needy received funds under this process, but the system seemed to work as intended in reducing any resentment toward the Government. While grappling with the above budgeting dilemmas, the federations could experience and appreciate the difficulties and conflicting demands decision-makers must confront and possibly realize that not always is "politics" responsible for a program's final form. Kibbutz ha-Meuhad, for example, objected to the allegedly excessive generosity of some program terms to the Ihud. But when the criteria were revised, the resulting list was substantially similar to the original one.[22] Committee decision-making seemed to succeed, therefore, at least in facilitating allocation of benefits while averting jealous reactions.

Group cooperation or competition to secure benefits could occur across or within party perimeters. Claims by one group or sector almost automatically generated claims from another. Often kibbutz federations affiliated with different parties banded together versus moshavim. Conversely, when kibbutzim pressed for debt relief, moshavim entered claims, though their need for conversion was not as urgent. Exploiting that very point, moshavim argued that any resources devoted to financing kibbutzim correspondingly reduced funds available for their development, and they should not be penalized for practicing fiscal responsibility.

Little "logrolling" occurred among groups. This was especially true between kibbutzim and moshavim, and kibbutzim often remained silent on issues important to moshavim. The picture of the interest group subsystem developing was one of spokes on a wheel with the Government or party at the center. Requests focused upon Government, and a Government minister either bargained with each group separately or gathered all together at one table, compelling the groups to equitably reconcile their demands.

The ostensibly "selfish" behavior of groups jealously spying upon others to secure an equal share of the pie becomes understandable when considered in the context of the extant political scene and decision-making procedures. The lack of explicit, mandated procedures for public discussion and the real possibility for political party abuse probably engendered group insecurities and suspicions. It may be argued, therefore, that group greed actually served to check potential political abuse.

Nevertheless, group demands for equality or parity presented the Government with distribution dilemmas. With groups so intently watching their neighbors and competing and clamoring for scarce resources, resolving such distribution dilemmas without arousing resentment is difficult. One method is to increase and extend the pie as much as possible, distributing something to everyone. Problems of more or less still may arise, but very vehement voices are quieted. Another option is to distribute according to Government decision, based upon whatever criteria it deems applicable. This method opens Government to accusations of political favoritism. A third method is to include affected groups in the decision-making process, compelling them to argue among themselves and make tough choices according to their consciences. By this procedure, Government greatly relinquishes direction over a program's purpose, and group determined distribution may or may not result in benefits proportionately reaching the place of greatest need. The Government of Israel combined methods one and three. Sensitive to accusations of party-based favoritism, officials attempted to give something to everyone, including, as in the case of the Manufacturers' Association, even those groups not politically close. By so doing, they limited accusations of party influenced distribution to issues of "more or less." Via bodies such as the conversion committee and the Agricultural Center, the Government transferred to the groups themselves major responsibility for distribution dilemmas and relied upon their judgments and power balances to make the appropriate decisions.

Reweaving the Network

To the Ihud's regret, Gvati decided to step down in 1958 as director-general of the Ministry of Agriculture. His replacement by a moshav person, Yitzhak Levi, was taken by the Ihud as a signal to start reweaving its network of members within the governmental apparatus. One of its responses, in addition to "claiming" the Agriculture Ministry and reinforcing its positions in the Jewish Agency, was to reinvigorate its Kneset presence.

Considering that the Ihud comprised only 12,000 voting members, of whom 11,500 voted for Mapai in 1959, its contingent of two or three Kneset seats seemed amply generous. The Ihud now decided to tighten its tie to this contingent. This consolidation was related to putting its party affairs in order. In both sets of relationships the Ihud sought to be the controlling factor.

When designing political structures appropriate for its new status as a Mapai region, the Ihud charged itself to "preserve our independence and non-dependence on the party."[23] Opinions differed whether this purpose best could be fulfilled by placing party affairs within the Secretariat's purview or by establishing a separate structure. Ihud leaders decided upon a separate structure for party activity but with important connecting links to the Secretariat.

Formally, member kibbutzim sent delegates to a special Council, and the Council chose a Secretariat and Secretary of the region. The Ihud Secretariat maintained some input, although the mechanism varied over time. At one point, the Ihud Secretariat selected members of the region's directing body, and in later years, the Ihud Secretary served as Chairman of the region in addition to a separate Secretary of the region. Membership between the two Secretariats always overlapped.[24]

For composing all party institutions, the Ihud permitted an assembly of the Ihud's party conference delegates to decide. For choosing Kneset members, however, the Secretariat reserved greater authority. It designated an appointments committee to recommend candidates for approval by an enlarged assembly. For filling Ihud positions in state institutions, the appointments committee likewise was empowered to prepare suggestions, in this instance for approval by the Ihud Secretariat. As an added measure of control, the Secretariat appointed a public action committee to discuss and decide upon political or party policy issues and party-related problems.[25] Via these structures and procedures activities containing a potential for party influence over the group were relegated to separate structures, but areas where the group could influence the party were retained under central group control. The Ihud thereby indicated that the Kneset would have special status and significance.

The Ihud used the process for the selection of Kneset candidates for the 1959 elections to express the renewed importance it attached to the legislature and to reassert its authority over its delegation. Both the appointments and public action committees composed a list of candidates for approval by the Ihud's Central Committee, as contrasted to the Secretariat which previously carried out this function. For this voting procedure, the Central Committee was augmented to include Ihud delegates to the party conference who were not Central Committee members. Using a broader based body for delegate selection would, Ihud leaders hoped, impress upon the delegation that the Ihud viewed "our representatives who go to the Kneset as Ihud representatives in the Mapai list" and "increase the feeling of the representatives that they are more obligated to weigh the feelings of this community."[26] Urging even greater authority over the Kneset delegation, one member proposed placing Kneset members under Ihud direction to the extent that "they can take instructions even when it is not comfortable and against the coalition."[27] Though this proposal was not endorsed, the Ihud nevertheless sent a strong message to the party with this Central Committee meeting.

Despite this muscle-flexing, the Ihud lost the top posts in the Ministry of Agriculture after the 1959 elections when Dayan, considered a moshav representative, became minister, and Levi moved up to deputy minister. Some observers wonder why the Ihud tolerated losing the agriculture ministership. The answer probably lies in the moshav's numerical superiority. Though the Ihud had contributed considerably to the election effort – 4,000 members worked on election day and 130 members worked more longterm – Ihud leaders admitted that their absolute numerical votes had declined.[28] The kibbutz sector, although not the Ihud, still retained one person in the upper echelons of the Ministry of Agriculture, Brum of the Kibbutz ha-Meuhad federation, and as tension among the federations had decreased by the end of the fifties, there was no Ihud animosity toward him. Rather than fight the party about a route that inevitably would close or narrow, the Ihud rerouted its affairs.

The Ihud did not move drastically, remaining within the party. Ideologically, the Ihud still could not leave Mapai and align with either of the other two leftist parties. Moreover, those parties were no longer solely kibbutz based but had accrued a worker's element, and if due to numbers, the Ihud's influence was waning within Mapai, certainly it would have had little bargaining power and even less institutional representation if it abandoned the party. Hoping to bolster kibbutz strength vis-à-vis moshavim, however, the Ihud urged including the leftist parties in the coalition after the 1959 elections, a change from its initial trepidation in 1955. In addition, most Ihud members favored unification among the three leftist parties and supported greater cooperation among the kibbutz federations, hoping that unification on either the party or kibbutz plane would effect unification on the other. Members increasingly pointed to party distinctions as the cause of fragmentation in the kibbutz movement and an obstacle that groups had to overcome.[29]

Special Politicization

A major weakness the Ihud was intent upon correcting derived not from the pull of various parties and inter-party differences but from disputes within Mapai itself. The question is how does a party-affiliated group assure its interests, which include group cohesion, in the face of factional disputes within the party. A crack in party leadership can extend its destructive faultline to all parts of the party, and an affiliated group must suffer the consequences or act to prevent them. Although its formal situation was quite different from that of the Manufacturers' Association, the Ihud's response was strikingly similar: it attempted to inure itself from party disputes by containing party affairs in organs apart from group activities. Perhaps the Ihud did not consciously intend to relegate politics to a separate realm, but that was the unintended result of the intra-Mapai and Mapai-Ihud tension. The Ihud now considered politics as consisting of power and personal struggles which were not necessarily related to achieving specific group goals. Separating political activity was the Ihud's defense mechanism for maintaining control over its political organizational life. The task was difficult, however. The Ihud was a group related to Mapai, and as such, it sought to influence party policy and maximize any benefits from that relationship while minimizing the dangers. Ihud members recognized the deleterious aspects of the ardent political atmosphere and their own penchant for becoming embroiled in party peccadillos and sought to contain this self-destructive inclination. A by-product of this decision was to push the overall Israeli political system toward one characterized by interest group power and influence.

The Ihud's reaction to intra-party power conflicts is comparable to the position taken by a group or political club in the United States system when it declines to endorse a candidate in a party's primaries or nominating procedures because (1) it may not be able to enforce a decision upon its members and therefore tries to avoid appearing embarrassingly weak and (2) it does not want to alienate anyone in the party and thereby endanger future relations. To an extent, such behavior admits weakness because if a group is sufficiently essential to the party to command attention from any winner, it might allow itself greater leeway in political activity. Conscious of its limited leverage, afraid of party and group splits, and aware of its dependence upon Mapai for maintaining its network, the Ihud sought above all to preserve its own coherence, as illustrated by its conduct during the Lavon Affair of 1960–61 and the Rafi challenge in 1965.

The Ihud and the Lavon Affair

Pinhas Lavon, who was Defense Minister in 1954 at the time of an abortive, clandestine Israeli attempt to create tension between the United States and Egypt, requested a statement from Prime Minister Ben Gurion in 1960 exonerating him of responsibility, based upon new evidence. Ben Gurion refused a personal statement, and relations between these two Mapai personages deteriorated, becoming quite bitter. The Cabinet established a Ministerial Committee of Inquiry, although Ben Gurion did not favor the panel. When the committee cleared Lavon, Ben Gurion claimed the committee had exceeded its authority by becoming judicial in function, and he resigned the premiership. An ugly, contentious intra-party crisis ensued, involving not only Ben Gurion and Lavon but other ministers as well who had been impugned by Ben Gurion's attacks on the committee. To resolve the conflict, Eshkol assumed a mediating role and concluded that Lavon's removal from his Histadrut post was necessary. Mapai's Central Committee so acted. The atmosphere still was not conducive to reconstituting a coalition, and new parliamentary elections were called.[30] Groups and individuals faced the dilemma of either endorsing Mapai's list headed by Ben Gurion or withholding support to punish the party for its treatment of Lavon.

When such crises occur in Israel, groups and individuals do not sit as idle spectators, but animatedly and at times virulently discuss events in all the nooks and crannies of society—in coffee houses, personal social gatherings, morning religious services, and even elevator rides. Such an atmosphere entailed a serious threat to the unity of the Ihud, especially because Lavon came from Kibbutz Hulda, a veteran Ihud settlement. The earlier decision to isolate its political activity did not allow the Ihud to ignore the Lavon Affair. Even remaining aloof required an explicit decision. Thus, the Ihud was compelled to confront and contemplate the matter when Ihud members sympathetic to Lavon resigned from Mapai party bodies. The kibbutz group faced a threefold task: to maintain a link to Mapai; to allow members with different views to express them; and to accomplish the first two tasks while maintaining unity within the kibbutz federation. A majority of the Ihud regarded a Mapai link as beneficial and worth maintaining. Yet, they wished to respect the right of a minority to express itself while not jeopardizing the group's standing with the party.

The Ihud Secretariat had to decide upon a stance toward the Affair and to decide whether or not to endorse Mapai in the elections. As for the Ben Gurion-Lavon dispute itself, the Ihud Wider Secretariat declared neutrality and banned all assemblies and organizing activities by Ihud members on behalf of either person. Nevertheless, despite declarations of good intention, many Secretariat members themselves were taking sides in the matter. Groping for some way to avoid a severe organization rift, the Ihud Wider Secretariat met to decide upon a course of action for the 1961 elections.

Although all knew who among them backed either side and who was neutral, discussion in Ihud leadership bodies did not deteriorate to personal recriminations and did not dwell upon the issue itself or the actors involved. Discussion centered on the party-group relationship and how the Ihud should handle internal divisions and organize its political party life. Gvati believed that to prohibit and suppress discussion of the Affair was both impossible and detrimental to the Ihud's stature in the party and the state. Anticipating argument, he sought to pre-empt damage by setting clear rules for the Ihud's internal discussion of the Affair. Certainly concerned about the Ihud's future relationship with Mapai and possible party retribution, Gvati reasoned that reaching an Ihud position and fighting from within would strengthen the Ihud vis-à-vis the party with which it still maintained a symbiotic relationship. Paramount to all members was preserving the Ihud federation, but Gvati viewed that unity "conditioned by the unity of the party." Pragmatically, he urged, "Therefore, with all the criticism some of us have with the party, it is our party, and we must be concerned to increase the strength of the Ihud with a concern for the strength of the party."[31] Similarly, others argued for "accepting a party ruling even if we don't agree." They advocated supporting the party in the elections in order to "have a say in the formation of the coalition" and to "enable the future Government to accomplish the previous policy that we agreed to."[32]

For the very purpose of preserving Ihud cohesion, other members disagreed with Gvati's suggested course, doubting both that calm debate could be conducted within the Ihud and that specific political direction could be imposed upon members. Therefore, they argued for neutrality "in order to preserve the Ihud framework."[33] They advised that loyalty to Mapai must yield to the higher value of group survival.

Unity in the face of conflict was not maintained simply by voting on different opinions and accepting the outcome. In fact, in political matters, the Ihud generally required unanimity, and when a majority-minority split occurred, did not necessarily follow the majority view. Rather than decisively conclude the debate, therefore, the Ihud sought to arrange a compromise within the party satisfactory to Lavon supporters that would enable an Ihud decision backing Mapai. A committee was established to seek such a solution and prepare suggestions for the Wider Secretariat.

To achieve a compromise, committee members met with Eshkol and party Secretary-General Yosef Almogi, and Gvati met with Ben Gurion. Reporting back to the Secretariat, the committee recommended that the Secretariat mobilize settlements for elections, allow structures of the Ihud's region to organize activities, declare a preference for including Lavon on the Mapai list, and publicly note that two party leaders had promised to try obtaining a party decision not to mention the Lavon Affair during the campaign. Gvati urged some decision so the Ihud could move onto other business neglected during the turmoil. Other members favored deciding because by postponement or a non-decision "it will appear as if the Ihud doesn't see itself tied to the party wagon," and the "public will get the impression that Mapai doesn't have a kibbutz movement."[34] To what extent the Ihud was tied to Mapai and to whose benefit was exactly the issue for the group. At an impasse, the Wider Secretariat postponed a decision, ordering the committee to try again to draft an acceptable formula. Indicative of the divisiveness of the issue, even the decision on a non-decision was close, with a majority (24–22) actually desiring a decision at that session.

During the three weeks provided until the next session, a subcommittee met with Ben Gurion, obtaining his promise not to mention the Lavon Affair in the campaign. The formula reached transferred to the "region of Mapai in the Ihud all activities connected to elections."[35] Satisfactory to those who preferred to regard the Ihud as not identified with Mapai by "authoritative decision," the solution also allowed those preferring a closer party connection to consider it tantamount to endorsing Mapai because many members on the region's directing body were chosen by the Ihud Secretariat.[36] Although several members contended the Ihud had abandoned Mapai, everyone finally endorsed the tactic, believing their power would not be diminished and that the Ihud Secretariat still would be the body designating members for state positions. Actually, in the election campaign itself the Ihud region was bypassed, and a special campaign headquarters for Mapai was established to ensure unhindered activity by Ihud members who supported Mapai. Judging the maneuver successful, Gvati claimed the Ihud thereby had managed simultaneously "not to hurt Mapai" and "not to have any negative occurrences."[37]

The Rafi Incident

The Ihud had a similar aim toward the 1965 elections as it had during the Lavon Affair, although by then the issues dividing the party and confronting Ihud members had become even more complex. With Gvati having replaced Dayan, who resigned as Minister of Agriculture, the Ihud again faced the task of maintaining a group link with Mapai in order to preserve group benefits while permitting freedom of political action for members and averting group disintegration. This time the situation was reversed, the anti-Lavonists under Ben Gurion's tutelage were pitted against Mapai, leaving the party in the summer of 1965 to form a new party, Rafi. Partly due to the Lavon issue, Ben Gurion and Rafi became rabidly anti-Eshkol. Eshkol, who had become Prime Minister when Ben Gurion retired in June 1963, attempted a rapprochement with Lavon's supporters early in 1964. This infuriated Ben Gurion who waged a campaign against Eshkol, including attacks on his qualifications as a leader, to prevent Mapai from readmitting the Lavon faction.

Rafi adherents were linked together on other issues besides the Lavon Affair. Rafi represented the young generation within Mapai which was fighting the old leadership for positions. This inter-generational competition became intertwined with the attacks on Eshkol, who was considered part of the old guard. And Rafi opposed the proposed union between Mapai and Ahdut ha-'Avodah because it threatened the young generation's rise. Rafi also advocated increased statism. Ihud members drawn to Rafi, including many prominent old timers and even Mapai activists, were attracted by a mixture of loyalty to Ben Gurion, agreement with the young generation's aims and belief in statism, and an opposition to union with Ahdut ha-'Avodah.

As the 1965 elections approached, the Ihud had to take a stand. Fearing that "debates conducted in the dining hall" would expose too clearly the division among members and could "turn men into enemies in one night,"[38] the Secretariat recommended that settlements not permit politicking on their kibbutz premises but rather convene or participate in assemblies outside the settlements, where larger forums hopefully would obscure the individual's perception of his neighbor's position. Preparing for all contingencies, the Ihud permitted a Rafi region to organize alongside the Mapai region and decided to contribute funds to both election campaigns according to the proportion of Ihud votes the parties received, although it eventually increased its contribution to Mapai.

Resolving the Lavon Affair in an ambiguous manner and responding to the Rafi challenge by attempting to accommodate all sides was the Ihud's signal to the parties that it would not be drawn into destructive party feuds. On the whole, the Ihud did not suffer internally from much political fallout, although one Ihud member has noted that two

Lavon supporters were, in effect, banished from the Ihud Secretariat.[39] Nevertheless, other Lavon supporters, important to the Ihud for their expertise, continued to participate in Ihud meetings. During Rafi's three year separate existence, Rafi members served in prominent Ihud roles with some, but manageable, friction with Mapai members.

While personal animus was minimized, the Ihud experienced anguish in relating to a turbulent party system. One occurrence during the Rafi interlude illustrates the group's travail. Ihud members of the Mapai region met and, though not authorized by the Ihud, took positions in the group's name on economic matters relevant to settlement interests. This party meeting was held prior to and in the same week that the Ihud's Secretariat and economic committee were scheduled to meet. The Ihud economic committee was headed by a Rafi person, Yosef Perlmutter, who regarded the Mapai meeting as an attack upon his ability to conduct the committee impartially. Ihud Rafi members protested the incident, calling for a Secretariat discussion.

At that session, members attempted to clarify the Ihud's relationship to the party system. Perlmutter, aside from feeling personally insulted, perceived the party meeting as group submission to party direction. Barukh Aznayah (a Mapai adherent), however, interpreted the meeting as an admirable group attempt to influence the party. He favored group activity within the party, contending that the Ihud should not limit its topics or venues for discussion, for "then we decree upon ourselves a lack of influence in important places."[40]

Although all clearly were dissatisfied with the ambiguous state of party-group relations, they did not make any alterations. Aznayah's remarks referred to Mapai, but by extending his logic, the Ihud could have considered formulating positions and exerting influence upon several parties, as the Manufacturers' Association had attempted and as Gush Emunim more successfully would accomplish. Interkibbutz forums existed where the Ihud could launch independent initiatives, but this strategy was not then embraced. In the highly charged political atmosphere, a group's position, even if independently reached, frequently was perceived as politically motivated. Perlmutter, for example, felt compelled to defend his conduct at the interkibbutz table as having been solely in the interests of the Ihud and not party inspired. To avoid any party taint, the Ihud temporarily remained aloof from decisions with a divisive potential, deciding, for example, that the Ihud's next Central Committee meeting would concentrate on internal problems.

Both the Lavon and Rafi episodes highlight the special pitfalls that party related interest groups may encounter. Truman's discussion of group cohesion and overlapping memberships is helpful in understanding the dilemma that these party disputes presented to Israel's group subsystem.[41] Overlapping memberships in groups, or, for the purpose here better understood as conflicting pressures or loyalties, create dilemmas for individual group members, and depending upon how widespread and intense the conflict, can threaten group cohesion. Ihud members were faced with setting priorities among their loyalties to the Ihud, to Mapai, to Ben Gurion and his followers, and to Lavon and Eshkol and their followers. As an example of the contradictory choices confronting a kibbutz member, Rafi included Dayan, whom many kibbutz members had viewed as unfriendly to kibbutz interests during his tenure as Minister of Agriculture. An Ihud member supporting Rafi would have to deem the Dayan aspect as less important than other factors. The Ihud always had been affiliated with Mapai in some way, and that affiliation, as well as group coherence, was threatened when Ihud members were attracted by other political currents.

Maintaining group cohesion, according to Truman, is a task of group leadership. The Ihud leadership had to prevent competing party pressures from overriding kibbutz and Ihud interests and dividing the group. The Ihud did this by diminishing or diffusing its political party activity. It maintained the group intact by repelling politicization and not compelling members to choose between group and party. Citing P. F. Lazarsfeld's study of the effect of conflicting group loyalties on voting behavior, Truman notes that individuals cope with conflicting pressures by escaping and "withdrawing in effect from participation in the campaign."[42] The Ihud's group response in these two instances conformed to Truman's observation. While not completely withdrawing from the political fray, the Ihud qualified its support, and by allowing members freedom of party choice, prevented conflicting loyalties from becoming a dilemma for its members. The group tried to obtain the best possible position for itself in all its political party relationships, developing a unique response of supporting all relevant sides to some degree. Its reaction in both instances revealed the Ihud's remaining dependence upon Mapai's apparatus and patronage but also gave notice that the kibbutz interest was paramount and that the group would not permit party and personal feuds to shatter its organizational unity. The group took the initiative in determining its party support, thereby reaffirming kibbutz priorities and group cohesion.

As a perhaps unintended consequence of the interaction between group and party systems, Israel's political model appeared more pluralist in nature, where groups operate autonomously of parties, demarcating themselves and claiming for themselves a certain set of priorities. Although the Ihud did not declare independence from all parties and did not yet attempt to become the independent variable extracting benefits from several parties by causing them to compete for group support, the Ihud continually distanced itself from the party plane. With its connection to the Mapai apparatus made more tenuous (but not severed) by these political brouhahas, and in view of its uncertain hold on the Ministry of Agriculture, the Ihud in the sixties had to reevaluate its position of influence. It had to decide upon channels it wished to recapture and compensatory channels it would seek to open, and how it would conduct this activity, either within or outside the party system.

Chapter 9

Growing Group Consciousness and Government Relations

Upon losing the Ministry of Agriculture in 1960, the Ihud searched for other channels. Meeting to decide upon the Ihud's and Gvati's future after Dayan had refused to return Gvati to the ministry or to appoint any other Ihud member as director-general, the Ihud pondered whether it was best to direct its efforts on strengthening the Agricultural Center or on enhancing the Ihud, and concomitantly where best to place Gvati. "Fearful of the Ministry of Agriculture," Gvati argued forcefully for revitalizing the Agricultural Center as a strong front to negotiate with a tightfisted Government.[1] He implored the Secretariat to assign him there. Unheeding, the Secretariat chose an unwilling Gvati to head the Ihud, accepting several members' assessments that the Ihud alone could not reinvigorate the Agricultural Center and that agricultural problems would not be solved there. It was believed that first priority should be given to fortifying the Ihud's own political leverage vis-à-vis ministers and governing institutions.[2] Since Gvati, the technocrat, was still in good standing with party and Government, selecting him to head the Ihud seemed to serve that priority.

Whether the Ihud's skeptical evaluation of the Agricultural Center was a self-fulfilling prophecy is difficult to ascertain, but the Agricultural Center did decline in effectiveness in the early sixties, paralyzed by moshav-kibbutz tension. Increasingly, the Center's party based structure was perceived as irrelevant because "ninety-nine percent of its problems [were] not on the party plane."[3] Thus, its structure could not provide a basis for renewal. Several reorganization plans were designed during this decade, but none was implemented.

True to his convictions that the Ihud alone could not counter moshav influence, Ihud Secretary Gvati soon set out to foster greater cooperation among kibbutz federations. Several meetings of the three kibbutz federations were held to explore economic and social cooperation that would not require political unification of their respective patron parties. Gvati sought to unify certain committees then existing separately in each federation. As of May 1960, Gvati already could report some progress to the Ihud Central Committee, such as formation of a joint committee that would examine the financial situation, economic matters, planning problems, and land and water issues, as well as a coordinating body for kibbutz members participating in Ministry of Agriculture area planning boards. Steadily expanding areas of cooperation, the kibbutz federations established the "Alliance of the Kibbutz Movements" (Brit ha-Tnu'at ha-Kibbutzit, hereafter referred to as the Brit) in December 1963 with Gvati as its first Secretary.

Undoubtedly, measures taken by the new Minister of Agriculture spurred increased kibbutz cooperation. Paradoxically, policies pursued by a minister from the group's own party impelled it to act outside. Confirming some of the kibbutz sector's worst fears, Dayan, upon becoming Minister of Agriculture, immediately raised one of the most explosive issues in the Middle East – the allotment of water. Dayan sought to change the standard for water ceilings and reallocate already designated amounts from kibbutzim to moshavim. But he met with resistance, and the struggle illustrates the Ihud's developing mix of modes for interest organization and expression.

The system for allocating water for agriculture until Dayan's time differed for kibbutzim and moshavim, resulting in what seemed to Dayan as discrimination against moshavim. At their establishment, kibbutzim were assigned an annual amount of water based upon a certain number of agricultural units regardless of initial population size, and that amount was to suffice for their growth; kibbutzim would not request additional allotments if their membership increased. Moshavim, on the other hand, received an allotment per agricultural unit existing at their founding, and with any population increase were entitled to receive additions. When Dayan became minister, there were kibbutzim that had not yet reached full population capacity but were receiving water based upon potential size, and in comparison with moshavim actually received more water per capita. Dayan sought to reallocate that water according to the existing rather than the potential number of units. He proposed the change in the Kneset. Criticism and cautionary statements immediately emanated from several sources. The Ihud was concerned that Dayan's remarks would incite resentment among new immigrants (who tended to prefer moshavim) who would blame the kibbutz sector for their water shortage.

The kibbutz federations went into action on several fronts within and outside party forums. Their committee on land and water criticized the Dayan proposals. The Agricultural Center was notified. Ihud's Gvati alerted Mapai's Secretary-General Almogi to the danger of a "civil war" among farmers.[4]

To ascertain the facts and figures, a Government committee was established composed of representatives from the kibbutz and moshav sectors and chaired by Peretz Naftali, a former Minister of Agriculture. Although Kibbutz ha-Meuhad was not satisfied with the kibbutz sector's counter-attack, and one Ihud member viewed Dayan's speech as a "declaration of war against the kibbutz" and urged a party inquiry, Gvati discouraged such extreme measures and advised awaiting the Government's report.[5] The tone thereby was set for resisting unfriendly policies and for resolving group disputes: greater kibbutz cohesion and a preference for Government committees. This is not to state that the water issue was settled quickly or smoothly. For several years, the Ministry of Agriculture continually proposed water reductions opposed by kibbutzim, and other Government committees which included group representatives were established to devise a reallocation plan, implement it, and hear appeals. Eventually by 1964 all groups reached an agreement.

The water allocation issue provides insight into the slowly changing relationships among groups, parties, and decision-making bodies. Stymied by the moshavim at the Agricultural Center, the Ihud paid only cursory attention to it. The Ihud then had two alternatives—to appeal to the party and/or to find a way to deal directly with Government. While not completely ignoring the party route, the full panoply of party organs was not called upon as a decision-making forum, and the party was only one of several channels. The appeal to party was a mild one, to the party Secretary who would be concerned about any dissension among collective and cooperative farmers and would probably personally speak to the Minister of Agriculture. Though a Mapai settlement committee was established in 1960, the Ihud shied away from utilizing it, believing that moshav-kibbutz tensions would be replicated there and that the Ihud would not have the backing of kibbutz groups affiliated to other parties. Participating in a Government committee, however, afforded the Ihud greater leverage, as it could sit there with other kibbutz federations. Paradoxically, though Mapai was powerful and dominant, holding many portfolios, neither the party apparatus nor the group's party members were much invoked because "when ministers were members of the party, why should you go to the party, go straight to the top."[6]

The Party's Limited Role

The party was not entirely out of the picture. However, it usually was invoked by a minister, not a group. In these instances, the Ihud was well equipped with Gvati to voice its concerns. The continuing campaign for loan conversion as well as pricing and subsidy policies further illuminate the party's limited role.

As of 1960, despite the first loan conversion, kibbutzim still had not entirely resolved their financial problems for two reasons. One, kibbutz leaders contended that the original sum provided had not been sufficient, and two, they acknowledged that several kibbutzim had used the money for additional investment rather than for settling outstanding debts. A plea for additional conversion had been made late in 1959, while Luz still headed the Ministry of Agriculture, and had been restated to Dayan when he attended an Ihud Secretariat meeting early in 1960 in his new role as Minister of Agriculture.

Perceiving that Dayan, while not opposed to kibbutzim on all issues, was not the advocate of their interests that previous ministry officials had been, kibbutz federations coordinated to press their views with Gvati in the lead. Starting with a self-help effort, kibbutz federations established a committee of kibbutz treasurers to analyze their financial problems.[7] Soon thereafter, going "straight to the top" and bypassing the party apparatus, kibbutz federation representatives met directly with Finance Minister Eshkol. This was a change from past practice of seeking the accompaniment of other Government officials. Apparently, Gvati as head of the Ihud was considered sufficiently influential with Eshkol. And that meeting resulted in some welcome news: twenty million lira for conversion previously had been discussed, and though the kibbutz federations claimed that the sum was insufficient, Eshkol promised that all the money would be directed to kibbutzim, not moshavim. (Later, however, Eshkol qualified this offer.)

While kibbutzim could not expect Dayan's automatic support, he recognized his responsibility for improving the agricultural sector. (Eventually, he was to be dubbed the "Minister of the Farmers.") Moreover, Dayan was sensitive not to be tagged as the moshav benefactor exclusively and understood the necessity of negotiating with other societal groups, such as the Histadrut, particularly on issues such as pricing. Somewhat surprising, given the emphasis Dayan supposedly placed upon statism, he regarded the party as having jurisdiction on various economic matters. As a new minister, he was not about to be a precipitous innovator of decision-making processes.

In the summer of 1960, therefore, Dayan raised within the party a need for improving the agricultural sector.[8] A committee was established composed of Ministers Eshkol, Sapir, and Dayan plus David Horowitz, Governor of the Bank of Israel, Uzi Finerman, representing moshavim, and Gvati for kibbutzim. Although ostensibly a party designated committee, participants were ministers and leaders of Mapai affiliated interest groups. The party apparatus as such was not involved, and the entire enterprise could be regarded almost as a bilateral Government-group forum. Theoretically, though non-Mapai groups could have sought representation through "their" party spokesmen, they expressed themselves via the Mapai affiliated groups. This perpetuated the pattern of the Ihud and other Mapai related groups as lobby leaders. The topics discussed were of varying importance to those involved. Finance Minister Eshkol was the figure to be persuaded. Concluding the meeting, he confirmed the twenty million lira to kibbutzim and appointed a committee to make specific suggestions on the other issues. At the close of the meeting, the moshav representative said to Dayan: "Moshe, do you know what we succeeded in doing today? In giving twenty million lira to kibbutzim." Dayan responded, "Uzi, do you want that they say I am the minister of the moshavim?"[9] A party sponsored committee thereby aided a minister's need to appear fair to all the ministry's constituents.

Bargaining among different groups' needs usually resulted in a compromise. Farmers, particularly kibbutz farmers, for example, argued for lower subsidies, requiring only a limited amount to plan production, whereas the Government preferred subsidizing a higher percentage of the price, calculating it as cheaper than paying all workers a cost of living allowance. At the party forum, some figure ultimately was reached because "Mapai then was always the party that makes compromises. If we said twenty-five, and the Government said fifty percent, then it was decided on thirty, thirty-five."[10]

Limiting the bargaining to affiliated groups enabled the party to temper issues and reach other groups as well because "after an unofficial forum like this reached an agreement, then the people of Ihud and the moshavim came to the Agricultural Center and said to Kibbutz ha-Meuhad and to ha-Shomer ha-Tza'ir, 'Listen, we sat on the side with Eshkol, and we reached a compromise like this.'"[11]

Such party meetings were not widely publicized. "One didn't need to know that the party appointed a committee like this. The committee was an unofficial forum."[12] The party merely provided the moral authority and an additional forum for ministers and groups to sit together once again.

Ihud members, in fact, did not regard such a party designated committee as an ideal decision-making arena precisely because negotiation rather than expert planning occurred. "Where are all the organs and organizations," queried one member who objected to turning "a party committee into a committee that decides prices."[13] He argued that policy should not be made in such an "improvisational" manner.[14]

These observations on "unofficial" party meetings leading to compromise suggest insights into Israel's political culture and the developing role of parties and groups. In a country where groups have existed and proliferated, Israelis are reluctant to acknowledge that development. Parties and politics are supposed to be ideologically based, and interests as particularistic demands are therefore suspect and not admitted to exist. For these reasons, Mapai did not project itself as, nor want to be regarded as, a non-ideological or an ideologically nebulous party. Nor did it want to reveal that differences of opinion occurred within it. While composed of groups, the party would not acknowledge that these groups deserved a role in decision-making because that may have required explicitly formulating ideology and addressing comprehensive policies. Though known as the party of compromise, it was only ex post facto so described. The party did not arrange compromises out of true belief in the process; it was not pragmatic for pragmatism's sake. Therefore, secrecy surrounded party supervised bargaining sessions. However, the party was composed of diverse groups, and therefore, bargaining was necessary. And bargaining occurred but to avoid addressing ideological issues or dealing with comprehensive policy, not as a positive method of resolving differences. Bargaining was considered somehow distasteful and improper political behavior.

Groups, especially those party affiliated which inculcated the same conception of politics, easily conformed to the party's process but in so doing also took steps, perhaps unwittingly, which contained a potential for system change. The Ihud participated in the "secret" party sessions and became a particularistic bargaining partner to party and Government but simultaneously started to expand beyond party bounds and sought to separate interest group activity from the party plane. By its actions, the Ihud may be considered a catalytic force for pragmatism and pluralism upon Mapai and the Israeli political system.

It may be noted that group leaders referred to Mapai and Government interchangeably. The substitution is significant for two reasons: it indicates that Government was assuming many functions previously performed by parties and that both party and Government were led by the same small group of officials. From the group's perspective, especially a group affiliated with the dominant party, whether or not a decision was taken under party or Government auspices made little difference in the group's choice of targets. The actors were the same, primarily ministers. The Ihud directed itself to them in either arena.

While the Ihud did not bargain on the party level as a primary tactic, neither through its party nor via another party concerned with kibbutz affairs, when benefits were available through that route, the group did not hesitate to take advantage of the offer, as the continuing campaign for fiscal relief demonstrates. In 1964 demands for aid again were raised, with special emphasis on older kibbutzim that had experienced the split and subsequent financial difficulties. Simultaneously, in 1964, the labor parties, particularly Mapai and Ahdut ha-'Avodah, were negotiating an alliance. As part of the bargain and to make the alliance palatable to Ahdut ha-'Avodah's kibbutz federation, Yigal Allon, an Ahdut ha-'Avodah leader and alliance negotiator, secured from Mapai minister-negotiators a promise for another conversion which was started in 1965. In addition, in September 1965, a sum of money was promised for a kibbutz credit fund.

Although the coincidence of increased funding for kibbutzim with the 1965 formation of the Alignment cannot be ignored, Ihud members argue that the programs objectively were justified, the result of longstanding and oft-repeated demands, and politically linked only insofar as funds for settlement were more easily obtainable since Ben Gurion's resignation had removed him as an anti-kibbutz force.[15] Nevertheless, those same members acknowledge that Ahdut ha-'Avodah's Allon was a key fighter for the funds. Granting these funds may be viewed as similar to the Finance Minister's inability to refuse a COLA claim in an election year, and certainly, the monies strengthened Ihud members' ties to Mapai, perhaps preventing greater Ihud defections to Rafi. While the Ihud was not sufficiently cohesive to use its support as a bargaining chip, it could allow itself to be wooed. In a multi-party or dominant party system, groups hold implicit power over parties, as surely parties must consider possible defections and attempt to maintain even marginal superiority over other parties. Groups caught in political turmoil may not themselves initiate negotiations with parties, but they are not adverse to accepting offers from the parties and attempting to maximize group benefits.

All the group maneuvers on water and financial issues occurred on the background of the Lavon Affair and the formation of Rafi. However, groups did not directly link interests and politics. From the group perspective, parties were perceived as arenas appropriate for ideological issues, questions of leadership, and the like. Policy-making and struggles for material demands preferably would be conducted elsewhere – in a ministry, in the Government, or in an interministerial committee. The Finance Minister was a central figure, appointing many committees. The connection between pressing for a party to gain office and obtaining certain rewards was weakening. A growing dichotomy was developing between interest groups and parties with Government acquiring a separate role.

Developing Government-Group Relations

Kibbutz groups increasingly oriented themselves toward Government, and Government became intimately involved in farm affairs. Government involvement in group affairs was a natural development since the settlement federations from their inception always were dependent upon an outside agency for start-up loans and other aid and were to some extent Government directed. Therefore, the Ihud, as other groups, made demands upon Government and regarded Government as the "great provider," even in contradiction to several of the kibbutz group's founding principles. Despite declarations of devotion to egalitarianism and a mutual help ethic, kibbutz federations regarded Government aid as their due, just as, if not more than, interest groups in any political system. Though kibbutz federations maintained a fund for financially aiding their poorer members, their largesse was not unlimited, and they began enlisting Government aid in financing struggling settlements. Such assistance, the Ihud believed, was a Government responsibility.

The Ihud became adept at appealing for and obtaining Government aid. For example, housing aid at times was more available for absorbing immigrants. The Ihud was not above appealing for housing aid for absorption purposes, and when the Ihud did not absorb an equal number of immigrants, it could utilize the housing received for internal expansion. While the Ihud would repay the aid on terms appropriate to the different housing category and therefore did not illegally take money from the Government, the group meanwhile succeeded in expanding its housing stock, for the housing could not be physically removed.[16]

Coping with adverse economic conditions in part generated a "take what you can" philosophy with little reference to ideological principles. To finance operating capital, for example, Yoseftal, as treasurer of her kibbutz, utilized a unique arrangement of "travelers' checks." "We had a bank account in Haifa, and a bank account in Tel Aviv and a bank account in Zikhron Ya'aqov. And post service was very, very slow. ... I wrote a check in Haifa to my own kibbutz in Tel Aviv and from Tel Aviv to Zikhron and from Zikhron to Haifa. And the checks went around without any money behind it."[17] Similarly, the first agreement for disengaging settlements from the Jewish Agency was an "in-kind" arrangement rather than in cash form, and as Yoseftal related, "We got irrigation pipes, but there was no water at all," and aluminum sheets to use for chicken coops and cow sheds in an extremely windy area.[18] So, she sold the pipes on the black market, and most of the siding blew away. Little reference was made to ideology to determine if such banking arrangements and black market dealing were permissible.

While originally most Government aid objectively was needed, once a precedent was set and assistance received, aid certainly was not voluntarily refused even when the need was not as grave. As long as credit was offered and available with Government backing, kibbutzim continued to borrow, although they probably could have financed themselves. Actually, very rational financial principles were involved, for in an inflationary economy, borrowing made financial sense. In this process, groups became accustomed to Government support.

Having Ihud persons in administrative positions not only helped the group to obtain funds but also served to increase Government involvement over group affairs, making the Government and group partners in administration, as the method devised for implementing credit programs demonstrates. When the several conversion schemes were not completely successful, kibbutz federation leaders and officials in the Ministry of Agriculture became worried. Though claiming funds were insufficient, kibbutz leaders admitted financial failure was "their fault" in many cases because kibbutzim continued to invest improperly.[19] The situation spurred Brum of the Kibbutz ha-Meuhad federation working in the Ministry of Agriculture to develop a "concentrated credit" program whereby the ministry not only would provide funds but would oversee the settlements' entire financial planning structure. In order to receive credit from the Ministry of

Agriculture, each settlement was linked to one bank, and together the three sides – ministry, bank, and settlement – drew up and supervised a financial investment plan for the kibbutz. Kibbutzim were required to submit semiannual progress reports. With this program, popularly known as the "Brum Club," initiated by a kibbutz person and enthusiastically embraced by the kibbutz federations, Government greatly augmented its direct involvement over group affairs.

Diversifying Targets

When Gvati became Minister of Agriculture in 1964, the Ihud conceivably could have established a very cozy relationship with him, and one would not have been astounded to discover the group receiving increased access and greater tangible rewards. Nevertheless, such was not the case, and paradoxically, the Ihud in this period exerted its independence and diversified its channels. Though Gvati attended Ihud meetings, often of a very detailed nature, the Ihud did not obtain all of its demands.

In fact, while Gvati was Minister of Agriculture and a kibbutz person headed the ministry's Planning Center, a dispute arose in 1966 between kibbutzim and the Government on allocating milk production ceilings for the following five years. Concerned to limit milk production overall as well as to guarantee a livelihood to settlements dependent upon milk as a main source of income, more moshavim than kibbutzim, the Planning Center's suggested production ceilings allowed moshavim a greater increase than kibbutzim. Because many kibbutzim already had reached amounts set for 1971, the Ihud and other kibbutz federations complained the ceilings were too low and even discriminatory against the kibbutz movement.[20] Furthermore, they predicted that moshavim would be unable to meet their quotas, resulting in milk imports. But Gvati stood firm and refused to modify the ceiling allocations.

Gvati's conduct in this case was an example of "rising to responsibility" and internalizing his new role as minister. Ihud members serving in public positions had to consider the general interest, or more accurately, the interests of all groups. Proud of this phenomenon, Ihud members boast that "every kibbutznik, the moment he received a Government position, saw his first loyalty to the Government and not to the kibbutz movement."[21] Such statements are largely true. Ihud member Naftali Ushpiz related that when he worked in the Jewish Agency during the fifties, Yoseftal accused him of not adequately favoring the Ihud with financial aid; Ihud members complained that their members did not always vote for the Ihud's benefit in the Agricultural Center; and Avneri pointed out that when he distributed funds at the Jewish Agency in the sixties, the Ihud did not receive the largest share.

To fulfill the functions of guarding every group's interest and protecting the Government's, the Ministry of Agriculture under Gvati relied and expanded upon two methods previously used: (1) committees were employed to resolve problems, and (2) groups were encouraged to participate in the ministry. For example, in the early seventies when the Government's water authority sought to raise the price of water and farmers protested, the ministry established a committee which included members of several groups. Also, groups, including private sector farmers, were represented on public councils within the ministry's Planning Center which convened to set food production ceilings. "Setting ceilings was not just a matter for bureaucrats. ... Each year through this forum they set the ceilings. Before, there were arguments on principle but afterwards, they sat at the table and made a compromise. ... All these battles that you read about ... in the end the matters were settled at the table without anyone from above having to force anyone. ... The Government built its policy on cooperation."[22]

In addition, the Kneset became an important advocacy center for the Ihud and the rest of the kibbutz movement. Kibbutz delegates conducted the interest group's case, but they did not focus only on Mapai/Labor Kneset members. In fact, according to one Ihud leader, the Labor Party did not always champion the farmers' interests because the party often gave higher priority to the interests of consumers who comprised a larger voting bloc. Therefore, "if we [the Ihud delegation] saw there was no majority in the Labor Party, then we tried to make use of the other members of the Finance Committee ... even under the Labor Government ... and if the farmers of the Labor Party could not convince the other Labor Party members of the committee, they went together with the other farmers."[23] Needless to say, Mapai/Labor was not "enthusiastic" about this development. The Kneset contingent did not have to act extremely by voting against the party because "a compromise was made before, but the party was more ready for compromise if the pressure was stronger."[24]

Seeking particular interests, the Ihud exerted whatever pressure necessary upon its party, the Government, and even upon its own members. In so doing, it expanded the arenas for pressure and decision-making and affected procedures followed in the governing institutions. When the Likud came to office, the Ihud was prepared to further expand these arenas of activity.

Operating Under the Likud: Of Perceptions and Politics

Although the Ihud had been dissatisfied with some of the policies pursued by Mapai/Labor Governments, had developed a protective distance from the party plane, and had developed independent channels of activity, it could chart those paths feeling secure that Mapai/Labor would direct the Government. Ihud members compare their struggles to a family quarrel. Loyalty to Mapai/Labor and consequently to the Government tempered the group's tactics and fostered a willingness to cooperate in resolving problems without "embarrassing" Government or party. The Likud's accession to office in 1977 came as a shock to the Ihud. After all, keeping the "fascists" out of power had always in the past rallied the Ihud behind Mapai/Labor. Now, with its "family" out of office, the Ihud had to confront the feared "fascists," and at first it floundered.

The Ihud's ideological blinders hampered its ability to view Likud policies objectively, calling into question whether the Ihud could continue to develop independently and expand channels opened under Labor. Many measures proposed by the Likud actually were extensions of policies already initiated or contemplated by Labor and even considered by the Ihud: (1) as early as December 1973, the Labor Government had intimated it would aim to reduce milk subsidies; (2) in January 1977, the Labor Government had considered differentiated subsidies according to the economic viability of farms; (3) in January 1975, the Government had suggested changing criteria for subsidized credit in order to direct larger sums to kibbutzim in greater need; and (4) also in January 1975, the Labor Government had planned reductions in the agriculture budget. Moreover, for years, the Ihud had contended it could manage without high subsidies. Thus, when the Likud after 1977 proposed reducing subsidies on milk and other commodities, establishing differentiated prices, reducing subsidized credit, and directing credit to weaker settlements, it was not really innovating new policies. Proposed by the Likud, however, these measures were perceived by the Ihud as aimed at the kibbutz movement's demise, and consequently, the group's response differed from its reaction under Labor.

While not always agreeing with the Mapai/Labor Governments' suggestions, the Ihud had been cautious in expressing its opposition.

When, for example, an Ihud kibbutz in 1967 had threatened to sue the Minister of Agriculture in order to obtain a higher milk production quota, the Ihud Secretariat dispatched Yoseftal to admonish the kibbutz not to act against "our minister."[25] In this instance their discretion may have been prompted more by loyalty to Gvati than to Mapai, but when the Government at the end of 1974 proposed a COLA payment and cancelling certain subsidies, though the Ihud disapproved, the group decided to follow one member's suggestion that "toward the outside, the Ihud must support the Government plan," and pursue its demands privately.[26]

Under the Likud, however, no party, minister, or group member provided a cushion of confidence that matters could be resolved satisfactorily in private or otherwise, and the fact that measures emanated from the Likud clouded the group's perceptions. Early in the Likud period, Ihud members were divided in their assessment of the Government's motivations and intentions as well as the required group reaction. Some believed that considering Government proposals and negotiating with the Likud amounted to acquiescing in their own demise. Others did not "think that the [Government's] suggestions are intended to destroy the kibbutz movement" but rather were "a response to problems that arose" and therefore "it is legitimate to argue over them and to suggest our viewpoint."[27] Unconvinced whether the Government was ideologically or pragmatically motivated, the Ihud reserved judgment, deciding to develop counter suggestions and to negotiate on the Government's specific proposals as well as to discuss formulating a socio-economic strategy for the entire settlement movement. No longer constrained by a need to protect "their" Government or minister from embarrassment, however, the Ihud engaged in more public pressure tactics than had previously been deemed appropriate. Whereas under Labor, the Ihud had discouraged member kibbutzim from going to court, under the Likud, judicial proceedings became a regular occurrence.

The Ihud now prepared itself for operating in a perceived alien environment. Anticipating Government scrutiny and charges that kibbutzim had received a disproportionate share of benefits, Yoseftal suggested public relations steps downplaying any image of selfish or particularistic kibbutz motivations, specifically to "publicize that the kibbutz movements invested in development fifty percent from its sources and did not raise the standard of living [of its members] ... but invested in development and did not receive gifts."[28] Parallel to this public relations posture and somewhat negating it, Ihud leaders acknowledged kibbutz inclinations toward consumption and took steps to restrain them. They advised kibbutzim to invest or save, rather than consume, monies available from redemption of security and employers' loans recently permitted by the Government. Conscious of past success in obtaining benefits, they designed tactics to protect them. In the housing area, for example, Yoseftal advised not altering criteria for meriting new housing to include absorption of new members lest it be "clear that we received more units of housing than we absorbed."[29]

Not allowing its predispositions and preconceived notions to paralyze it, the Ihud attempted to accommodate itself to the Likud's governing arrangement. The group's experience in adapting to previous Governments' and Mapai/Labor's operating modes served it well in dealing with the Likud. As this Government perceived itself besieged by demand-making groups, the Ihud took its place as one. Understanding that the Labor Party was now without leverage against the Likud, the Ihud realized the necessity to fend for itself and negotiate with the Government. It attempted to do so by meeting with the Finance Minister, with the director-general and other members of the Ministry of Agriculture, and with the Minister of Commerce and Industry.

The Ihud's dispute with this Government developed as much over method as over money. The Ihud opposed Government subsidy reductions, for example, not only because of the monetary loss but because the cuts upset production planning and eliminated the rationale for Government participation in that planning. The Ihud valued the "concentrated credit" program not only for the sums involved but for the Government oversight. Without adequate funding, Ihud leaders feared there would be no incentive for kibbutzim to comply with Government supervision. Concentrating on more equitably distributing a reduced pie, the Government ignored the programmatic implications of its actions, and this troubled kibbutzim. To compensate, the kibbutz federation itself sought to install its own supervisory arrangement.

The Likud's proposed changes challenged not only implementation procedures but the established decision-making process itself. Previously, I outlined three options for Government when dealing with group distributive demands: (1) Government decision to distribute something to everyone; (2) distribution according to ministerial determined criteria while disregarding and defending against criticism; and (3) including affected groups in decision-making. Choosing the second method, the Likud now opened itself to accusations of politically motivated favoritism. Unburdening themselves to the Ministry of Agriculture's director-general, Ihud leaders expressed their feeling that kibbutzim were being discriminated against in favor of moshavim. Denying the accusation, the director-general explained that the ministry was concentrating aid on weak settlements of which moshavim were a large proportion. Ihud leaders were dubious. Not part of the process, they viewed Government decisions as capricious, that "now the kibbutzim and moshavim are dependent on the good will of the agricultural ministry. If they [the ministry] like a certain settlement, they may give them from different funds, and if they don't like, it could be very poor, but it will not get."[30] Dismissing their fears, the Minister of Agriculture did not contemplate any attempt to incorporate the kibbutz sector into his ministry's decision-making process.[31]

Not called upon to cooperate with the Government, the Ihud sought other means to influence it, turning to the Kneset. In the Kneset, finding Labor members and Labor-led committees to be largely ineffective, the Ihud relied again upon the agricultural caucus, noted for its "special feature" of containing farmers from all parties and including the private sector.[32] Especially helpful was Likud member Pesah Grupper, a wine grape and citrus farmer who chaired the subcommittee for water prices, because "he has much more direct communication with the Government than we [and] it's very convenient sometimes to send him for negotiation."[33] Through such flexibility in cooperating with its ostensible rival, the Ihud became "successful in using him."[34] Interest triumphed over political preconception, and the Ihud thus took another step toward consolidating an interest group subsystem in the country.

As in previous periods when the Ministry of Agriculture was relatively closed to the Ihud, the group again sought to increase its leverage by strengthening its alliance with other kibbutz federations. The Ihud and the Kibbutz ha-Meuhad federation joined and formed the United Kibbutz Movement (ha-Tnu'ah ha-Kibbutzit ha-Meuhedet, acronym Takam) in 1979. Full structural unification still is in process. The Ihud also moved toward "closing ranks"[35] with moshavim, in contrast to its distance during the Mapai/Labor governing era. In the first three years of Likud Government (1977–1980), Ihud members expressed concern for moshav interests and cooperated with moshavim far more frequently than in the twenty-six years of Ihud existence under previous Mapai/Labor Governments: (1) when evaluating new contract terms from the Jewish Agency for establishing settlements, the Ihud, while favoring acceptance, deferred its desires in order to act jointly with moshavim; (2) Ihud members expressed concern that reducing milk subsidies would cause a problem between kibbutzim and moshavim; (3) when kibbutzim opposed a raise in land rent, they decided to make every effort to cooperate and appear together with the moshav sector; (4) although kibbutzim had little interest in the branch of eggs for consumption, they discussed cooperating with moshavim in demanding an adequate price system; and (5) the Ihud acknowledged its "moral responsibility to be concerned about the [moshav] movement that is ideologically close to our movement."[36]

By 1980, the sum of Likud procedures and policies affecting kibbutz interests seemed to fulfill the Ihud's pessimistic expectations, crystallizing its opinion that "the Likud as such was interested in making it difficult for moshavim [and] kibbutzim to exist."[37] The Ihud regarded Government decision-making as "erratic," noting that "several times in the last year ... the Minister of Agriculture announced that prices are going up, and the next day the Minister of Finance announced that the prices won't go up."[38] Addressing the Ihud Central Committee (then called the Central Committee of the United Kibbutz Movement), Yehudah Sa'adi, the Ihud Agricultural Center representative, denounced a whole litany of Likud policies: Government measures had ended agricultural planning; this Government "succeeded in ending the argument between the Histadrut and farmers on the question of subsidies," reducing subsidies to such a level that even farmers admitted their necessity; Government had cancelled all the credit systems; Government policies would harm industry; development budgets were half the amounts allocated by previous administrations; the Minister of Commerce and Industry had imported meat at cheap prices so that "all we are doing lately is submitting lawsuits and we are winning"; and the Government had reduced milk subsidies causing a milk surplus and a 25 percent reduction in demand for dairy products. All these measures revealed "the clear purpose of the Government is to reduce agriculture and settlement."[39]

Such accusations were hyperbolic. After all, would any Government deliberately seek to destroy an entire economic sector of its country? A communication failure on both sides was responsible for the rapid deterioration in group-Government relations, a residual element of the ideological culture where, blinded by preconceptions, people posture and speak past each other rather than to each other. Anticipating a Government attack upon kibbutzim, Ihud members interpreted all Government actions accordingly. Therefore, this Government lost credit with the group much sooner than another Government pursuing similar policies would have.

The Government, too, was plagued by preconceptions and misperceptions. Although ministers and bureaucrats met with group representatives, the Likud's governing pattern provided no place for group participation in decision-making. Probably regarding a Labor Party affiliated group as ipso facto inclined against the Likud, ministers, especially the Minister of Agriculture, did not believe cooperation to be possible or potentially productive. Initially, the Government was uncoordinated and did not understand the confusion that this caused to groups, the need for projecting an image of stable decision-making, nor the connection between procedure and policy. Misinterpreting a group demand to retain the Government-group arrangement to supervise farms as an unwarranted politically motivated attack, the Government made no attempt to include groups in making decisions. Certainly, Government-group relations were impeded. Given past Ihud behavior of acting in its own interest regardless of party preferences as well as Ihud expressions favoring Government involvement in agricultural affairs, the group probably would have cooperated with the Government had it been given the opportunity. However, no such call was forthcoming from the ministry. Moreover, while groups such as the Ihud often press ministries to act on behalf of their "constituents," many group leaders admit that "one of the big problems" of Israel's governing system is that ministers see themselves as agents of their special departments and do not view the Israeli economy as a whole."[40] While not volunteering to sacrifice, these leaders imply they would accept an offer and opportunity to cooperate, and await an invitation.

The Ihud in the Eighties

The events of the eighties—economic crisis, war in Lebanon, and a unique National Unity Government—posed potentially divisive issues for the Ihud. Dealing with them required reflection, reorientation, and vigorous action.

With the formation of the Takam (United Kibbutz Movement), the Ihud partially realized its long held aspiration of unifying the kibbutz sector within a unified party. However, the union required the Ihud to modify its arrangements for political affairs. Kibbutz ha-Meuhad would not agree to separate structures for politics, and therefore, a compromise arrangement was found. The Takam comprised a Labor Party region, and the Takam Secretariat and Central Committee were responsible for both political and internal kibbutz matters. In addition, wider and smaller political forums, but with connections to the federation's central administrative structures, were established for political discussions. The smaller body consists of forty members elected by the Central Committee. It includes, among others, the Secretary-General of the Takam, kibbutz Kneset and Government members, and kibbutz members active in the Labor Party. This body convenes every two weeks, sometimes discussing issues with the Secretariat, and is responsible for political decisions throughout the year.

The larger forum consists of the Takam's Central Committee, kibbutz members of the Labor Party's Central Committee, kibbutz Kneset members, and kibbutz members on the Executives of the Histadrut and Zionist movement. This body convenes only for major matters such as formulating the Takam's position on a joint Labor-Likud Government and electing the Takam's candidates for the Kneset. There also is a political, ideological committee, not entitled to make decisions, which functions to educate and activate kibbutz members on political affairs.[41] Indeed, since the establishment of this new arrangement, discussions of state policy questions such as the war in Lebanon do appear more frequently in Secretariat sessions. The movement still accommodated diverse political opinions, however, by allowing members to organize for parties other than Labor especially during election campaigns.

Several prominent kibbutz movement leaders were not comfortable with these arrangements, contending that discussions and decisions on state policy were more appropriate to a party arena and that concern for values would be better expressed by increasing volunteer work in the kibbutz movement and party. The old debates arose over what political matters were permissible for kibbutz deliberation and whether such discussions enhanced the movement's power vis-à-vis the party.[42] It remains to be seen if more centrally located political activity creates a problem for the kibbutz movement as the Ihud component had always feared.

These arrangements, however, did not permit greater Labor Party control over the kibbutz group. On the contrary, on both policy issues and specific party matters such as representation, the Takam sought to be influential. The Takam blamed Labor's poor showing in elections on the party's failure to articulate an ideology, reiterating its past laments about the party abandoning kibbutz values.[43] On one policy question, extending Israeli law to the Golan Heights, Takam Kneset members, in fact, voted differently from their Labor Party colleagues.[44]

Even as a united kibbutz movement, the Takam was a small segment of the Labor Party, and it continually struggled to maintain its share of party and political positions. In the Kneset list for the 1984 elections, for example, Takam was promised six places with a realistic potential for entering the Kneset, but only four were so placed. This was a real decline in the kibbutz group's Kneset representation. Attempting to resolve representation disputes, the Labor Party and group agreed to 20 percent representation on party bodies for kibbutzim and moshavim, split 60 to 40 percent, respectively, between the two settlement types. The Takam was ever alert to prevent the agreement from eroding when the party increased an organ's overall size.[45]

Increased attention to policy issues did not diminish the group's material concerns, and it mobilized to press for a Government loan conversion program. The National Unity Government adopted anti-inflationary measures, intensifying with an austerity program in July 1985. Loans were linked to the dollar, and interest rates rose. Kibbutzim continued taking loans, found they could not roll them over or repay them, and became financially distressed. The Takam tried to cope with the situation, tightening expenditures and arranging an internal movement loan whereby stronger kibbutzim aided the weaker. These steps also enhanced the kibbutz's case for requesting Government help.

Takam leaders noticed the dangers and contemplated such a request already at the end of 1984. One Takam Secretary-General, Yosef Perlmutter, and the chairman of Takam's economic branch met in early 1985 with then Prime Minister Peres to request aid.[46] Takam wanted a low-interest, long-term Government loan so kibbutzim could pay off their costly short-term debts, i.e., a loan conversion program. Although later in the negotiations, the Minister of Agriculture and Finance Minister were involved, Takam initially targeted Peres. On such a vital issue, Takam leaders appealed to the person deemed most interested, powerful, and sympathetic to their cause. Peres had taken on a leading role in the country's economic affairs, and contacting him was a logical first step. By not requesting the Minister of Agriculture to intermediate, the kibbutz group acted as it had in the past when the Minister of Agriculture was a moshav person. Moreover, the Finance Ministry was in Likud hands, and Takam estimated it would need maximum clout. Peres promised to press their case, and indeed, he pursued it even after the rotation.

The persuasion process was long, through 1987, with Takam altering its demands to include a partial debt cancellation. An agreement actually was reached in 1986, but Takam had to continue struggling for its full implementation. To make its case, Takam pulled out all stops. It (1) recounted the contribution of the settlement sector to the country, (2) argued that allowing the settlement sector to fail would destroy all Israeli agriculture and change the character of the state, (3) demonstrated opposite the Kneset with the other kibbutz and moshav movements and supported by the Histadrut, and (4) blocked crossroads in the north of the country with farm vehicles.[47] As in the past, these demonstrations were supported by a Government official. Deputy Minister of Agriculture and Takam member Avraham Katz-Oz reportedly joked that the amount of a kibbutz's debt relief would depend upon its appearing at the demonstration.[48] No longer was Takam concerned about not embarrassing the Labor Party, which it felt was neglecting the kibbutz movement.

Takam faced several obstacles: (1) getting action from this split Government was complicated; (2) Likud headed the Finance Ministry; (3) both parties recognized the need for economic recovery and were determined to lower inflation and curb expenditures; and (4) several revelations about Takam's financial practices had tarnished the movement's image and even damaged its self-confidence. (It lost money in the Israel stock market crash of 1983; Takam also had placed money with a speculator, an episode that became public in January 1985; and two Takam persons allegedly accepted bribes from that same speculator.) A limited plan for rescuing kibbutzim eventually was implemented. Given the obstacles, achieving anything at all attested to the residual power of the kibbutz group.

Conclusion

Ironically, the Ihud, the group that supposedly desired to do away with interests and denied having them became, perhaps, the most particularistic of all. But irony only states a condition, it does not explain it. And once a condition is explained, then the irony loses its sharpness and ceases to astonish. Ihud behavior under Labor and Likud Governments illustrates and explains how interests develop, how groups organize, and how different interests may be recognized and reconciled within a decision-making process, in turn affecting the development of that process. Not originally designed as an interest group, the Ihud especially illuminates the genesis and development of groups in Israel generally, their interaction with other parts of the system, and the limits set by the ideological political culture.

While mindful of minority opinions within, the Ihud on the whole ideologically identified with Mapai. Most of its social, economic, and political aims matched those professed by the party. In response to the party's efforts to broaden itself by including organized groups, the Ihud began, at first reluctantly and with a great deal of guilt and regret, to identify itself as an interest group with material concerns and to adapt to the party's preferred procedures. Realizing that its ideology would not be adopted en toto by party or country, in reaction the group assumed an attitude that "Okay, you don't want to go our way, then we'll behave just as you wish and get the best for ourselves." Hardships encountered in everyday life additionally contributed to its coalescence as a group. Improvising to meet the challenges, the group was compelled to adjust and reorder its aims. The Ihud's particularism suited the party's bargaining procedures. In effect, the party had signalled its approval of particularism, and the Ihud conformed. Both group and party put ideology in abeyance; concerning ideology, both party and group varied together.

The Ihud took its place and behaved as an economic interest group, demanding financial aid, resources, tax benefits, and compensation for any services it provided to party or country. It represented kibbutz settlement interests, first making demands on agricultural and other matters related to the kibbutz lifestyle and then on industrial issues as well. The group projected itself as representing the entire kibbutz sector. It competed mainly with the moshav slice of the agricultural sector and then the worker/consumer element of the economy.

Though not always approving Government policies regarding other economic sectors, the Ihud did not articulate a comprehensive policy. It did not even chisel away for systemic change as the Manufacturers' Association attempted, but rather strove to secure its portion. I have outlined three possible levels of group demands: very particularistic, for or against a certain policy or portion thereof; more systemic, for alteration of the very system or mechanism by which demands are processed; or particularistic but with consequences for systemic change. Of these, the Ihud falls into the last category. By pursuing its particularistic demands, the Ihud unintentionally affected the governing process and the system's institutional development.

The group's primary and continual tactic was an intense form of personal politics conducted through the party. It placed persons in relevant public offices, using its right via the Mapai/Labor Party to do so, and then appealed to them. For this purpose, the group attempted to cultivate persons of some expertise. The Ihud also appealed to other personal political contacts. Ministers became its main targets for demands. These demands usually were presented privately for several reasons: personal access made publicized protests unnecessary; out of consideration for the party, the group refrained from openly criticizing it; and in an ideological system that denies the legitimacy of narrow interests and the need for organized groups, not publicizing demands suggests that they do not exist. It is noteworthy that public protest was permissible and occurred when necessary to demonstrate that a demand actually was widespread and not particularistic.

In pressing its points, the Ihud cooperated with other kibbutz groups, even across party bounds. At first, it served as a spearhead for them to party and Government and then soon required their added pressure. Acting in concert with the other groups, the Ihud continually separated interest from party politics.

Moshav ascendance was a main impetus to the Ihud's developing interest group consciousness, affecting its choice of arenas for action. Viewing the moshav as competitor, the Ihud was impelled to strengthen contacts with other kibbutz groups and therefore required other than party arenas for action and decision-making. The Ihud impinged upon Government, preferring Government rather than party forums. When the Ministry of Agriculture was occupied by a moshav person, the Ihud directed itself to another minister, the Finance Minister. Though the party was not eliminated as a decision-making forum, it served as such most often at a minister's request. The Ihud had a qualified advocate there as well. All the Ihud's activities continually reinforced its status as an economic interest group and contributed to the development of an interest group subsystem with greater autonomy from parties.

Though preferring personal politics and kibbutz appeals to ministers, the Ihud participated in broad decision-making forums when directed there either by party or Government. Ihud members are fond of referring to their relationship with important Mapai and Government officials as a "family." Expanding upon this image, I would observe that as children in a family, groups required and invited parental discipline. Such discipline was imposed via Government and party committees and quasi-official institutions such as the Agricultural Center where groups were compelled to sit and exhaust themselves talking past each other until arriving at some solution. Ihud member Avneri recalled how Finance Minister Eshkol used to convene a committee meeting, charging the participants to be concerned that a "moshavnik in a new moshav will have an income." Then he would exit, letting his bureaucrats and the farmers' representatives work out a solution satisfactory to all groups as well as the Government.[49] Similarly, Government committees of experts provided necessary discipline and solutions welcomed by groups unwilling or unable to arrange their own bargains. Decision-making thereby acquired certain corporatist features.

Government became a main decision-making arena both as a consequence of group activity and due to separate imperatives that lead ministers and bureaucrats to enlarge spheres of activity and influence. Government always played a prominent role in Israel's agricultural development, especially in the cooperative sector, by owning the land, overseeing the establishment of settlements, providing and guaranteeing loans, supervising production quotas, operating the water system, etc. All agricultural and settlement groups, as recipients of loans and other Government provided resources, were highly dependent upon Government decisions for their existence. Each ministry was regarded as the guarantor, if not of one single group, then of the members of one economic sector: the Ministry of Agriculture existed to protect the interests of farmers; the Ministry of Commerce and Industry, of industrialists; the Ministry of Education and Culture, of teachers. When Dayan, suspected of moshav leanings, demonstrated he supported farmers, the Ihud could deal with him. Toward the outside, a minister was expected to negotiate on behalf of the component groups together, and within his ministry's jurisdiction, he was expected to mediate among them. The public or general interest was considered either by ministers sitting in the Cabinet or in a committee or by the Finance Minister. At times, ministers rose to responsibility, acquiring a general outlook. Gvati, for example, was concerned about regulating milk production for the entire country, not only ensuring each group a quota. Inevitably, a certain amount of tension developed between group and ministry. When even Ihud members in the Ministry of Agriculture proved unsatisfactory to the group, the Ihud turned to its Kneset contingent, thereby enhancing the development of that institution and individual Kneset members and contributing further to a decline in party discipline.

What, one may ask, is the role of parties in mediating interest group competition? Mapai leaders expected that by including groups within the party framework, preferably an extensive united labor party, they would be able to control and mitigate group demands and foster inter-group agreements both within the party and through them in the country. On conversion, for example, Eshkol warned the Ihud not to vote against the moshavim at the Agricultural Center, but Eshkol also instructed the moshavim to vote for conversion. To an extent, this policy was effective with the Ihud, influencing group tone and tactics. Party affiliation had enabled it to establish a network and earned it easier access.

Nevertheless, the group continually acted as a centrifugal force upon the party, finding the party insufficiently inclusive, efficient, or knowledgeable to serve as a decision-making forum and certainly not as an instrument for policy implementation. In seeking its particularistic objectives, the group sought to broaden its group base, sought new alliances, and impinged upon new targets. Even after the Left coalesced and kibbutz groups united, the Ihud continued pioneering new paths. The party and party affiliation became increasingly irrelevant for interest group mediation.

When the Likud came into office, though the Ihud maintained its Mapai/Labor links, it was prepared to protect its interests by cooperating with the new Government in policy-making and implementation. Possibilities existed for either finding a modus vivendi with the Government or retreating into an even closer connection with the Labor Party. Much would depend upon how oppressive the group perceived the Government's policies.

Structures for cooperative policy-making and implementation were in place and ready for activation, but the Likud declined to avail itself of them. Following its philosophy of governing for the whole and aiming to redress past discrepancies which it perceived had occurred for political reasons, the Likud sought its own way for decision-making, developing a minister-centered pattern. At the same time, the Ihud diversified its tactics and targets under the Likud, allying wherever necessary to achieve policies appropriate to its situation: it drew closer to moshavim, and it even allied with private sector, Likud-linked agriculture. Whether under Likud or Labor, the Ihud as interest group continually pressed its claims and as a result, perhaps unwittingly, contributed to the development of an interest group subsystem, continually pioneered new paths for pressing demands, and finally, fostered broader forums for decision-making.

In the introduction, I outlined three models for government—strong party, pluralist, and corporatist—and aimed to understand the contribution of groups to system change. Israel's political system in the early period may be considered as falling within the strong party rubric and the Ihud as a party affiliated interest group. Groups in a strong party model are understood to be very dependent upon the party as a client to a patron. Accordingly, Mapai's leaders believed that by distributing benefits and positions, they could balance off and control the groups comprising the party. Ideology, and the opprobrium attached to narrow interests, it was hoped, would discipline the groups and aid in attaining a measure of cooperation.

To some extent, these aims were fulfilled, but there were unforeseen changes. Inherent in a strong party model are weaknesses that potentially generate greater group independence. When a group is affiliated to a party, factionalism within the party or party system affects group cohesion. From the very beginning of its relationship with Mapai, therefore, the Ihud took a wary stance, structurally inuring itself from the party. This was a defensive action. The group did not then use its independence to extract favors from other parties. Although such distancing did not directly strengthen the group, and the group still could be considered electorally "in the party's pocket," the possibility of group disintegration or defection carried an implicit threat, endowing the group with a measure of influence upon the Mapai party. Despite the fact that the group itself did not seek to be wooed by other parties, Mapai of its own volition offered it incentives to remain loyal. One Ihud member recalled that Prime Minister Eshkol more readily extended benefits when Rafi's establishment was pending and he still hoped to forestall it. Moreover, the factors by which the patron party hoped to control the clients became elements of strength for the client: (1) the group represented an entire segment of the economy and could negotiate with other similar groups and obtain agreement to Government or party policies; (2) the group cultivated experts in economic affairs required by the Government and party; and (3) the group contributed money and manpower to the party even without a formal structural tie. Taking its place as a party affiliated group and exploiting these elements to attain its interests, the Ihud compelled first the party and then the system to become more aware of group power and activity, thereby enhancing pluralist features of the system.

As Government and group sought appropriate forums for expressing and reconciling competing interests, they experimented with corporatist arrangements. Admittedly, this development occurred within the confines of the Left. Whether or not these experiments would continue became a question for the Government of the Right after 1977. While the Likud Government might have preferred applying a philosophy of governing for the whole, it had to relate to groups. Groups which asserted themselves would remain a permanent feature of the political scene.

Both the non-party affiliated Manufacturers' Association and the party affiliated Ihud acted in ways which intentionally and unintentionally created an independent interest group subsystem where groups expressed particularistic concerns as well as demands for procedural change. They managed to accomplish this development from a defensive position vis-à-vis the party plane. To what extent the system could be further changed now bears examination. Gush Emunim illustrates how an idea group could capitalize upon the inter- est group subsystem already established and expand the newly opened paths by acting more aggressively and impinging upon the party system.

Part IV

Gush Emunim

Chapter 10

Gush Emunim in the Labor Era

The characterization of the settlement movement Gush Emunim, Bloc of the Faithful, as a threat to democracy, a charge usually made by the group's opponents, actually bespeaks how much the group was perceived as challenging not only policy itself but policy-making procedures as well. The group's activities exposed incoherence in the political system's decision-making process, especially the difficulty officials had in working collectively. Consequently, the group proved problematic for all Governments, regardless of party composition, that attempted to deal with it.

Genesis of the Group

Although sentiment for settling the West Bank surfaced after the 1967 war, the settlement movement of Gush Emunim did not form during the euphoria after 1967 but out of despair following the war in 1973. Like for the rest of the nation after 1967, for those desiring to attach the West Bank to Israel, sights were raised and horizons widened, and all expected some major transformation in the country's path. Perhaps visions were just as conflicting as when the state was created, but now, all desired clear-cut decisions to resolve many of the outstanding issues. The Mapai/Labor Government's response on the territories was ambivalent. Between 1967 and 1973, several small groups, in effect embryonic Gush Emunims, arose to nudge the Government out of its alleged static position and onto what they perceived as the correct path. Using what would become one of Gush Emunim's most famous tactics, Rabbi Moshe Levinger led a group in a "semi-legal" act of establishing a base in Hebron which, after capturing the attention of the Government, resulted in construction of a

Jewish town nearby. Other groups developed the Gush 'Etzion sector near Jerusalem and a site on the Golan Heights. Another group, called the Group for Settling Shekhem, requested permission to settle near that town. Because the town was located in the densely Arab populated northern West Bank, further from Jerusalem than the other settlement spots, settlement there necessitated a comprehensive Government discussion and decision. Unable to undertake such a debate, the Government refused the request.

The 1973 war began to raise the nation's consciousness, especially among religious-oriented persons, that the country's indecisiveness about the territories was not, as many had hoped, regarded by its neighbors as an invitation to peace, but as a sign of weakness. How these persons came together with those already involved in settlement activity and acted on the political party scene begins the story of Gush Emunim.

Soon after the war, several religiously observant young men, some of whom already were living in settlements on post-1967 territory and who shared the same religious school background, simultaneously experienced "fear for the moral crisis in Israel, that all the processes of the redemption of Israel—building the land, the ingathering of exiles—[had] declined."[1] They countered their despair with the idea of "Eretz Yisrael" (The Land of Israel). The term "Eretz Yisrael" expresses a broad, somewhat mystical concept, referring not only to the physical borders of the country but also to a moral and religious lifestyle for persons within those borders. Having explained this, however, it should be noted that these persons did not plot a religiously oriented revolution. Rather, they concentrated on the more narrow, nationalistic aspect, that of securing the expanded borders of Israel, those resulting from the 1967 war, and did so by encouraging a Government backed settlement policy.

In pursuing this aim, they first acted upon the National Religious Party (NRP). Although the initiators of Gush Emunim were predominantly religiously observant and were close to segments of the religious party, the movement was not established or controlled by that party nor by a faction of it. From the beginning, Gush Emunim was an autonomous, activist group, calculating its own moves and impinging upon the political scene in various ways. Ideological reasons coincided with political considerations to make pressure upon the religious party a logical first step.

To understand why the National Religious Party was so crucial, one must refer to the coalition Government system that had existed in Israel since the beginning of the state and to the role of parties. As Mapai/Labor's perennial coalition partner, the religious party was very influential. In 1973 it still seemed inconceivable to the ordinary observer that the Labor Party would be voted out of office, and therefore, if any change were to be made in Government policy or perhaps in Government composition, it would have to be achieved through the religious party. In addition, the religious party, as most parties in the state, was a comprehensive organization, providing education, health, and other services to members. These ancillary organizations provided opportunities for members who were not professional politicians to apply pressure on the party. Many Gush Emunim adherents, while not party activists, were connected to the party as educators, and these politically dormant members started becoming more politically active in order to influence the party's settlement policy and its decision about entering a new coalition Government. In this activity, they coordinated with two professional politicians of the party known as the Youth Faction leaders.

The Youth Faction leaders, Zevulun Hammer and Yehudah Ben-Meir, shared the same educational background and agreed ideologically with the new activists and joined them in establishing Gush Emunim. However, these politicians also had more purely political motivations. The NRP had been dominated by a few, by now older, members, and the party's limited number of portfolios left little place for the younger partisans. The Youth Faction wanted to expand the party's purview to include all aspects of the nation's life, not just those pertaining to religion and the religious community, and they wanted a personal place in that expanded role. The notion of Eretz Yisrael in its broad and narrow connotations provided pegs for their activity. They therefore worked closely with the developing group of non-professional party persons. In pressing the idea of Eretz Yisrael within the party, they, too, at first concentrated on settlement policy.

Thus, as the 1973 war ended, there were four, sometimes overlapping, strands that eventually would coalesce to become Gush Emunim. There were persons living in post-1967 territory, some of whom became more active within the religious party and some of whom pressed the idea of Eretz Yisrael but without a party connection; there were the professional politicians within the religious party; and there were peripheral party members living within Israel proper who were drawn to become more active both in the nascent Gush Emunim and in the party. Early activities by members of the budding group included pressuring for a plank on settlement policy within the party platform and pressuring the party to make settlement policy part of its bargaining package for joining any forthcoming Government.

To this end, several persons had appeared before the party's platform committee, and persons of the Group for Settling Shekhem (later called Elon Moreh Nucleus) met with NRP leaders and ministers of Government. These contacts resulted in platform planks on settlement policy as well as guidelines on such policy to be followed by NRP officials in the next Government and in state institutions. Authorized by NRP leader and Minister of Interior Yosef Burg and dated prior to the elections, the guidelines document, in the form of a letter to settlers on the West Bank, restated two principles of the party platform – that the NRP would not agree to any plan which yields parts of Eretz Yisrael and that the NRP would act to settle liberated areas of Eretz Yisrael. The guidelines affirmed the right of every Jew to settle in every area of Eretz Yisrael, and for this purpose, promised to establish a ministerial committee to plan and carry out wide ranging municipal and village settlement in Judea, Samaria (names used in Israel for the West Bank), and the Golan Heights with priority given to establishing settlements in the heart of Samaria such as at Shekhem. The party further promised to work for extending state sovereignty to Judea, Samaria, and the Golan Heights so Jews could purchase land.[2]

Although this material seemed to indicate the NRP naturally would participate in the next coalition, the Youth Faction and nascent Gush Emunim persons pressed the NRP to demand a national unity Government and to refuse to join a Government other than a grand coalition. This activity intensified after the elections. The Group for Settling Shekhem, which prior to the war had had contacts with Government members and officials of several parties, realized it would not achieve its aim quietly and became more publicity minded. The group therefore published the letter received from Burg along with a review of its activities, timed to coincide with NRP discussions about composing the next coalition.[3]

Paralleling all these activities, since the end of the war there were several meetings of persons from the diverse strands concerned with settlement policy in order to establish a more organized framework. Shortly after the war, a meeting was held in the home of Rabbi Hayyim Druckman, significant for it illustrates how the different streams of individuals came together. Rabbi Druckman was the head of a *yeshivah* (religious school) and an NRP member but not especially active in its political sphere. However, he was a widely respected individual who identified with the concept of Eretz Yisrael, and he therefore was approached by others more active in both settlement activity and the party to volunteer his home, thereby bestowing his prestige upon the affair and attracting people to attend. Continuing the organizational effort, in January 1974 persons representative of the Youth Faction, party-associated activists for settlement, as well as party affiliated intellectuals from Israel proper agreed to participate in, and lend their names to a notice calling for a meeting in Tel Aviv of the "religious-national community for the purpose of establishing a national emergency Government and guarding our sovereignty over Judea and Samaria."4 Then these settlers, sympathizers, and party activists, together with the Youth Faction of the NRP, organized a larger meeting held early in February 1974 near Jerusalem at the post-1967 settlement Kfar 'Etzion. At this meeting, the name "Gush Emunim in the Mafdal" (Bloc of the Faithful within the NRP) was adopted, formally inaugurating the group. It should be noted, however, that the Group for Settling Shekhem remained a separate entity, although membership of individuals overlapped.

Youth Faction member Ben-Meir's recollection of the origin and early role of Gush Emunim differs from that of other participants, including his faction partner Hammer, but is interesting because it highlights some of the political motivations present at the birth of the group. Ben-Meir attributes the group's founding to his efforts together with Hammer after the December 1973 elections in order to prevent the NRP from joining the Meir Government. According to Ben-Meir, the Youth Faction began organizing "citizens' groups who were affiliated within the NRP–intelligentsia, spiritual leaders, professors–a pressure group within the NRP."5 Some of these persons had votes on the party's Central Committee which the Youth Faction calculated would help their effort against joining the Meir Government.

From conversations with Hammer and others, a slightly different picture emerges. Hammer acknowledges that the Youth Faction attempted to attract fresh party activists in order to broaden the party and its concerns but does not tie this activity to the individuals and efforts involved in establishing Gush Emunim in which he refers to himself as a "participant."6

It is possible to reconcile these differing accounts. While sincerely identifying with the objectives of Gush Emunim and promoting these aims and others, the Youth Faction also had their own agenda. It would seem, therefore, that the Youth Faction and Gush Emunim worked on parallel lines and that all–Youth Faction and new and old

Gush Emunim and party members regardless of how they were brought into the party–merged to exert pressure on party leaders.

Starting its pressure effort, Gush Emunim placed ads in newspapers calling upon NRP leaders to demand a national unity Government and a Government policy not to relinquish Judea, Samaria, and the Golan Heights. Gush Emunim also sought to make these provisions party policy. For several months, most activity occurred within the NRP and to a large extent in cooperation with the Youth Faction. The Youth Faction allied with another party faction in order to keep the party out of the Government, and with the votes of the Gush Emunim persons, pro-national unity Government forces obtained 40 percent of the vote in the party's Executive, still insufficient to prevent party leaders from joining the Meir Government.

Although the party entered the Meir Government in March, the Youth Faction appealed the decision to the party's high court which ruled that entrance required ratification by the party's Central Committee. Youth Faction and Gush Emunim persons then lobbied the Central Committee. There they obtained 42 percent of the vote, which in effect retroactively approved the party's decision to enter. The combined Youth Faction-Gush Emunim pressure, however, succeeded in obtaining a pledge from Meir that any agreement negotiated with a foreign country that provided for returning parts of the West Bank and Gaza Strip would not be signed until new elections were held in Israel. (Ben-Meir denies that Gush Emunim played any role in obtaining this condition, that even before the Kfar 'Etzion organizational meeting, the Labor Party had sent an emissary to meet with the Youth Faction and offered this proposal hoping it would remove their objections to the party's entering the coalition. Despite Ben-Meir's interpretation of events, it is difficult to make such fine distinctions in pinpointing a source of pressure. Most likely, the same atmosphere that fostered the formation of Gush Emunim and the Youth Faction's resolve to keep the party out of the Government gave rise to the suggestion and imposition of this condition.) Although this clause in the coalition agreement has been regarded by some observers as a concession and sign of weakness by the Labor Party, it was not considered strong enough by Gush Emunim persons who had wanted to prevent the Government from even starting negotiations without new elections.

The Meir Government fell within a month. The Youth Faction-Gush Emunim forces continued pressuring and succeeded in keeping the NRP from immediately entering Rabin's Government which took office in June. The entrance of the party to the Meir Government, however, had signalled to Gush Emunim that it was necessary to consider changing course. The decision involved Youth Faction members as well.

While contemplating its future, Gush Emunim quickly clarified its distinctive group character. To all those who had answered Gush Emunim ads requesting support, the group's organizers sent a newsletter in which they pointed out that the Youth Faction's extensive backing of their aims, while gratifying, had obscured the distinction between them. They acknowledged support received from other elements of the party as well, thereby clarifying that the group was not identical to the Youth Faction nor part of it. The message despaired of further activity within the NRP under the then existing leadership, although the group believed the times demanded a strong national religious force. Undecided about a future course, the newsletter suggested supporters hold parlor meetings in order to expand the organization in preparation either for working for changes within the party or for establishing a new framework.[7]

While Gush Emunim worked within the NRP, the Group for Settling Shekhem continued acting separately for the limited aim of establishing a settlement or any type of presence near Shekhem. To this end, group leaders wrote to members of Kneset and to ministers of both the Meir and Rabin Governments, not confining themselves to any party. Actually, they were perceptive in realizing that open association with the opposition could be detrimental to their cause. Letters went to NRP Minister of Interior Burg reminding him of his promise to give preference to settlement at Shekhem, to the Defense Ministers, to the head of the Government's Settlement Committee requesting to appear before that body, and to the Prime Ministers. While becoming skilled at letter writing and at selecting proper targets, they did not advance at all toward their objective. As the Rabin Government was about to take office, this group realized the futility of these "quiet" approaches and decided upon a more drastic public method. They would engage in illegal action, physically entering the West Bank and attempting to erect a settlement. Their new tactic suited Gush Emunim's purposes as well, ending its search for a new mode of action, and the two groups merged.

An enlarged Gush Emunim sans appellation "in the Mafdal" emerged. The group of independently minded individuals who had come to work within the NRP and in consort with the Youth Faction now decided to separate itself and become a truly autonomous, single-purpose interest group. Although Gush Emunim documents hint at the possibility of establishing a new political party, most Gush Emunim persons disdained any party connection, hoping to attract adherents, both religiously observant and secular, from all parties and the general public and to impinge upon the parties as well. Ben-Meir claims he encouraged the new framework, but Hammer concedes he was not as comfortable with the notion. He had envisioned some NRP link, that Gush Emunim would be a settlement movement with an educational function within the party framework similar to the arrangement between the party and its school network or youth movement. Paradoxically, the group's efforts to expand caused a certain narrowing of purpose. Although biblical notions of borders and the broader concept of religion as a lifestyle still provided a raison d'être for many of the group's leaders, as they attempted to attract secular persons, expended energy organizing demonstrations, and became involved in policy issues that some observers considered extraneous to the settlement issue, the religious aspect receded. The Youth Faction's concept of a religious party was broader than the cause of Gush Emunim. Nevertheless, the subtle change in emphasis and the organizational break did not entail complete disassociation from the Youth Faction, which in most cases remained ideologically compatible with and supportive of the group's activities.

Amorphous Structure

Although Gush Emunim still deemed a change in Government desirable, it left that struggle to the professional politicians. The group tried to maintain a very delicate relationship to the party system, a more sophisticated but difficult approach than the Manufacturers' Association had pursued. Judging that a "politics is dirty" attitude pervaded public opinion, the group's founders decided that outright alignment with a party would tarnish the group's image and automatically repel members of any other party. On the practical level, they concluded that support of existing party leaders would be difficult to obtain if they were considered competitors. Although there were differences of opinion within the group about political activity, those who counselled against any party label prevailed, and neither did the group become a party itself. Similar to the Manufacturers' Association, Gush Emunim adopted a non-allied position but not only as a defense against fracturing a group composed of affiliates from several parties. The decision was a deliberate tactic enabling the group to attract adherents of all parties and further, to take the offense and impinge upon the parties.

Emphasizing its distinction from parties, Gush Emunim maintained no official membership rosters and was not highly structured. Membership on a Greater Secretariat was about twenty-five persons, and while a total of thirteen persons over time participated in a Small Secretariat, at any given time, about five persons comprised the smaller body that made decisions and planned events. A General Secretary/spokesperson also was chosen to coordinate events and public relations. (At times, these roles were separated and conducted by two persons.) Adopting a "minimal framework" and remaining unburdened by organizational details, the founders reasoned, would allow them to "express the idea."[8]

They were not naive ideologues, however. On the contrary, the amorphous structure was a clever device, allowing those who argued for greater political involvement to operate on the party scene. When more direct political action beyond lobbying ideas was deemed desirable, the enterprise usually was undertaken by an offshoot group as individuals. Gush Emunim "would say the Secretariat doesn't get involved in these matters, but if you invite me to a meeting, I come." Similarly, "if someone came and said they wanted to work so that ... Druckman [for example] would be in the Kneset, we said, okay, but don't do it in the name of Gush Emunim." Such a method permitted Gush Emunim to uphold its untainted character, and members could continue asserting that "Gush Emunim didn't take a decision if the Mafdal [NRP] should join the Government or not, didn't take a decision on the type of relations with the Youth Faction."[9]

The amorphous structure and consequent lack of a specifiable base opened the group to accusations that it represented no one, as Prime Minister Rabin discounted it for "not representing the settlers like the manufacturers represent all the manufacturers in a democratic process in accordance to a voluntary group [with] rules. Gush Emunim pretended to represent those who did not want them to represent them."[10]

Such accusations Gush Emunim leaders believed was the price to be paid for retaining flexibility of action, but other factors may have been considered. Perhaps they indeed feared not attracting wide support and therefore adopted the non-party, loose framework as a Gideon type tactic for appearing stronger and more influential than they were. If this were the case, it attests at least to their ingenuity. Or, they may have perceived the populace's reluctance to align formally with a new structure, and therefore designed a framework to allay that fear. And they may have made a political calculation that a new party would not obtain many seats. Moreover, by innovating with a new type of organization, they could counter the tendency in Israel to view groups as party controlled. Most likely, all of these reasons entered into their assessment.

Admitting that they could not claim a specific constituency, they contended that the large turnout at their activities indicated support and conferred representative, albeit informal, authority upon them. Likewise, they considered the size of their decision-making body unimportant because "if the group of five decides on something ... and ten thousand people come, then that shows they support [us]."[11]

Autonomous Interest Group Into Action: Settlements as Demonstrations

Taking a cue from the Shekhem group, Gush Emunim acted upon all political forces in order to obtain a Government settlement policy, both in word and deed. Dramatizing its aim and showing that its support derived from various political sources, Gush Emunim organized efforts to enter the West Bank and erect settlements. Capitalizing upon the growing cross-party nature of Gush Emunim's aim and on an increase in politicians' independence, these demonstrations were successful as intended for attracting political figures to its banner and gaining publicity for the group. Reused many times, these "settlement as demonstration" efforts became a finely honed instrument for Gush Emunim.

Moving toward the Shekhem group merger, Gush Emunim's first activity, appropriately, was to attempt to establish a settlement in that area. Located deep in the northern part of the West Bank, Shekhem came to symbolize the course of all settlement policy. Although active in other areas, Gush Emunim would continually return to Shekhem. Shekhem became almost a curse for the Rabin Government, and although blessed by Begin soon after he succeeded in the 1977 elections, caused his Government some concern as well.

Two days after Rabin assumed office in early June 1974, the Group for Settling Shekhem, accompanied by some Gush Emunim members, went to "squat" at a site in that area. Disbanded by the army, they re-grouped and gathered more supporters for another effort in August. These two attempts were mere forays, testing the ground for a much more dramatic, lengthy, and widespread campaign in October dubbed Operation Haqafot[12] which marked the first major public effort by the newly organized Gush Emunim. Over several days, a barrage of settlement groups, totaling a few thousand persons, entered the West Bank to squat in areas they had designated for future settlement. Based upon a settlement program they had drawn up in July, the campaign was a testimony to their organizational and planning ability not only in the logistical sense necessary for this particular action but in policy formulation as well.

Although critics tried to detract from the group by pointing out that participants were not prepared to reside in the area but were merely demonstrating, demonstrating was precisely the campaign's purpose. "When a garin [settlement nucleus] went up to an illegal site, it was a demonstration with the central function of bringing the matter to discussion among the public and in the Government."[13] They engaged in unauthorized settlement but aimed to obtain Government approval, prod the Government into proposing a comprehensive settlement program, and raise the nation's awareness to the need for such a plan. They did not intend to intrude upon the Government's jurisdiction, not yet seeking or desiring any place in the decision-making process. The same persons who thought it prudent to remain aloof from party politics, demarcated their role and that of the Government. They wanted the Government to accept responsibility for designing and implementing settlement policy, believing Government authority necessary to imbue policy with legitimacy.

In marked contrast to the group's display of vision and planning ability, the Government seemed hesitant, frustrating the group which longed for a definitive Government position, whether positive or negative, and spurring it to further action. As one Gush Emunim activist explained, "They never told us no. ... They never informed us that the Government discussed the matter and decided not to establish a settlement. They didn't decide. We thought if we would bring a great deal of pressure, they would decide and decide in favor."[14]

Decision-Making by Deception: Incident at 'Ofrah

Gush Emunim continued pressuring via rallies within Israel proper, additional settlement demonstrations, and a Government approved Passover march through the West Bank. Nevertheless, not one civilian settlement at a Gush Emunim desired site resulted from these activities. Realizing it would not achieve an overall Government policy direction, Gush Emunim settled for a more piecemeal approach.

Claus Offe has noted that

> political parties seem no longer to be the main authors of program-
> matic policy decisions. Such policy decisions tend to result not from
> intraparty deliberations and consensus building but, rather, from
> interparty negotiations involving the parties in coalition. Or else the
> proposals emerge from and are advocated by clearly identifiable
> segments, wings, and factions within the party and fail to get
> approval of the party as a whole.[15]

These observations certainly applied to the Israeli case. Not only were
the leading Labor Party and Government divided about the future of
the territories, but individuals within the Government and of the same
party were not above imposing their views by less than open means
and not by discussion and persuasion. The rift provided an opening
for an interest group to promote its aims. Although Gush Emunim did
not cause the Cabinet discord, the group certainly was aware of its
existence and exploited it. The first Gush Emunim settlement, 'Ofrah,
resulted from this effort.

   In the Rabin Government, Defense Minister Peres, a political rival
of the Prime Minister, was known to favor a stronger Israeli presence
in the territories. Besides personal animosities and differences of
views between these two ministers, a crack existed in bureaucratic
responsibility for the territories. The Defense Ministry was
responsible for maintaining security and administering the areas,
whereas a Ministerial Settlement Committee headed by Minister
without Portfolio Yisrael Galili held authority for any new civilian
type development. Settlement activists could exploit the overlapping
authority arrangement and yet deny any intentional deception.

   Gush Emunim, seeking to establish a foothold by any means deep
in the West Bank, devised a scheme to persuade the Defense Minister
to acquiesce in the aim. Gush Emunim activists planned to obtain
employment in the area, preferably under military auspices, and then
seek a way to remain in the area at night. And this they did. They were
hired by a private building contractor working at a military installation. After several months, according to their literature, they "sensed"
the Defense Minister was seeking a means to approve their settling in
the area and then attempted to stay overnight.[16] Nearby was an abandoned, half-built Jordanian military camp. The workers entered the
buildings, while at the same time several of their supporters were at
the Defense Minister's office in Jerusalem, requesting permission for
them to establish residence at the site. The Defense Minister at first

denied permission, but after an emotional entreaty by one Gush Emunim leader, instructed the military governor of the area neither to aid nor hinder the group that night. Following appeals by members of Kneset on the group's behalf, the directive was extended. Thus, the "'Ofrah Work Camp" was founded.

Since the entire enterprise was connected to defense work, technically, the Defense Minister was empowered to make such a decision, and leeway existed for all to disclaim any intended deception. The group could claim that the Defense Minister in his capacity as the official in charge of affairs in the territories was the legal and relevant channel to approach with their request, and the Defense Minister could claim that he was well within his authority. Defending Peres against the charge of collusion with the group, one Gush Emunim member insists that "Peres didn't give us any promise that there would be a settlement here and that he would support. The only thing that he agreed was that if there wouldn't be a Government decision, he wouldn't evict the settlement."[17] Peres, in fact, claims that he brought the decision "before the Government and the Government approved it. ... Civilians were supposed to operate the military installation. ... Even if it was a civilian group of people that's supposed to serve the military, it was clear this was going to become a civilian place. ... Maybe some members of the Cabinet didn't want to understand what we were deciding, but it was approved by the Cabinet."[18]

Prime Minister Rabin, however, contends "this ['Ofrah] was brought to me directly by the Minister of Defense because it was not settling settlements. The establishing of military installations anywhere was not subjected to this committee [Ministerial Settlement Committee]. ... When I was approached by the Minister of Defense, I was told that the idea is to build some military installation in this area and to save time there will be a labor camp for those who would work in the building of an installation. And it might be that I made a mistake by believing him."[19] As MK Ben-Meir summarizes, "The Defense Minister here did something without fully bringing it to the attention of the Prime Minister knowing that had he brought it to the attention of the Prime Minister maybe the Prime Minister wouldn't have been in favor. In other words, he used the latitude which he had to push this thing."[20]

Certainly, Peres's explanation notwithstanding, something is amiss if a decision can be taken without all participants being clearly apprised or aware of the full consequences of their act. At the very least, one must wonder about the nature of discussion and procedure followed in Government sessions and communication among Government members. A Government minister took measures that could have widespread consequences for the country's foreign policy without directly or fully informing the Cabinet. The divided Cabinet made a minister approachable in the first place. A group could capitalize upon that division while remaining within legal bounds. A decision was made not as an outcome of rational discussion but as the result of group game-playing. Such decision-making by deception opens a Government to ridicule and could very well lead to doubts about the Government's stability and even legitimacy.

Paradoxical Purposes

While pleased with its success at 'Ofrah, the group was not so easily appeased. It accepted piecemeal gains but did not abandon its quest for a definitive Government policy to promote settlement throughout the West Bank. Ostensibly for this aim, the group organized demonstrations against U. S. Secretary of State Henry Kissinger who was in Israel in March and August 1975 to negotiate a second interim agreement between Israel and Egypt on further Israeli withdrawal from Sinai.

By these activities, the single-purpose interest group seemed to signal more expanded sights and yet, paradoxically, a narrower purpose, departing further from the religious motif and distancing itself further from the ideology of the religious party's Youth Faction. Youth Faction leader Ben-Meir observes that "in August '75, here was the first clear, serious difference of ... approach. In my opinion, I think the downfall of Gush Emunim began at that time. ... We knew about it and we were definitely not in favor of it. ... They were turning into, instead of the struggle for Eretz Yisrael, a type of political organization ... against, in any area, any concessions. ... In other words, they left the issue of settlement."[21] Although Gush Emunim members demur, the demonstrations marked a turning point in the non-party nature of the group.

Both Kissinger visits prompted Gush Emunim organized demonstrations, but whereas the demonstrations during March took the form of settlement attempts, the August demonstrations were of the mass crowd variety, converging upon Jerusalem where Kissinger was present. The distinction is significant because settlement type demonstrations seemingly would support one of Gush Emunim's arguments, that they were compelled to protest a Sinai pullback to ensure against setting a precedent for the West Bank. However, by raucously demonstrating against Kissinger and the negotiated agreement in August, Gush Emunim appeared to acquire a different dimension. The group's spokesman from that period acknowledges that although all Gush Emunim leaders agreed upon the demonstrations, "there was great difficulty to explain this because it didn't speak about settlement but about an interim agreement in Sinai. ... People didn't understand what this caused from the moral point of view. ... And also people who were in Gush Emunim who saw the things in Judea and Samaria, Sinai was for them a bit out of the picture." Gush Emunim attempted to allay these doubts with three points. "The first point was that the symbolic pressure on Kissinger was very politically and ideologically important. The second thing, we explained that the interim agreement, as it was, is not good for Israel. And the last thing, that I think is the most important, is that it is a precedent ..." They also argued that Sinai could be regarded as part of Eretz Yisrael, "that Sinai is at least not Egyptian."[22]

The nationalist strand of Gush Emunim ideology seemed to be overtaking the religious, and Gush Emunim had difficulty confining itself to settlement policy. Pursuing the nationalist strand to its logical conclusion eventually would affect the group's character and perception of its role in the political process.

Of Politics, Parties, and Perceptions

Deriving from the ideological dimension's veneration of principle and intolerance of independence, Israelis often tend to categorize individuals and groups, usually devaluing them by attributing to them some party label or political motivation. Groups that cannot be readily stamped into a familiar mold may seem threatening. Moreover, because parties have often designed demonstrations to embarrass the Government and because groups often were party appendages, it is difficult for Israelis to change their view for a group that claims to be nonpartisan. Gush Emunim adopted a non-party stance and amorphous structure to avoid being typecast, but because it did not completely sever and eschew all political associations, it could not entirely escape the stigma. Perceptions merit consideration because they often condition reactions and relationships.

Rabin's perception of Gush Emunim reveals to what extent the group represented a departure from the Israeli norm and could be accepted as such by the Government and political system. Rabin perspicaciously "regarded Gush Emunim in accordance with their decisions and their actions as an exparliamentarian body [outside parliament]." He realized that "they tried by demonstrations and other activities to carry out the policy of the whole Eretz Yisrael, and they were supported by the Mafdal [NRP] and the Likud because in a way they were the means and the extreme means of the implementation of what the Likud then and the Mafdal believed in." "Therefore," Rabin explains, "I had to bear in mind both first that they were an independent body that was not controlled by either party and in a way was the leading part of sharpening the differences between the Labor Party and the Alignment on the one hand and of the Likud and the Mafdal on the other." His view of the group under the Likud Government further illuminates his view of its role in the past. Noting a confrontation between Gush Emunim and the Likud Government, Rabin explains that "therefore, at least no major parties support them in the way they used to, as an instrument against my Government."[23]

Although Rabin could not completely divest himself of traditional political notions and avoid the temptation of categorizing Gush Emunim with his political opposition, to a large extent his view reflected the group's position within the political system. Gush Emunim members admit they often served as an "instrument" for the opposition and regarded opposition support useful for attracting attention and generating publicity. While not directed by a party, several times they cooperated with the Likud in planning and conducting protest activities. Warned by the Youth Faction against even a thin political cloak, Gush Emunim shrugged off the criticism, risking the association in public opinion as long as its cause was served.

From the parties' perspective, the prospect of changing the Government may have prompted the Likud and the Youth Faction to support Gush Emunim activities, further confirming Rabin's view. When asked whether the Youth Faction had hoped the Gush Emunim demonstrations of 1974 would weaken the Rabin Government, Youth Faction leader Hammer replied, "I wouldn't say that we planned this. But it is clear, when we opposed things touching upon Eretz Yisrael ... that these demonstrations would awaken our community first of all against the Government but not that we initiated it, pushed it, but it went together."[24]

Nevertheless, granted that Rabin's view was abetted by the group itself, his understanding of Gush Emunim as closely associated with the opposition and intent upon bringing down his Government is exaggerated. Members of his own party supported the group, but he minimizes their significance. (Gush Emunim's Labor Party supporters became known as the 'Ein Vered Circle.) Gush Emunim members assert they did not plan their demonstrations in order to topple Rabin's Government. Although they would not have been unhappy had the Government fallen, evidence confirms that any demands for changing the Government were pressed via the NRP during coalition nego- tiations. Representing the attitude of many members, Uri Elitzur explains, "I never saw that one of our purposes was to bring down the Rabin Government. I didn't act for this. ... We wanted to advance the idea of Eretz Yisrael, of settlement, and everything that advances this is good. But I don't see myself as connected to politics that I can say I have to bring down this or that Government."[25] Others recognize that Rabin may have misunderstood their motives since they made a settle- ment attempt so soon after he took office. Indeed, according to Rabbi Yohanan Fried, "There were months when we thought that the Government of Rabin is not Zionist because it is against settlement, because it speaks about Shomron as if it were a Palestinian state, and therefore, we thought that the first thing is that the Government has to fall ... but," he asserts, "not in a *putsch*, not in Sebastia [Shekhem area]."[26]

When focusing on Gush Emunim as a group per se, Rabin con- siders it "a threat to the democratic process in Israel." Although, according to Rabin, "in every democracy you can have protest movements" and "protest movements are justified for certain pur- poses," he believes that "exparliamentarian [outside parliament] bodies are not healthy to the democratic process." Seemingly threatened by the group's non-party form, Rabin would have preferred that they fit into understandable old political molds. Couching his fear in terms of preserving democratic processes, Rabin explains, "If they want in accordance to our kind of democracy, they've got all the rights and the freedom to convince people to support their views, but they have to put it to the test of the democratic voting system. If they would like to form a party, fine. Then we'll see, but they believe that G-d has given them a mandate which doesn't need to be tested by the mandate that the people would give them."[27]

What Rabin apparently does not comprehend is that a group's organizational framework and mode of operation by themselves do not threaten democracy, but rather the challenge comes from the system's failure to counterbalance any destabilizing aspects of group activities with structures and procedures for discussing issues and making decisions. In many instances, this failure caused Rabin's Government to appear inept and weak. Moreover, Rabin's understand- ing of the group as associated with his opposition, although not unfounded, may have prevented him and his Government from considering the group and its issue seriously and caused him to obsess over the group's political motivations. Gush Emunim, while not directly demonstrating for the Government to fall, certainly exploited the Government's fear of falling when planning the most propitious timing for the group's activities. The case of Qadum is illustrative.

Crisis at Qadum: Deficiencies in Decision-Making

Prepared long before but held in abeyance for the most effective timing, Gush Emunim's settlement attempt at Sebastia (near Shekhem) in December 1975 exposed the difficulty Israel's Government and political system encountered in reaching a consensus on settlement policy and in establishing procedures for dealing with groups. For Gush Emunim and the Government, Shekhem symbolized the struggle over settlement policy. Approval for a settlement near Shekhem would be considered a significant breakthrough for settlement throughout the West Bank.

Having attempted to settle several times since 1973, the group seized the moment after the United Nations resolution equating Zionism with racism to try again. Following their usual tactic, Gush Emunim members made a small preliminary effort and were removed by the army. Then, they organized thousands to enter the West Bank, encamping at an abandoned railway station west of Sebastia. The timing was right on the mark, effectively concerning and constraining Rabin who noted that

> it [Sebastia settlement attempt] coincided with a high wave of feeling in Israel and in the Jewish world in response to the decision taken in the General Assembly against the Zionist movement. ... Therefore, many people in the Likud leadership and in Mafdal all joined, maybe twenty thousand people, in Sebastia. ... At the same time we had here the Jerusalem Solidarity Conference of leaders of Jewish communities all over the world. And the problem that I was faced with was that during this period if I would have used the armed forces, it would have created sharp confrontation and division amongst ourselves, and instead of solidarity it would have shown to the world unfortunately sharp divisions and who knows to what it might have led.[28]

The group's well timed action placed Rabin in a tight bind. Any decision would have drawn criticism. From Rabin's vantage point, forcibly compelling the group to leave could possibly cause violence and bring accusations that the Government was unconcerned for its citizens and insensitive to Jewish feelings. Letting the settlers remain could invite criticism that the Government was weak and indecisive. The compromise reached indeed raised the latter charge.

The incident indicates the important role of perceptions in policy-making. Apparently, Rabin believed the group capable of violence, although one may question the basis for such an assessment. Considering the prevalence of weapons in Israel, compared to groups elsewhere, Gush Emunim's activities had been relatively benign. During the Kissinger demonstrations, described as the most violent in Israel, some burning tires were rolled, but the most damaging objects thrown were eggs. And, although Rabin could not know it, group spokesmen refer to the disputes lightly as a "family" fight. Gush Emunim, however, perceived Rabin's dilemma and dismay and did nothing to dispel them. Exploiting the publicity to the fullest, Gush Emunim persons such as Rabbi Levinger treated the public to dramatic emotional displays. Evoking tragic images of the Jewish past, Rabbi Levinger tore his clothes in a sign of mourning and screamed about the Government pursuing a White Paper policy. (A British White Paper issued in 1939 restricted settlement of Jews in Palestine.) Gush Emunim brought participants in the Jerusalem Conference to the site. Capitalizing upon Rabin's premonitions of violence, and moreover, calculating that the Government would be apprehensive and reluctant to fall over this issue, group members adopted a stubborn stand and refused to evacuate the site.

Emissaries from the Government including Sharon, who was a military adviser to the Prime Minister, Defense Minister Peres, and a self appointed mediator, writer Hayyim Guri, visited the site to negotiate either moving the settlers out or into some compromise arrangement. NRP ministers appealed to the Prime Minister to allow the settlers to remain, and NRP Minister of Social Welfare Hammer especially prevailed upon Rabin to arrange a compromise and not use force. Opposition Kneset members came to the site offering moral support, and in the Kneset opinions were voiced about dealing with the situation.

Authorized by the Government, Peres played the primary public mediating role. According to press and private accounts, the Government, adopting a suggestion by Sharon, permitted the settlers at Sebastia to enter a nearby military installation, Camp Qadum. They would be allowed to remain there temporarily, working in their regular jobs as well as for the army. The Government did not promise the camp would become a permanent settlement and undertook to discuss settlement policy within two to six months. Thus were Government ministers reduced to conducting shuttle diplomacy and negotiating with groups.

Rabin thought the compromise would allow the crisis atmosphere to cool down, but it actually permitted the situation to simmer, as all awaited the Government's decision about a final status for Camp Qadum. The Cabinet discussion was delayed until May following unrest on the West Bank and municipal elections there. Gush Emunim used the period to press its cause and regarded the delay advantageous because "at every Government meeting there were questions concerning Qadum put to Rabin" that gained publicity for the group.[29]

In the interim period, attention focused on the prominent divisions and difficulties in decision-making within the Government as well as within the Alignment and Labor Party. The Alignment Kneset faction met but did not vote on the Government compromise. The "no-vote" session, although not rejecting the Government action, neither was very supportive. Peres and Rabin were quoted in the press indicating different positions on settlement policy, on a final dénouement for Qadum in particular, and on relations with Gush Emunim. (Peres denies he ever supported a permanent settlement at Qadum or widespread settlement in the northern West Bank called Samaria, although he acknowledges perhaps having supported one or two sites there.) The Labor Party did not reach a consensus on settlement policy in general or on Qadum in particular, which Rabin understood as undercutting his credible options for action, as he explained, "I said it's impossible that the party would not come out [against Gush Emunim] and that the Minister of Defense would describe them as idealistic pioneers and at the same time will use only the violence of the armed forces against them."[30] Gush Emunim approached various ministers for support. NRP Kneset members visited the site during this period, and Hammer hinted about leaving the Government if the settlers were evacuated from Qadum.

The eventual Cabinet decision permitted further procrastination. The Government decided that Camp Qadum would not become the site of a permanent settlement and that at a date in the near future the group would be transferred to a permanent place within the framework of the Government's approved program. However, a final site never was selected, and the issue still was in limbo when Rabin dissolved his Government in December 1976.

Continually attracting press attention as the Government proposed alternate sites, the situation did not bring credit upon the Rabin Government for decisiveness. Apparently, Rabin determined that an ineffectual public image was the price to be paid for peaceful relations with Gush Emunim. There is some reason to speculate that when arranging the initial compromise, Government officials had expected Camp Qadum would remain "permanently temporary." One Gush Emunim leader claims that, although a different story was released to the press, Peres had assured them they could remain at Qadum or at another site in the area and that the Government's future discussion would not concern Qadum but rather additional settlement in that sector.[31] Rabin indicates that, in contrast to the 'Ofrah episode, this time he did not feel deceived by the Defense Minister and actually anticipated the group would remain quite a while at Qadum, as he explains, "... I made a compromise that moved them to a military camp on a temporary basis. ... Indirectly, not openly, I made it clear to Gush Emunim that if they tried to settle one settlement more in Judea and Samaria, the armed forces would not be used only to the new attempt but also would be used to get rid of those on a temporary basis in Qadum. As a result of it, for one and a half years, Gush Emunim did not try to do anything in terms of settling settlements, from the beginning of '76 until the elections."[32]

Thus, Rabin achieved some group quiescence and prevented unbridled settlement but at the expense of his Government and party appearing indecisive on a particular incident, unable to set a comprehensive program, and subject to group pressure. Qadum raised more questions about the system than it resolved, revealing many lacunae in the decision-making process. Regarding group relations, the main question was not whether groups could be heard, for certainly the dramatics brought them publicity and guaranteed that some official would at least pay attention, but rather how they would be heard. Sufficient and permanent channels proved dangerously lacking. The group's tactic of "lobbying" individual legislators and Government ministers irrespective of their official function, while effective for the group, pointed up the lack of prescribed channels or mechanisms for bringing a concern to the Government and legislative tables for review and decision. The incident also raised the question of whether decision-making could move beyond dealing with an immediate crisis and focus unemotionally on the essence of an issue. The prognosis seemed negative, as politicians ran to demonstrate in the West Bank instead of sitting and hammering out differences to formulate a settlement policy. These deficiencies in the decision-making process were inherited by the next administration.

Chapter 11

Elections 1977

Rabin believed the extra-parliamentary nature of the new group was destabilizing to the system and yearned for Gush Emunim to follow the customary and therefore reassuring pattern of establishing a party, but the group chose not to fulfill his wish for the 1977 elections. Although two major party blocs were developing, from the group's perspective the system still was multi-party, and many Gush Emunim members deemed it wise not to enter the labyrinth. Gush Emunim's relationship to the party system prior to the elections may be analyzed regarding the group's aims, its envisioned role for achieving those aims, and the organizational structure adopted for those purposes.

Continuing to perceive its aim primarily as obtaining a Government settlement policy in Eretz Yisrael and its role as pressing the parties and Government for such a policy direction, the group declined to seek a place for itself in Government or a formal part in the decision-making process. The group, therefore, did not succumb to the temptation of establishing a political party, remaining a fresh and unique phenomenon on the Israeli political scene. Some members more adamantly than others favored restricting the group's role and structure, as Gush Emunim founder Hanan Porat explains that

> Harav [Rabbi] Levinger was very strong about this. If it had depended upon him, for a certain period Gush Emunim would not have organized garinim [settlement nuclei]. ... He said the Government was obligated. I said, perhaps you are right theoretically, but in practice, the Government will not work in this sphere, and the result will be that there won't be settlements. ... In the sphere of establishing garinim, he agreed with my opinion, and in the political sphere, we agreed ... that Gush Emunim doesn't have to be active in

a direct way in anything that touches politics and parties. It is possible to influence policy lines, to meet with ministers, Kneset members, to bring them to our position but not to get into the question
of the composition of the parties.[1]

The approaching elections tested Gush Emunim's trans-party
stance. Not becoming a party itself did not preclude the group from
impinging upon the party system, but it had to decide upon an appropriate mode. Truman observes that "avoiding any commitment,
especially an open or continuing commitment, to a particular party
organization or faction is generally characteristic of interest group
politics."[2] Among the factors he cites for such behavior is the relation
between partisanship and cohesion. A group may be composed of persons of different party tendencies, and the group's interest may not be
sufficiently cohesive to override members' party loyalties. Therefore,
a group is careful not to align with any party because it may not be
able to deliver its members accordingly, and the party endorsement
may in fact become a divisive element. Although Truman refers
mainly to the American scene with two-party competition between
pragmatic, weak parties and has since noted that some interest groups
have aligned with parties, his original observation certainly applied in
Israel to both the Manufacturers' Association and to Gush Emunim.

In another context, Truman addresses the popular notion that
"politics is dirty" and how that view interferes with the public's
understanding of the role of interest groups. In Israel, moreover, the
concept of political activity as a stigma is very pronounced with a real
effect upon the system. Ideology is upheld as the main legitimate
rationale for party activity, and every politician therefore is under
even greater suspicion for acting in his own power interests and
engaging in "dirty politics" than in a pragmatic system. Cognizant of
this popular attitude, Gush Emunim persons rigorously avoided a formal party connection which might give an impression that they were
insincere in their aim and were just another group seeking a seat in
parliament. For these as well as other, more pure power considerations, they carefully calculated their involvement in party affairs.

Gush Emunim was more active in political affairs than the
Manufacturers' Association, however, and it was more attuned to the
multi-party system. In deference to members who counselled against
even limited involvement with parties, Gush Emunim craftily
designed a strategy that enabled it to preserve peace and unity within
the organization, maximize its influence upon several contenders,
avoid perhaps backing a loser, and mitigate its alienation of an unsup-

ported winner. Gush Emunim's official position called upon members to support any party sympathetic to settlement in Eretz Yisrael. Gush Emunim did not officially engage in specific campaigns, but the group did not restrict its politically inclined members. The group's amorphous structure allowed it to accept credit for any successful initiatives made by its members while avoiding any stigma that party alignment would entail. Practically, the policy meant support for three parties – the NRP, Shlomtzion, and Likud – and opposition to Labor.

Gush Emunim's opposition to Labor was subtly expressed. In a publication addressed to its members, Gush Emunim attributed the "main blame" for the lack of settlements upon present and previous Governments, which meant the coalition forming Labor Party. The group did not plan an attack on Labor, however, and instead sought to raise settlement as an election issue and pressure all parties about it. Apparently, the group expected again to press for a national unity Government and it did not want to absolutely alienate Labor, should Labor win a plurality.

For several reasons the NRP was the main target. First of all, a need for circumspection in party activity made the NRP the most available for Gush Emunim influence. Members of Gush Emunim already were active in that party and therefore could pressure the party without explicitly invoking the name of Gush Emunim. Second, the NRP was the party upon which the group expected it could exert the most influence because a large proportion of the group had developed within the womb of the NRP and a "family type" relationship continued to exist.[3] Third, of all the parties sympathetic to Gush Emunim's aim, past history demonstrated that the NRP was highly likely to participate in the coalition, and therefore, any influence on the NRP would reap great dividends. Backing the Likud still seemed risky and even more so would have been an endorsement of the new Shlomtzion Party, based essentially upon one personality, Sharon. On Labor's list, Gush Emunim as a group could naturally have little direct influence. Fourth, of all the possible parties upon which to act, the NRP was deemed the party most in need of influence. Settlement policy was the founding ideology of the Herut Party within the Likud and also was basic to Shlomtzion. The NRP was the most shaky, with the old guard still somewhat reluctant to prominently stress the settlement ideal and with the commitment of even the Youth Faction slightly in doubt after their qualified support regarding some of Gush Emunim's activities. Fifth, and most important, the candidate Gush Emunim members supported already was an NRP member, and therefore they could back him without appearing to affiliate the group officially with the party or subjecting the group to party authority. They always could claim either that the candidate on his own initiative had desired the spot or that the party had selected him.

Piecing together various versions of events, it seems that a group of persons with dual membership in Gush Emunim and the NRP cooperated with the Youth Faction in backing Druckman's candidacy for the party list and succeeded in placing him in the second spot. The difficulty in obtaining an exact picture of the group's party activity must be noted here. Group members and politicians relate different accounts, having different perspectives and motives, perhaps unconsciously, for doing so. Group members who believed that Gush Emunim should be circumspect in party activities would want to impart that impression to an interviewer and therefore minimize the direct party connection and influence of the group. Some members said the group was not involved in the initial selection, that the NRP desired to attract a segment of the populace supportive of Gush Emunim's ideas, but once Druckman was accepted by party officials, they admit to pressing for him to be in a high place. Other Gush Emunim members, despite their opinion that the group should keep aloof from party politics could not resist trying to impress the interviewer with the group's influence and power. They recall "nailing the Youth Faction to the wall" to place Druckman on the list.[4] Party officials, on the other hand, would not want to admit they were pressured by a group and therefore would seek to minimize the group's role in influencing them. Youth Faction officials explain they desired and initiated Druckman's candidacy, not because he was a Gush Emunim sympathizer, but because he represented the type of person they sought in order to enhance the party's image. Rather than blurring an understanding of the group and politics, the different accounts reflect the political culture to which groups had to relate.

It is commonplace in Israel to state that groups seek to influence the system by establishing a representative and spokesman, whether a party, a particular minister, or a Kneset member. Gush Emunim's methods demonstrate that this explanation of group activity is too simple. Gush Emunim never was content to rely upon one representative. In fact, as soon as Druckman was designated for a political role, the group eliminated his name from the wider secretariat so as to further obscure any identification between the two in public opinion. Consequently, the group's mode of political activity actually had the effect of not establishing an explicit representative. Gush Emunim's very circumspection in party activity permitted Druckman to regard himself as independent of the group, and therefore, the group's aloofness from party activity was not without a price, but one deemed minimal and necessary.

Gush Emunim's party activity did not lead to a patron-client relationship where the group was coopted into one party in return for a place on its list. Rather, Gush Emunim always tried to retain the initiative in political activity, and some members even pressed the NRP to consider their candidate for a ministerial position. In many respects, therefore, this group acted as an interest group within a more pragmatic system as described by Truman but with an extra dimension of flexibility and cunning to compensate for the ideologically charged atmosphere and multi-party character.

To understand the full dynamic between groups and party system, it is necessary to evaluate the reaction of parties to groups and the effect, if any, of the group upon the behavior of the system. Again, the difficulty of obtaining exact information must be mentioned. Party officials tend to deny making offers to groups, and groups, in order to enhance their importance, may exaggerate offers received. Moreover, generalizations from one group's case admittedly is flawed since that instance may be exceptional. Nevertheless, some observations may be ventured.

Political party theorists observe that ideological mass parties often compete in appealing to new groups of interests, not necessarily organized, that they perceive to exist among the voters.[5] In the process, the parties become less ideologically differentiated either in expressed purposes or in practice. Some observers of the Israeli system contend that this process has not occurred there and instead emphasize the system's equilibrium, depicting each party, composed of groups, either content or resigned to its portion of the electorate and consequent political position. The parties' relationship to Gush Emunim partly confirms and denies both explanations of party behavior and organization.

Whether or not a party vies for a group may be a function of party size as well as of group size, structure, and projected image of the group's influence. According to Gush Emunim persons, three parties – the Likud, NRP, and Shlomtzion – offered places on their lists to Gush Emunim persons and in different degrees of intensity encouraged Gush Emunim to formally affiliate and operate within the party framework. (Begin denies that the Likud made any such offer, and Sharon categorically denies having had any political designs on Gush Emunim.) The Labor Party made no such offer. In this case, therefore, the two major blocs did not compete with each other. Ideology or the ideological division within the Labor Party apparently was an impediment, and the party judged it could do without organizationally penetrating every group. Rather, parties closer together on the political spectrum competed for the group, with the greatest appeal made by the smallest party, Shlomtzion. It may be postulated that a small party seeks to expand its base by attempting to attach even a small group.

The parties were not complacent enough not to make any attempt. The desire to expand and project an image of a large organization still were important imperatives and apparently, parties preferred, if possible, to have a group inside rather than outside. The NRP, or at least Hammer of the Youth Faction, admits that despite the Youth Faction's disapproval of some Gush Emunim activities, "we always wanted, before the elections and always, Gush Emunim to help us."[6] When the group's response was not enthusiastic, and, in the case of the NRP, the Youth Faction realized that Gush Emunim's aims were incompatible with theirs, that "Mafdal is not Gush Emunim; it is a larger party," the parties desisted in efforts to incorporate the group as an entity.[7]

The parties' reduced efforts reflected Begin's view that "we don't like to woo people from another party."[8] The case of the Likud suggests an additional explanation for party behavior toward groups. Begin perceived Gush Emunim persons as predominantly supporting the NRP. At that time, the Likud and NRP were drawing closer together in anticipation of perhaps forming a coalition Government. Where a party foresees a need or possibility of cooperating with another party, it may instinctively institute a moratorium on competitive appeals to the same constituency or group. The Likud may not have deemed it necessary or prudent to compete very hard for Gush Emunim, whose members were perceived anyway as divided mainly between the two parties.

Although Begin did not consider Gush Emunim's electoral support as crucial for his party, it is interesting to note his comment that his party "came out first" in the election in Qiryat Arba' where there were many Gush Emunim members.[9] His comment underscores the difficulty politicians have in understanding or gauging the political impact of ideas or idea groups. They continually attempt to render the group relationship in more tangible terms, in this case in a geographical pattern. Moreover, in a country that is politically built as one constituency in a deliberate attempt to downplay geographical differences, it is interesting that some politicians nevertheless make geographical political analyses. The West Bank area subsequently would bear some political significance, but in 1977, the area was sparsely settled, and therefore, on the whole, parties responded to the amorphous nature of Gush Emunim.

Actually, the NRP and Likud accepted and reacted to the very image that Gush Emunim projected. Gush Emunim, which prided itself on an unstructured organization, lack of formal membership, and non-party position, may not have been attractive to the parties because there was no guarantee that linking it would produce substantial electoral gains. Parties received some campaign help anyway, as Gush Emunim members worked as individuals. Moreover, the group's leaders actually claimed not to have enough influence to dictate members' electoral preferences. Ben-Meir noted that "Hanan Porat did not have and does not have today legions that he can order how to vote, neither organizationally nor ideologically. We didn't ask them to take a decision one way or another because the decision wouldn't have meant that much one way or another."[10]

Any party appeals to groups were not motivated by a desire to control or subdue the group but rather by a desire for organizational campaign aid and any support from the general electorate which the group could muster. The party system was not a leviathan swallowing up any efforts for change. In fact, the parties realized the futility of any patronage type approach to an ideological group that proclaimed it could not be "bought" with jobs or positions, as Hammer discovered that "when Druckman was inside, it also wasn't enough for Gush Emunim to join in. This didn't help."[11]

Under certain conditions, then, parties accepted their portion, and it may be concluded that efforts to coopt groups have waned. However, these conclusions apply only when considering groups as organized entities. Parties did not necessarily cease modifying their positions to appeal to unorganized groupings or opinions in the electorate. Indeed, Gush Emunim persons attribute the establishment of settlements before the elections to Labor Party recognition of the settlement sentiment and to the party's desire to retain the support of its hawkish element. The NRP's inclusion of Druckman may be considered as an attempt to enhance its image and its appeal to a broader segment of the electorate. As explained by Ben-Meir, placing Druckman on the list "actually was aimed ... to attract supporters of Gush Emunim to support the NRP. Gush Emunim is an amalgam of people that is not membership but these people would be supporters of Gush Emunim to support the NRP at the polls."[12] If the Likud did not seek to attach Gush Emunim, a reason may lie in Gush Emunim's seemingly wild tactics which the Likud may have deemed a liability when

it was seeking to present a more moderate image. It may be concluded, therefore, that the parties were becoming less rigid in their
appeals and all along the spectrum were more competitive and sensitive to perceived public opinion than previously assumed but not in
a manner of structurally incorporating organized groups.

When considering groups as organized entities, the hypothesis
that ideological parties compete for group support does not apply to
the Israeli situation, at least regarding Gush Emunim. The two major
parties did not compete with each other to attach the group, but for
different reasons. The Labor Party was stymied by ideology, and the
Likud, attempting to project a more moderate image, did not make
extraordinary efforts to link the group. Also when considering groups
as organized entities, the second hypothesis appears partly true: Parties did not compete to attach groups organizationally, but the system
was by no means static. Rather, to understand development in the
system, groups must be viewed as unorganized groupings of attitudes.
Then, the first hypothesis to a certain extent is confirmed, and the
second is false. Parties began reacting to the ideas which groups
represented insofar as the parties perceived the group influential
among the voters.

These developments do not indicate the futility of organizing nor
the unresponsiveness of the system to interest groups. On the contrary, if a group seeks to alter a party's policy, it may organize, thereby
signalling to the parties the existence of another viewpoint. Groups
may play a role in raising issues and drawing attention to just those
unorganized opinions. In fact, Gush Emunim capitalized upon the
perception that there was an unorganized but numerous part of the
electorate holding a certain viewpoint, a so-called "silent majority."

In summary, an examination of the interrelationship between
group and party reveals a decline in party pervasiveness and in the
need for party alignment in order to express an opinion or demand a
policy change. Group activity was a factor in bringing about this subtle system change. Party activity was not the only route for influencing
decision-makers. Otherwise, a group such as Gush Emunim would
have been compelled to gamble on aligning with a party, and this did
not occur. However, despite group declarations of non-alignment and
differences of opinion within the group about party activity, the group
did not ignore parties but regarded the party system as one channel
of activity. The important change to note is that a group took the initiative and acted among several parties. Although parties in response
tried to attract groups, they did not necessarily aim to incorporate
them but to attract the vote of the group's potential supporters in the

electorate. Actually, the group's steadfastness against having an overt party connection, its refusal to succumb to party direction, and the group's loose structure may have spurred the parties to rethink their group relationships, abandon any ideas of cooptation, and instead concentrate on more general appeals.

Chapter 12

Gush Emunim, the Likud, and the Eighties

Summer of Discontent, 1977

The Likud formed a coalition with the NRP and Shlomtzion, all parties with which Gush Emunim ostensibly had sympathized.[1] Now that the group no longer had to hedge its bets and the Government parties no longer were in an objectively competitive position vis-à-vis the group, several scenarios for Government-group relations became possible: some very close, perhaps consultative relationship could develop between the entire Government and group; the group could decide to align with one coalition party and receive a position within a ministry; or the group conceivably could disappear, confident the Government would fulfill its aims. Indeed, for a short time some group members anticipated the group might become superfluous. Expectations of achieving their aims were raised high when soon after the elections, but before taking office, Begin attended a celebration at a West Bank settlement, promising many more similar settlements and an open door to his office for discussion with group members.

The group soon would learn, however, the cost of having taken a tangential party position. The main connection between the new Government and group was an ideological affinity; there was no mutual indebtedness from the election campaign. Just two months after the elections, group members had an inkling that their advice would not be automatically accepted and their goals would not be achieved so effortlessly. Gush Emunim remained, therefore, as an entity, organizing groups (called settlement nuclei) for eventual settlement in the West Bank, monitoring Government policies affecting settlement, and constantly pressing the Government to hasten the pace. The Government did not discourage the group but also did not attempt to incorporate it, finding a distant relationship at times allowed the group to fulfill important tasks that the Government could not risk undertaking itself, similar to the Manufacturers' Association's role under a Labor Government.

The Prime Minister was scheduled to visit the United States in July 1977. Gush Emunim, anxious that President Jimmy Carter would not be amenable to Israel's settlement policy, tried to persuade the Prime Minister to initiate settlements before his trip in order to build a firm bulwark against United States pressure. The Prime Minister disagreed and postponed starting a settlement effort until he returned.

Government and group differed on how the election victory should be interpreted. In Gush Emunim's view, the Likud's success presented an opportunity similar to Israel's victory in the 1967 war. Psychologically, according to the group, the country anticipated and expected great changes, and this was the time to seize the opportunity, quickly changing the course of events. The Prime Minister and his aides understood that the nation, as well as the world, anticipated changes but were not certain the nation would tolerate them. To allay fears of a revolution, the Government proceeded slowly. Although the Begin Government listened to Gush Emunim – both the Prime Minister and the minister in charge of settlement met with Gush Emunim leaders – by no means did the Government feel compelled to comply with their every wish.

The United States role also was a factor considered by the Israeli Government. Begin was relatively new to a leadership role. Although he had participated in a National Unity Government, this was the first time he and his party had primary responsibility for the country's leadership. One has the impression that immediately after taking office he perceived himself as a neophyte and was somewhat awed or anxious by an upcoming meeting with the leader of a superpower. He wanted first to learn exactly what to expect from the United States as well as to explain to the United States what to expect from Israel. He was conciliatory or cautious rather than confrontational, and perhaps naively, believed he could convince Carter of the correctness and advantage of his proposed course.

Gush Emunim believed that the Prime Minister had promised President Carter not to make "any surprises" about settlement. Although Begin denies having made any such promise, apparently his horizons and considerations were widened during his U.S. visit. The U.S. was attempting to reconvene a Geneva Conference by October aimed toward achieving a comprehensive peace settlement for the

Middle East, a major topic of discussion between the two leaders. It also is possible that there already were intimations of some dramatic declaration or move from Egypt. The Prime Minister had to consider the impact of any aggressive settlement effort on prospective peace talks.

Upon Begin's return from the U.S., Gush Emunim urged immediate implementation of a plan to settle about eleven sites throughout the West Bank. Gush Emunim leaders threatened, or considered, settling without Government approval, but this situation was not exactly comparable to their settlement campaigns under Labor. During the Labor period, they pressed for a policy initiative, but in this case, they felt Begin was reneging on a commitment because they had worked closely with administration officials in preparing the settlement program and had organized groups of potential settlers.

Begin sought a way to satisfy the settlement group as well as his own ideological inclinations while not arousing the ire of the U.S. or any potential peace partners. He first attempted accommodation. Similar to previous Governments that had bargained and made deals with groups on a less than global level, the Government approved and moved to settle one site, Yatir. Gush Emunim expected a much more comprehensive effort from a Begin Government and would not agree to postpone the broader settlement program. Another option Begin briefly considered was permitting the groups to settle privately, supposedly without Government foreknowledge, and then he would proclaim that he could not prevent Jews from settling in any part of the land. However, he realized this would reflect poorly on his leadership ability and prestige and would bear the same, if not worse, consequences for the Government as a Government backed policy.[2]

Pressing the issue to a climax, on the eve of the Jewish holiday Sukkot in September 1977, Gush Emunim directed the settlement nuclei to pack their belongings and wait on roads leading to the West Bank sites. Tension throughout the country mounted as the media focused on the situation. Would they carry out an illegal settlement attempt as they had under Rabin, would they obtain Government approval for settling, or would they back down?

Although the situation was highly dramatic, a solution was possible. Most of the group, disappointed about the alteration in the Government's course, still felt deferential to this Government, especially to Begin. From the Government's perspective, just as Rabin had hesitated to use the army, so did Begin, and moreover, this Government wanted to preserve the group, considering it a helpful and controllable factor in any future peace negotiations.

Negotiations were conducted on a very high level between core Gush Emunim members and the Prime Minister himself. During the summer and especially during September and the night of September 27, several times a Gush Emunim delegation met and spoke by telephone with the Prime Minister. Sharon, head of the Ministerial Settlement Committee, visited the group's headquarters in Jerusalem. Begin offered a compromise solution, to settle six groups over several months within military camps in the West Bank. The proposal for settling civilians in military camps had been outlined to President Carter by Foreign Minister Dayan in the U.S. that September, and according to the Prime Minister, "President Carter liked the idea."[3] To help persuade Gush Emunim leaders to accept the scheme, Begin also spoke to Rabbi Druckman, then an NRP Kneset member. Although Druckman reemphasized to Begin the need for settlement, he accepted the military camp arrangement and attempted to influence Gush Emunim not to act against the Government. Interestingly, Kneset member Druckman was not designated by the group as a representative but rather acted as an honest broker, and his presence at the discussions was more valuable to the Government than to the group. Neither was NRP Youth Faction member Hammer, then Minister of Education and Culture, involved in these talks. The group still had its own access to the top, and therefore, did not yet seek to establish or utilize "representatives" or intermediaries in Government, parties, or legislature.

By dawn, the military camp proposal was accepted. The compromise provided that no group would be disbanded, and groups for which there was not yet a military installation available would be adopted by an already existing settlement until a site could be found. The message was relayed to the waiting groups not to move that day. Before receiving the notification, one, more rambunctious, group moved and was intercepted by the military. The military action underlined the Government's resolve to impose its will. Gush Emunim leaders apologized in writing to the Prime Minister, demonstrating their willingness to cooperate with and not undermine the Government despite the group's pressure tactics.

The solution was satisfactory to the Government. The Government could appear as having resolved a crisis without resorting to the army; to the world, it could appear flexible and pragmatic on the settlement issue; it could appear as fulfilling its promises to a group; and it still could keep the settlement issue alive, maintaining these groups in reserve to be settled when deemed appropriate and necessary. To the group, however, still predominantly respectful of the

Government, the compromise signalled that the Government was swerving from the settlement path and required considerable guidance.

Government Divisions and Decision-Making, the Likud Version

Two months after the September crisis was resolved, Anwar al-Sadat made his famous visit to Jerusalem, and Begin was offering autonomy to Arabs of the West Bank and Gaza. Gush Emunim mobilized to oppose the autonomy plan and press further settlement, utilizing every opportunity to publicize the settlement issue and opposing any hint of Government "softening."

Actually, Sadat's peace initiative placed Israel in a quandary about settlement policy. The ideology of the Likud now had to confront possible peace with Egypt and other Arabs, the necessity of expanding the coalition to include parties not ideologically aligned, limited resources for settlement development, competing claims on resources from various groups, continuing pressure of Gush Emunim, as well as foreign pressures. To fully comprehend how the Government could handle these different pressures, the procedure involved in establishing a settlement requires a brief explanation.

Several stages were involved when the Government established a settlement. A Government decision and announcement designating a site did not immediately usher in bulldozers and contractors to erect huge cities overnight. The Government made a high level, rather general decision, and then the Minister for Settlement took over long term planning and development. Especially when Gush Emunim or another group was eager to settle, the first stage of implementation usually involved entry of a small number of persons to a campsite or abandoned structure. Then, prefabricated structures were set up to accommodate the group and perhaps additional persons followed by longer term planning for more permanent structures, including determining available land. While a site was in the early stages, sometimes it was categorized officially as a military encampment and not a permanent settlement at its final location.

Each stage conceivably could be manipulated to meet some internal or external purpose. The Government, for example, could schedule the announcement of a site for its maximum impact on the diplomatic scene and then stall on developing the area, permitting its negotiating counterpart to react. Or, an announcement could be timed to reassure a domestic group clamoring to settle, and then development could be delayed to meet some international imperative. Or, many announcements could be made followed by quick positioning of small groups in scattered spots in order to stake a claim to territory with development slowed until appropriate resources could be gathered or an international agreement reached. Finally, all three stages could be collapsed together as quickly as possible.

After examining the Government decisions regarding settlement, progress in the peace talks, and disputes with the group Gush Emunim, I originally intended to argue that Israel considered all these elements and actually "fine tuned" the stages to the ultimate purpose of making peace with Egypt. One also might claim that Israel always intended to retain the entire West Bank and calculated all its moves to that end. It seems, however, that such procedures would be too sophisticated and calculated to ascribe to decision-making in Israel. In classic Israeli fashion, similar to the Labor Government, this Government's response was not to take an explicit and public decision. In fact, as the Labor Government never officially adopted the Allon or any other plan, this Government examined but never officially adopted Sharon's plan. Although a majority in this Government was predisposed to promoting settlement and retaining control over the West Bank, not officially announcing a detailed plan allowed members to avoid confronting their principles while leaving room to adjust when pressured. The decision-making model to bear in mind is that of a Government subject to pressures internally and externally, experimenting with all approaches at one time or another depending upon the extent of the pressure or the persuasion of a particular individual.

Following Sadat's visit, the first Likud Government was divided regarding territorial compromise, and even within the same segment of the political spectrum among members not basically opposed to retaining the West Bank, there were differences about the extent to which settlements should be placed and paced to achieve that end and to facilitate negotiations with Egypt on terms most favorable to Israel. The Democratic Movement for Change was the most intent on slowing the settlement effort, and as a condition for entering the coalition in October 1977 was allowed to appeal any settlement decision to the full Cabinet and then to the Kneset Foreign Affairs and Security Committee. As peace negotiations proceeded, differences among ministers became more pronounced and were reinforced by overlapping authority for the territories and split responsibility for the different stages of the settlement process. The minister in charge of the settlement committee, Agriculture Minister Sharon, was known to favor forging ahead with settlements, creating fait accomplis wherever and whenever possible, and Defense Minister Ezer Weizman came to support a slower approach. Until the winter of 1978, the Ministerial Committee on Settlement was responsible for deciding upon settlements, with its decisions having the delegated authority of the entire Cabinet. However, Weizman's Defense Ministry supervised the military government in the territories and, therefore, had some jurisdiction or voice concerning activities by Israeli citizens in the area. At the least, policy had to be coordinated with the Defense Ministry because in any case, the Defense Ministry soon would observe any occurrences in the area. In the winter of 1978, responsibility for designating settlements was transferred to a Ministerial Security Committee, but the Ministerial Settlement Committee, which included representatives of the World Zionist Organization, continued to exist for developing settlements decided upon, and therefore, coordination between the two bodies still was necessary, and conflict was possible.

Regarding the group Gush Emunim, the Government also was ambivalent, reluctant to oppose the group outright because some officials found the group-created commotions helpful to negotiation efforts. The sporadic crises allowed negotiators to try extracting concessions from the other side by claiming they faced tremendous domestic pressure. The Government also considered it expedient to utilize the group's organizational ability for populating the area. However, the Government was not always able to control the group.

Gush Emunim judged, probably correctly, that any hiatus in development signalled Government swerving from the settlement course. In this period, while the group did not initiate crises on the scale of previous settlement campaigns, it took advantage of any friction between ministers and gaps in the decision-making process, ever ready to cooperate with any authority that abetted its efforts. Gush Emunim refused to accept control over the timing of the settlement enterprise, and in pressing its agenda, aggravated and exposed the developing differences within the Government as revealed by the incidents at Shiloh and Nebi Tzalah.

As a result of all these competing pressures and jurisdictional and opinion cleavages, especially about the relationship of settlements to peace negotiations, the Government's settlement policy appeared to seesaw. By December the Government had kept its part of the September compromise with Gush Emunim, and at least six groups had been settled in or near military installations. Early in January, following calls by the Egyptian Foreign Minister to liquidate settlements as soon as possible, Israel's Cabinet decided to encourage additional settlers to move to existing settlements in Sinai and also to establish three sites in the West Bank but did not yet specify them. Although appearing spiteful, this decision was rather cautious as the Government chose not to follow Sharon's urging to establish completely new sites in Sinai and left open designating the exact West Bank spots. The announcement also appeared as appeasement of Gush Emunim because it followed Gush Emunim protests of Begin's autonomy plan and its pressure, which it openly stated would test the Government's determination regarding settlement, to settle groups that had been residing at established sites as per the second part of the September agreement. In accordance with that agreement, Gush Emunim's Qarnei Shomron group was permitted to settle, and, mindful of Israel's promise to Carter to settle within a military context, a site was staked out that could be construed as a military camp. Shiloh was designated an archaeological dig, and a number of Gush Emunim persons were permitted to work at the excavation.

At the outset of the Shiloh operation, it seems Gush Emunim intended to erect a settlement gradually, as it had at 'Ofrah, but then it changed course and attempted to compel the Government to take an explicit stand on a full-scale settlement program. Gush Emunim went public, stressing to the press that its members at Shiloh were settlers, not archaeologists, and thus invited controversy. The issue became a cause célèbre, greatly discrediting the Government.[4]

Whether or not the Government or some Government ministers collaborated in the group's aim is uncertain. One naturally must wonder why the Government would have resorted to such means when it was possible to declare sites forthrightly, as it had been doing. There are three possibilities: (1) the entire Government may truly have intended it to be an archaeological expedition; (2) certain members of the Government may have deemed another settlement by any means so important that they deceived their colleagues by presenting it as an archaeological site while secretly hoping or intending to transform it; or, (3) the Government approved the archaeological expedition thinking that if somehow the site should eventually evolve into a permanent settlement, so much the better. (One Gush Emunim member claims that Begin, Weizman, and Sharon all intended to establish a settlement at Shiloh and devised this method to circumvent DMC opposition.)

The incident erupted at an unwelcome time for the Government. On the peace negotiations front, political committee sessions between Egypt and Israel began on January 17 and broke off on the 18th, and the military committee also was discontinued. The Government took a cautious stand toward Shiloh. Although not banning a Gush Emunim cornerstone laying ceremony there on January 23rd, the Jewish holiday of Tu' be-Shvat, the Government refused to recognize the ceremony as indicating a permanent site, and Government officials did not participate.

The issue would not fade away, however. Shiloh was discussed in the Kneset and the Cabinet and reached American news media. All speculated on the Government's motives, internal rifts, and intentions. The United States accused Israel of having reneged on Dayan's promise not to establish civilian settlements for a year and settle only within military areas. Dayan defended himself, denying the promise was for a year but rather for the rest of 1977, and by so doing, he appeared nitpicking and deceptive. Several ministers insisted Shiloh was an archaeological dig, while the press printed reports that structures were being built for a yeshivah. Other ministers gave an impression of not being well informed. Whether or not the Government had acted surreptitiously, it was portrayed in the media as divided and deceitful. The incident was a classic example of the dysfunctions of the ideological dimension as Government members continually avoided deciding upon a settlement policy. Instead of debating and arriving at a coordinated settlement policy, the governing institutions let themselves become embroiled in an uproar over the development of one site.

From any perspective, the Government's image was tarnished, appearing disingenuous at worst or at best weak and conflicted over policy and lacking control over events. If the Government had planned a quiet settlement attempt, it would mean the Government had felt pressured by world opinion and had hesitated to declare a firm public stand. It also would have been considered wily and untrustworthy for having reneged on an understanding with the United States to settle in military camps. If the Government as a whole had not decided to locate a settlement there and it was proved that one was developing, then the Government would appear as internally divided and out of control, with ministers able to deceive their colleagues. If the Government did not stop further development, it would appear weak and outmaneuvered by a group. Certainly, as at 'Ofrah and Qadum, at the very least the Government's decision-making procedures could be questioned. Whether or not the Government had conspired with the group, it certainly learned that group control could go awry and that synchronizing settlement with the negotiating process could become extremely complicated.

While Gush Emunim encouraged the Shiloh situation, it exacerbated a ministerial showdown at Nebi Tzalah. An initial group was settled at the military camp there in November 1977 and awaited further development, at least the provision of prefabricated structures. Early in February 1978, Gush Emunim slightly shifted its strategy—in addition to pressing for new sites, it pressed for fully developing the military camps where members were confined, thereby pushing the Government to address the problem of land acquisition and future sovereignty over the area. The Government determined a final spot for the settlers at Nebi Tzalah but without stipulating a starting date for preparing the land and positioning the prefabricated structures. Always seizing opportunities to extend its inroads, Gush Emunim, supported by Sharon, obtained equipment and began work early in March just prior to Defense Minister Weizman's trip to the United States to negotiate an arms package for Israel. Contrary to Sharon, who then thought no circumstances justified slowing settlement, Weizman thought it would be prudent to downplay settlement and certainly did not view his trip as the propitious time for expanding West Bank sites. Taking the media into his arsenal, Weizman phoned the Prime Minister from New York with a member of Israel television as witness and threatened to resign if development at Nebi Tzalah continued. At Weizman's request, the Prime Minister convened a meeting of the Ministerial Security Committee, and after a "bitter debate" with Sharon, the Government decided to halt development until Weizman's return.[5]

Gush Emunim did not defy the decision but continued complaining to the press about the settlement slowdown and unsteady Government course. These views were endorsed by Sharon who claimed that the winter 1978 settlement halt had not advanced negotiations between Israel and Egypt but actually had the opposite effect, encouraging Egypt to escalate its demands and speak about Israel's withdrawal to 1967 borders and about establishing a Palestinian state.[6]

The Shiloh and Nebi Tzalah incidents were merely two examples of Government and group disagreement over all settlement policy and development in 1978, including sites in Sinai. In all cases, the Government's decision-making procedures were discredited as policy seemingly was set through the media after publicity and pressure by ministers and groups instead of by discussion. Problems of overlapping ministerial jurisdiction for settlement were revealed. In the Nebi Tzalah episode, Sharon actually had not breached a Government decision regarding work there; rather, it was Weizman who requested a change or modification. Regarding development of sites in Sinai, however, Sharon was criticized by his colleagues for having exceeded Government authority. The group's pressure and activities did not instigate but did exacerbate the different ministerial positions. Though the group was not included in the decision-making process, its aims and actions certainly affected the Government's stop and go settlement program.

What the United States and Egypt regarded as excessive, Gush Emunim regarded as piddling. Although adapting to the Government's piecemeal procedure, Gush Emunim never abandoned its quest for a comprehensive settlement policy with full scale construction and development not hidden behind rationales about security and a military camp façade. "We wanted from the Government a plan, to know what the Government considers, where to settle, where not to settle and when. And that we never received, not from Rabin and not from Begin."[7] Though accusing both Governments of holding back on settlement, Gush Emunim activists were less willing to tolerate an ad hoc approach from Begin. Expecting the Government to "build highways and devote billions to develop the area," to their dismay, they got "caravans and huts."[8]

Settlement Movement

Despite Gush Emunim's vociferous heightened anti-Government rhetoric and demonstrations, in 1978, the Government took a seemingly anomalous step and recognized Gush Emunim as a settlement movement. Technically, this meant that Gush Emunim would be the legal representative body for a network of settlements similar to kibbutz and moshav movements that had existed in the country since the pre-state period. Just as the other movements were supervised by and eligible for financial aid from the Jewish Agency's Settlement Department, so, too, would Gush Emunim. In one aspect, however, such recognition was novel. Most other settlement movements were affiliated with a political party, but Gush Emunim was a non-affiliated organization. Conceivably, had the Government desired stronger control over settlements, it could have compelled various settlements to affiliate with one of the existing movements. (Indeed, Kfar 'Etzion, established prior to the existence of Gush Emunim, is affiliated with the NRP kibbutz movement.)

One might well wonder why the Government would take such a step which seemingly rewarded a group opposed to the Government. I do not think there was a premeditated decision to temper the opposition and coopt the group. Begin was astonished at that suggestion. Rather, one might argue that the group's anti-Government expressions and pressure prompted the Government to reaffirm its adherence to the settlement cause and to try persuading the group that the settlement issue could be separated from the peace process. The step was taken, therefore, as MK Ben-Meir explained, "not to regularize them, but on the contrary, to go towards them because Begin liked them, to show them his Government was in favor of them..."[9] The Government, according to Ben-Meir, wanted to show Gush Emunim that at least on the "practical issues" the Government was willing to help them and was "not against them because of their opinions." Though not "buying them off," the Government hoped the group would express its opinions in a "more proper way."[10]

Government intentions notwithstanding, Gush Emunim's acceptance of the designation had far-reaching organizational consequences, eventually modifying the group's character. Even without imposing a political connection, the Government's move somewhat routinized the group. What had been an arm of Gush Emunim, the settlement committee, now became ascendant. As a movement responsible for decisions affecting the housing, livelihood, and future of thousands of persons living in settlements, Gush Emunim as a settlement movement, called Amanah, necessarily became more formally constructed with regularly and democratically elected organs.

Shekhem Revisited

Gush Emunim's elevation to a settlement movement did not prevent the Government from exerting authority over the settlement process nor preclude Gush Emunim from challenging that authority. Settlement underwent another slowdown when new outposts were postponed until after the Camp David meeting, and then new settlement was ceased for three months as per Begin's promise at Camp David. Gush Emunim's reaction to Camp David was to stage immediate settlement attempts, all promptly dispersed by the army at Government direction, thus preserving Begin's promise. Apparently to assuage criticism and to indicate its resolve on settlement, in October the Government decided to strengthen existing settlements in the West Bank, Gaza, and the Golan Heights. Gush Emunim, however, was not satisfied.

As soon as the freeze expired, Gush Emunim tried again in January 1979, resurrecting its old aim of settling a site near Shekhem, to be called Elon Moreh. Managing to circumvent the army, Gush Emunim members stationed themselves on a road in the area, and this time were not quickly dispersed. Noting that the Government did not have to cope with a provocative emotional issue comparable to the anti-Zionist U.N. resolution that Rabin had faced, one naturally wonders why Gush Emunim's action was tolerated even briefly. Camp David still was not consummated by a peace treaty, the negotiations having undergone some rough passages, and therefore, one might conclude that army action was not ordered against the group because the Government wanted to use the opportunity to score some negotiating points. The Government wanted to emphasize to the United States and Egypt that it would not yield to a claim to the West Bank, that the promise for ceasing settlement had been only for three months until the expected signing of a peace treaty with Egypt and not, as the U.S. interpreted, for the duration of any prospective negotiations with other Arab parties, and that strong domestic pressure existed for Israel's position.

Having made these points, the Government had to extricate itself from the group imposed dilemma. The Government was not ready to forfeit a peace treaty for another settlement. Despite this general Government outlook, ministerial differences did surface. Hammer and Sharon supported the Elon Moreh group. Weizman and others opposed, although Weizman favored strengthening existing settlements. A third group did not oppose Elon Moreh but wanted the Government to preserve its prestige and withstand group pressure.

Again, the country beheld the spectacle of ministers and Kneset members shuttling to the group and arranging a compromise. Perceiving themselves to be in a weak position in public opinion, Gush Emunim mustered support from many sources, not only from those holding a portfolio directly related to settlement. The group concentrated, however, on coalition party members, finding it helpful to create an "atmosphere" within the coalition.[11] Therefore, Gush Emunim leaders now called upon NRP Minister of Education and Culture Hammer to become involved, and he did. Despite the NRP's differences with Gush Emunim on the peace process, the Youth Faction still supported the settlement effort, and on this, Gush Emunim could continue to count on their help.

Kneset members began playing a curious role in this crisis. Begin, stung by the anti-Government outcry raised by Gush Emunim since Camp David, did not meet with group representatives himself but appealed to Likud Kneset faction members with influence upon the settlers to persuade them to leave the roadsite in order to preserve the

Government's prestige. Usually, a group will apply to Kneset members to prevail upon the Government, and in this case Kneset members did send telegrams to the Prime Minister, but in a turnabout, the Prime Minister used Kneset members to prevail upon the group.

After nine days a compromise was reached. Minister Hammer probed possibilities for a solution. He realized the settlers were staging a demonstration and knew they would not remain without Government approval. Hammer also conversed with Sharon, and when they recalled that in November 1977 the Government had approved in principle a settlement in that area, they conceived of a face-saving arrangement whereby the Government could present any dealings with the group in the context of that decision without appearing to bow to group pressure. At a meeting of the Ministerial Security Committee, while the ministers discussed options and their various views on settlement, Dayan drafted a document wherein the Government recognized the group as a candidate for settlement in the near future, reserved the timing and exact location to the Government, and promised to consider the group's preferences as much as possible. Sharon and Hammer explained the decision to the group members, and they were persuaded to disperse.

Thus, at a time when the group was unable to affect the Government's position on the peace process, it demonstrated sufficient power to gain one more site by appealing to the ministers' loyalty to them on the settlement issue. The Government may have made its point concerning settlement on the international scene but at the cost of appearing coerced by a group, exposing internal divisions, and revealing an incoherent decision-making process.

Metamorphosis

Beginning in December 1977 when Begin outlined his peace ideas and crescendoing with Camp David and the Egypt-Israel Peace Treaty, Gush Emunim became more concerned with issues other than West Bank settlement. It increasingly opposed not only Government policies but the Government itself, unappeased by the Government's granting them settlement movement status and Government agreement to additional West Bank sites. Reminiscent of the anti-Kissinger era, the more nationalistic, non-religious nature of Gush Emunim was regenerated. The expanded activity raised questions within the group both about the appropriateness of its action and its structural expression. Ultimately, the group was transformed.

In the U.S., when Begin first presented Carter with his proposal on autonomy for West Bank and Gaza Arabs, two Gush Emunim leaders, who coincidentally were there on a speaking tour, met with Begin in New York and expressed their qualms about his plan. His "trust me" reaction did not allay their fears. In Israel, Gush Emunim leaders met with the Prime Minister several times and also organized demonstrations near his office and the Kneset. The issues were autonomy and the fate of settlements including those in Sinai. They convened protest meetings, one of which attracted settlers from all areas, not only West Bank residents and Gush Emunim members, and to enhance their strength, they established a joint staff with the Land of Israel Movement (a movement for retaining the territories that was established after 1967 but never acquired a religious and activist character like Gush Emunim). Turnout at the street demonstrations was relatively small, and organization was difficult amid the general euphoric atmosphere that still pervaded Israel in the wake of Sadat's visit, but rhetoric ran high as Porat spoke of "breaking" Begin.[12]

Notably present and active in organizing Gush Emunim protest meetings were Kneset members of coalition participating parties. As no comments were made by either the Government or the parties' leaders, this type of group supportive activity by Kneset members apparently was tolerated and considered legitimate. On the contrary, at times Kneset members were called upon by the Prime Minister to mediate between Government and group.

While Kneset members engaged in such "extra-parliamentary" activity, within the Kneset they did not invite the "idea" group to address a committee as, in contrast, they had invited the Manufacturers' Association. Struggling to account for the different Kneset methods, MK Ben-Meir distinguishes between an opinion group and an "interested" group, explaining that

> the Kneset gives a hearing in its committees to interested groups which appear, groups that have a specific interest in the issue....Gush Emunim does not have any special interest in the hit-nahalut [settlement] more than any other citizen has an interest. It's not going to affect his livelihood....Let's say we asked Gush Emunim to come. What would be the answer of the other people? "Why Gush Emunim?...Go to any street in Tel Aviv and ask a man to come." They have an opinion, they don't have an interest.[13]

Gush Emunim as a settlement movement might qualify for a Kneset appearance because the lives of the settlers organized by the movement could be directly affected by Kneset measures, but then, ironically, their views would be devalued because "when a member of Kneset gives a hearing to all these groups, in his mind he's giving a hearing to a special interest group.... He'll listen to them, and he may accept many things that they say, but always they're limited because he realizes they are concerned; they're not objective; they have their interests which are not necessarily the interests of the country."[14]

Idea groups were thus destined to voice their views in the streets, at protest meetings, or to any individual Kneset and Government members who might be sympathetic. Noticeably, and a bit surprisingly, absent from Gush Emunim inspired protest meetings were Cabinet members, unless they came as party leaders to explain policy. Considering that Cabinet members had publicly aired differing views, their presence would not have been astonishing. They seemed to draw a line, however, on directly supporting an opposition group, agreeing with Sharon that as a Kneset member it is a duty to attend group rallies and meetings, but a Government adviser or minister should avoid such a role.[15]

As peace negotiations proceeded during 1978, how Begin's plans would be finally cast was unclear. Uncertain about exactly what provisions would require counteraction and discerning a decline in public support, Gush Emunim concentrated efforts on the West Bank settlement situation, publicizing the Shiloh affair, Nebi Tzalah, etc. To Gush Emunim's chagrin, the ephemeral peace ideas were crystallized in the Camp David Accords of September 1978.[16] Regarded by Gush Emunim as the Government's ultimate betrayal, the accords marked a turning point in the group's political relations. As the Government attempted to become more pragmatic, a horrified Gush Emunim became more ideological, a redirection noted even then by Ben-Meir who claimed "what happened was not that we changed but that they changed."[17]

Rejecting Ben-Meir's advice to concentrate on West Bank settlement and remain aloof from other issues, Gush Emunim opposed the Camp David Accords. The group justified its action, arguing, "What use is making another settlement when the Government can come and pull it all away."[18] Though many contended that Sinai was part of Eretz Yisrael, they also offered more "logical" arguments such as withdrawal from Sinai setting a precedent for other areas and oil being important for "our life now."[19]

Begin agreed to the Camp David frameworks contingent upon a Kneset vote within two weeks ratifying Israel's abandoning the Sinai settlements. Gush Emunim swung into action. In addition to settlement demonstrations, the group, together with non-Gush Emunim persons from the Sinai settlements, mounted all night vigils outside the homes of Begin and other ministers, cooperated with other settlers and the 'Ein Vered Circle to persuade Kneset members to reject the accords, and mounted demonstrations in Jerusalem with Sinai settlers from Yamit, featuring a tractor brigade led by Porat. Together with Rabbi Druckman, they called upon the NRP to leave the Government.

Whereas Gush Emunim increasingly fused settlement to other issues, some coalition party members, significantly the NRP's Youth Faction who had helped found the organization, distinguished among issue areas. Explaining the widening "ideological dispute" with Gush Emunim, Hammer claimed "the settlements are important also to me. But it was a fact to lose the peace or not to lose the peace."[20] The Youth Faction rejected Gush Emunim's position on the peace process. Gush Emunim was unsuccessful in its new scope, as the Kneset, with each member freed from party discipline, voted its acceptance of Camp David on September 28. The group's latest pressure effort actually boomeranged because, as Ben-Meir believes, "Gush Emunim's big mistake was it thought it could dictate to the Begin Government, to the NRP. It failed in both."[21]

Not having prevented the Camp David ratification, many perceived that "the way of influencing and working within the parties...came to an end."[22] Those with party proclivities, who until then had been overruled by the rest of the group, reconsidered establishing a party, listening to Gershon Shafat who reasoned, "What use is it to work if on the crucial point you have no influence? You have influence on *hityashvut* [settlement]...but on the political case, you have no influence."[23] This time, a number of central Gush Emunim members joined with breakaway members of the Prime Minister's Likud bloc, plus a number of the country's intelligentsia who had been Gush Emunim sympathizers, to form the Tehiyah Party.

By moving to other issues besides settlement, Tehiyah and its Gush Emunim adherents actually narrowed the group's purposes and purview, futher distancing the group from its political party backers. As Ben-Meir explains, "The way that ha-Tehiyah [the Tehiyah] differs from us is that Mafdal [NRP] was never willing to adopt a position that was *'af sha'al'* [not one inch], neither was Herut. Mafdal was always in favor of basic, far-reaching retreat in Sinai for peace....That's not Eretz Yisrael."[24] Attesting to the group's more nationalistic tendency, Rabbi Druckman, who had helped found Gush Emunim and who had joined them in opposing Begin's autonomy plans and Camp David, did not enter the new party. He reasoned that the country still needed a religious-national party and that "Tehiyah operates only on the national side."[25]

Some Gush Emunim members argue that the group's political relationship had not drastically changed because Gush Emunim always had contained members of various parties, and Tehiyah members could be considered just another cluster. However, this change was significantly different because the initiative to form a party emanated from Gush Emunim, and many now chose not to work within the existing political configuration, rather forming a discrete addition to it. Ironically, the Likud Government's build-up of the West Bank may have contributed to the decision to establish a party. The settlers could provide a geographically delimited, identifiable electoral base. By the same reasoning, however, the settlers now provided a tangible target for competition by all parties. Only a future electoral analysis could determine the impact of the West Bank settlers on the political system and the influence of geographical considerations on parties.

Besides Rabbi Druckman, other Gush Emunim members disagreed with their colleagues' political assessment, and consequently, the group continued parallel to the party. However, Gush Emunim "has gone through a metamorphosis. The main effort today is on the strength of the settlements."[26] Becoming enmeshed in practical, physical settlement building, the group relegated the political realm to Tehiyah and became less activist as well. In effect, according to Ben-Meir, "Gush Emunim hardly exists anymore because the entire emphasis has gone over to the settlers who are living there."[27] Porat attributes the group's subdued character to the realization that the tension its activity had created might have become counterproductive. Never having regarded the organizational framework especially important, the group's leaders "reached the conclusion that...with quiet intensive work in the field [Gush Emunim] can contribute ideas [that] will be absorbed by 'Am Yisrael [Nation of Israel]."[28]

Leeway still existed for those who desired more activism but only on the settlement aspect, and they had to resort to the incremental method. Thus, the Elon Moreh action occurred in January 1979, and in an even more piecemeal move, Rabbi Levinger engineered a squatting action by Qiryat Arba' women in an empty, former Hadassah hospital building in Hebron. This seemingly small action had far-reaching significance. It attempted to open the way for Israel to settle in Arab populated centers, thereby nudging the Government one more step in considering a sovereignty declaration over the entire West Bank. The Government allowed them to remain, and step by step, eventually some work was permitted on the building, and husbands and families were allowed to join the women. Rabbi Levinger cleverly knew how to extract concessions from an indecisive Government. From one building, Levinger's band hoped to build a community of Israelis living within the city.

With part of Gush Emunim acting as a party, part concentrating on mundane, detailed, but energy consuming settlement development, and a part sitting in Hebron, the question arises whether Gush Emunim had begun to disintegrate and whether the concept of an idea interest group in Israel had died. Indeed, the vociferous voice of Gush Emunim in demonstrations has not been heard since the early 1980s when Gush Emunim settlers resisted leaving the Elon Moreh site in compliance with an Israel Supreme Court decision of October 1979; conducted a hunger strike in front of the Kneset to press the Government to survey and document land ownership in the territories; and protested the evacuation of the Yamit settlement in Sinai and returning the Sinai to Egypt.

Gush Emunim still maintained an informal structure and office in Jerusalem for discussing ideological matters, but much of its efforts went into developing Amanah, its arm concerned with the nitty-gritty details of building settlements. Under the 1984 National Unity Government there was an understanding not to start new settlements, and only about six were built in this period out of a planned twenty-six. According to Gush Emunim, even under Shamir's Likud Government, obtaining settlements still was a struggle, for Shamir, in the group's estimation, was hesitant in the face of outside pressure.[29] Nevertheless, Gush Emunim had achieved something from its years of effort and concentrated on consolidating its gains. Gush Emunim persons became involved in all the enterprises rising in the territories—yeshivot, museums, businesses, even motels. Moreover, while Gush Emunim retained its non-party posture and did not endorse any one party in election years 1984 and 1988, Gush Emunim members became further embroiled in the party system: Rabbi Druckman founded a party; Porat left Tehiyah and became active in the NRP; and Elitzur also became active in the NRP. Gush Emunim per se simply no longer was the single organization for the original members' energy.

Most activities pertaining to settlement moved to the actual settlers and their new, more formally organized structures, although the leadership of the organs was comprised largely of Gush Emunim members. Demonstrations and protests on security matters and even moves to press further settlement in Hebron, for example, were locally organized. Gush Emunim did not initiate these efforts but participated and supported them.

For governing purposes, the territories are divided into four regional councils, with large cities having separate organizations. These are governing bodies, similar to city councils, democratically elected and under the jurisdiction of the Ministry of Interior. Residents of the territories organized Yesha, an acronym in Hebrew for Judea, Samaria, and Gaza and also a word meaning redemption. Settlements and the regional councils are represented in this organization, and it elects its leadership. Yesha concentrates on matters of infrastructure and the quality of life in the territories.

Yesha maintains a lobbyist in the Kneset who, with one MK serving as liaison, organized a caucus of MKs from various parties including Labor who promote settlement matters. Although the lobbyist distributes literature and information on policy issues, his main task is to represent Yesha on specific matters such as budget, education, transportation, electricity, security, and so forth. The liaison, MK Yigal Cohen, arranges appearances for the lobbyist before Kneset committees. As Ben-Meir predicted, Gush Emunim through Yesha has become a regularized interest group, pressing and vying with other societal groups for specific benefits. This development again demonstrates both the importance that groups assign the Kneset and the larger role the Kneset seeks.

Another reason for Gush Emunim's lower profile was its need to deal with the discovery in 1984 of a violent Jewish underground which included prominent Gush Emunim members. Gush Emunim spokesmen all deny any prior knowledge of the underground's activities, and indeed, Gush Emunim first expressed incredulity and disavowed the violent actions. Nevertheless, after it became apparent that Gush Emunim members were involved, an argument over how to relate to the individuals and their deeds created a severe crisis in the group. One camp, led by then Gush Emunim General Secretary Daniella Weiss, supported the underground group and condoned their actions. Another camp, led by Porat, while acknowledging that Gush Emunim persons had participated in the underground, wanted Gush Emunim to condemn the activities and emphasize that it did not support the underground in fact or in spirit. Both camps, however, agreed that the defendants' families deserved financial help.

In addition to the dispute about the underground, the two camps also differed over harsh public statements Weiss had made about kibbutzim. The Porat camp felt that Weiss was not accurately presenting the consensus of the group but rather her more extreme views.[30] Some wanted Weiss to resign and accept other duties. At a tense meeting in May 1987, an arrangement was made for leading the group.[31] Weiss continued as General Secretary until her term expired at the end of July 1988, when she announced she would not hold it again. The position remained vacant, with no eager aspirant, until a reluctant Yitzhak Armoni of the Golan Heights began to serve in May 1989, which spokesmen contend proves the dispute was not a power struggle.[32]

By retaining the Gush Emunim umbrella, the group hoped to have the best of all worlds, an idea interest group as well as party and settlement work. Once so dispersed, however, one might doubt that the group could be reconstituted. By recognizing Gush Emunim as a settlement movement, although not intentionally, the Begin Government had succeeded in routinizing and taming the group. Zvi Slonim and Porat, however, disagree, the latter contending that "if, G-d forbid, there should come a time from the political or spiritual point of view, there won't be any choice but to bring it again to a strong and concerted expression."[33]

Conclusion: Group and System

Gush Emunim presented a new phenomenon to the Israeli political scene, that of an idea interest group. It eventually evolved, or rather divided, into three segments – a party for its ideological concerns, a settlement organization for its more tangible concerns, and a small remnant of activists headquartered in Hebron. Although the Gush Emunim idea group remained as an umbrella organization in Jerusalem, essentially Rabin's wish was fulfilled, and Gush Emunim became a more routinized organization, a type the system was more accustomed to accommodate.

In many respects, Gush Emunim behaved as a group in a pluralist system, but rather than enhance any pragmatic predilections, it exacerbated the ideological. Ever vigilant, the group confronted any attempts by either Government to modify, redirect, or supervise Gush Emunim ideas and plans. On the contrary, in the case of the Likud, originally akin to the group, Gush Emunim escalated its demands. Any corporatist arrangements conceivable for the Manufacturers' Association were not even contemplated for Gush Emunim. Neither did Gush Emunim request them.

The governing institutions under two politically different administrations encountered difficulties in coping with such an idea group because they had not formulated precise procedures for decision-making, allowing Gush Emunim to benefit from any lacunae. The legislator evinced greater independence and his realm encompassed many extra-parliamentary activities, practically inviting Gush Emunim to engage in its brand of "lobbying." The group's tactics included not only collaring legislators within parliamentary chambers and appealing for a tangible benefit but also acting outside parliament, attracting politicians to demonstrations. Gush Emunim always attempted to retain the initiative and was not directed by any party, but sometimes found it advantageous to associate with the opposition. Understanding the media as usually skeptical of and opposed to any Government, no matter of which party, Gush Emunim believed publicity would be more easily attainable when the opposition espoused the group's cause and enlarged its number. Via demonstrations, Gush Emunim offered politicians publicity stages and profited from them as well; Gush Emunim created a symbiotic relationship between politician and group.

Both Labor and Likud Governments experienced personal, psychological, and procedural problems that Gush Emunim exploited. Certain comprehensive and long-term decision-making distressed the Governments. The Cabinets were unable to maintain collective responsibility, and sitting to "reason together" was almost a foreign concept. And the Governments abhorred civil violence, vulnerable to its threat. Aware of all these attitudes, Gush Emunim developed effective, incremental, but activist methods and became adept at pressing upon individuals.

The response to Gush Emunim revealed a system—politicians, parties, and governing institutions—still striving to create a framework for considering and acting upon demands presented by both functional and idea groups. The system has not evinced an ability to cope with policy demands and ideological change in a more than ad hoc manner. Certainly, it is far from innovating with any arrangement for including idea groups in discussing and setting policy.

Part V

Conclusion

Chapter 13

System, Groups, and Change

Contrary to the popular perception of attenuated interest group development in Israel, actually groups flourished. The popular view does not reflect mass myopia but reflects the party-group arrangement that stamped its mark upon the country's consciousness. Those commenting upon the dearth of interest groups really mean that an ideological/strong party system rather than a pragmatic/pluralist system has prevailed. Impressed by party juggernauts, these observers doubt that groups arise from the "grass roots" level, view groups as formally attached to and subsumed within parties, and question the significance and effectiveness of groups that may exist within or outside of parties. In an ideological political culture, moreover, groups making specific demands are discouraged. Therefore, interest groups are not acknowledged or admitted to be in the picture and certainly not as independent entities. Groups are purposely tucked away, or they conceal themselves, within the borders of comprehensive, ideological parties. This study, therefore, has not focused upon whether groups have existed, for that was considered a given, but rather has concentrated upon their mode of existence and has inquired why that mode arose, what it bode for decision-making, whether it has changed over time, and why and how it developed.

Indeed, we found that a transformation has occurred in Israel's political system from an ideological/strong party model to one that is pragmatic and pluralist with some corporatist features. This transformation resulted from interaction and change among several aspects of the system with interest groups playing a leading role. Challenging the view of many political scientists that the established system determines the arena, means, and aims of interest group activity, groups in Israel did not merely accommodate themselves to existing institutional arrangements. Groups were creative forces, although at times

225

unwitting ones, stimulating change in the group pattern, in other institutions, and in the overall system. Nevertheless, Israel has not completely conformed to each model, change has not occurred en bloc,
nor has change been complete. In each phase of Israel's political
development, ideological politics has imbued the system with special
qualities. Comparing Israeli reality with the theoretical models set
out in Chapter 1, particularly the specifications for groups, should
enhance our understanding of variations in the models that may
occur, the array of relationships possible between parties and groups,
and how and why systems may evolve.

The Strong Party Model in Israel

The strong party paradigm postulates that parties are highly
organized, have defined visions or programs which they intend to
carry out once in power, and subsume groups to their structures and
programs. The party is the primary forum for resolving conflicts
among societal groups. In this pattern, we expected that the number
and type of interest groups would be low, that interest groups would
not be autonomous but rather would be politicized, that party
ideologies would condition how groups express their interests, that
groups would seek their aims mainly by bargaining with their respective party leaders, and that groups might convert to small parties.

In many respects, Israel's political system in the early years
resembled a strong party model, although the system encompassed
several such strong parties which also were highly ideological. Each
party had associated with it a number of interest groups for which it
sought to negotiate. As expected, the ideological and strong but multi-
party system conditioned (but did not necessarily directly cause) the
type of interest groups that emerged as well as the groups' party relationship and mode of expression. With parties covering the ideological
realm, groups, such as the Manufacturers' Association and the Ihud,
represented mainly occupational sectors. The formation of material
interest groups was a surprising phenomenon to discover in an
ideological system that is assumed to discourage specific interests.
These groups actually arose in reaction to, and despite, the ideological
environment, as groups felt and filled a need in the system for a less
doctrinaire and practical way of making decisions. More in line with
expectations of the strong party model, interests represented were not
highly cohesive. The Ihud, for example, represented only the kibbutz

part of the agricultural sector, and the kibbutz interest itself was fragmented among several parties.

Mapai, with the broadest configuration of groups, typified a strong party, and any analysis, therefore, starts with reference to it. Mapai sought to set policy by mediating agreements and arranging compromises among its component groups. It could hope to succeed in these efforts because many major societal interests were represented in the party. For example, of several kibbutz groups in the country, one was linked to Mapai; of several moshav entities, the largest organization was tied to Mapai; and though several parties competed within the Histadrut, Mapai effectively was in control. On different issues, Mapai negotiated among its groups or singly with each. Mapai could expect that agreements reached by negotiating with its component groups would be accepted by other similar groups that were not part of Mapai but perhaps were affiliated with other parties. On certain issues, Mapai negotiated with other parties on matters that affected those parties' constituent groups. To the extent that party-group relationships were so constructed and conducted, where parties negotiated with their respective groups and with other parties on behalf of those parties' affiliated groups, the system may be categorized as "strong party."

However, party-group relationships were not always so consistently ordered, and we find that variations may occur in the strong party paradigm for reasons deriving from both the party and group realms. What I would term a "governing imperative" operated. Mapai-in-Government realized it required cooperation from all groups in society. Moreover, it also realized that negotiating with its affiliated groups would not always produce an agreement that was optimal for the country. While the party-in-Government believed it had to support its constituent groups' aims, Mapai ministers recognized that the long held ideas of the party and its groups were not always applicable to reality. For these reasons, in order to govern, the administration deemed it useful and necessary to interact directly with groups irrespective of their party affiliation. In this way the party-in-Government could reach decisions and set policy without confronting and modifying its own ideology.

The administration governed by bargaining among the groups. In many instances, the Government negotiated directly with groups, affiliated or unaffiliated. In some cases, however, the Government encouraged an outside group to negotiate with an affiliated entity, and at other times, the Government relied upon an affiliated group to convince outside entities to agree to a program. To rule in this manner, the Government required strong organized groups which could aid in implementing programs and whose decisions would be respected by other similar, but less organized, entities. The Government looked to organized groups for bargaining partners. Thus, while different types of private businesses and employers existed, the Manufacturers' Association, as the most clearly organized entity among them, became the Government's preferred bargaining partner and employers' representative to negotiate with labor. The Government also frequently delegated power to groups to implement programs, since the Government did not always have either the manpower resources or the detailed knowledge necessary. For example, the Manufacturers' Association received control over a sum of money for making operating capital loans. Thus, in order to govern, a function that includes both mediating disputes and implementing programs, the Government relied upon groups. The Government's investiture of authority in groups encouraged them to organize further and enhanced their status. By selecting groups as negotiating partners, the Government contributed to the development of a pluralist system where groups become important bargaining agents, and by delegating administrative authority to groups, the Government fostered the development of corporatist tendencies.

As groups sought ways of organizing, expressing themselves, and pursuing particularistic interests within an ideological and party permeated milieu, in many respects the group configuration in the early period conformed to the specifications of the strong party model. However, in many ways groups confounded our expectations, strained against the system's bounds and thereby, intentionally and unintentionally, contributed to system change.

Reluctant to identify itself as a material interest group, the Ihud maintained a party tie and in the first instance pursued its demands through the party. By operating quietly within the party, the group could impart a public impression, and convince itself, that it was highly idealistic, while actually making very material demands. The Manufacturers' Association chose an unaffiliated route, but its choice nonetheless was influenced by the ideological, party permeated atmosphere. Initially, the Manufacturers' Association assumed an independent position as a defensive tactic to prevent the array of political forces from overwhelming it and causing its disintegration, not in order to exert its power upon the political system. The Manufacturers' Association had an especially difficult task of gearing itself to the strong, multi-party system. It had to take into account various parties on the Right and consider the ideology of the dominant Left.

Whether formally affiliated with a party or not, groups contoured the demands and issues they raised to the ideological environment and, more specifically, to the dominant socialist ideology. Accordingly, the Manufacturers' Association, sensitive to the dominant ideology that discouraged "selfish" anti-socialist interests, minimized any display of pursuing private gain and emphasized its aim of building industry for the country. The Ihud, while employing ideological rhetoric as a tactic for obtaining specific benefits, did not initiate doctrinal discussion.

Ironically, the dominant party's desire to preserve the prevailing ideology actually was conducive to the emergence of groups making material demands. The dominant Mapai party represented a Zionist/socialist creed. Applying that ideology to a developing economy inevitably entailed interpreting the doctrine. Various segments of the party – labor, cooperative business, kibbutz agriculture, moshav agriculture – while generally adhering to the creed, had different perspectives on appropriate interpretations. Party leaders attempted to maintain the status quo with respect to the party's ideology and its group composition. Therefore, the party avoided reviewing and discussing its principles. Groups were signalled to "know their place" and not to impose their views on the party or on society. Hence, even within party confines, groups such as the Ihud focused on seeking benefits for themselves and refrained from raising ideological issues or questioning overall economic and social priorities. Avoiding the task of ideological interpretation actually fostered the development of material interest groups, a phenomenon that socialism ostensibly disdains.

The dominant party sought to maintain the status quo by distributing benefits among groups, whether within or outside of the party. To maintain the status quo, the party implicitly limited the scope of demands that groups could make. Consequently, issues that implied any change in the extant interpretation of socialist doctrine, that disturbed the balance among groups within or outside of the party, or involved comprehensive change were not welcomed.

In face of ideological and party diversity, both the party affiliated Ihud and unaffiliated Manufacturers' Association reacted somewhat similarly vis-à-vis the party system in order to preserve group cohesiveness. With their membership spread over several parties or factions, both groups distanced party organizational activity, an action that seems especially surprising for a party affiliated group. The Ihud, though tied primarily to Mapai, feared the debilitating effects of party instability and therefore formally separated party organizational activity from Ihud structures. In instances when the Ihud became active in party affairs, however, the group attempted to maintain its control, centrally deciding upon its party emissaries. In the case of the Manufacturers' Association, it did not turn its independent position into a bargaining strong point. On the contrary, it placed a moratorium on political party discussion and organizational activity.

Group-party relations within the dominant party require closer examination, as even party affiliated groups were not entirely the passive party captives assumed by the strong party paradigm. While groups did not seize the initiative and overtly wield their support to bargain among parties, as long as group cohesiveness was not adversely affected, groups exploited any opportunities that arose to exert pressure on parties and gain advantages for themselves. These opportunities usually occurred at times of potential political instability. For example, in election years and after wartime episodes, unions pressed larger wage and COLA demands. As even the dominant Left party never took its portion of the vote in the Histadrut for granted, the party always experienced difficulty rejecting a labor claim and was vulnerable to pressure. Similarly, though at a later time, when Eshkol as Mapai's leader was endangered by the Rafi faction's possible defection, the Ihud, the majority of which supported Eshkol, was able to use its support to pressure him. Ultimately, however, group cohesion controlled the credibility of a group's threat. When, for example, Rafi defected anyway, and prominent Ihud members supported Dayan for Defense Minister in 1967, Eshkol no longer was so favorably disposed to the kibbutz group. The Ihud's unity was jeopardized by its members' involvement in party affairs, and it developed protective structures for party activity. Thus, to different degrees, within the strong party model, both party affiliated and unaffiliated groups endeavored to exert autonomy, to exert control over parties, and to limit politicization.

While groups adjusted their aims and struck a political posture that took into consideration the ideological and party permeated system, they did not press their aims in the manner predicted by the strong party model. Though certain distinctions may be made between groups affiliated with Mapai and those that were not, on the whole, groups did not feel compelled to adopt a party as patron. Instead, groups turned primarily to Government ministers and administration bureaucrats holding portfolios pertinent to the groups' concerns. Several reasons account for this unexpected, though not entirely surprising, behavior. The multi-party configuration actually prompted groups to circumvent the apparatus of parties and overcome party boundaries. Shifting party alliances and political infighting made the party route unreliable for interest groups. Coalition Governments were not all-inclusive, and therefore, groups realized that working through a party out of power would not be immediately beneficial. Moreover, in the early period, when the population was smaller and power relationships still fluid, groups contained and cultivated individuals who were personally acquainted with relevant officials or exceptionally qualified themselves to serve in the bureaucracy. Groups could bypass formal party organs and deal informally with administrators. Groups also soon perceived that one party was becoming dominant. Rather than undertake the long term effort necessary to change that situation, groups preferred to pursue their immediate interests and therefore worked within the evolving power structure. Even groups affiliated with the dominant party did not follow a precise party path. Within the dominant Mapai, ministers formed a leadership core, ironically reducing the need for a linked group with personal connections to operate through specific party offices.

Distinctions, however, may be made between groups affiliated with the dominant party and those which were not affiliated regarding the extent to which groups eschewed a party route. The Ihud benefited from its party affiliation, which enabled the group to position its own members in official spots. Therefore, the Ihud maintained its party tie while exploring additional means of access. The Manufacturers' Association, whose tie with the Right was tenuous from the outset, was quicker to cultivate other targets. Though there were variations within the ideological/strong party model, all groups sought to increase their access points and reduce their dependency upon parties. Coinciding with greater ministerial control over their offices' affairs, the groups' activities served to redirect the locus of decision-making to the Government arena.

Since groups increasingly dealt with ministers and could address them successfully on issues that were not ideological and involved only partial policy changes or particular benefits, groups had to develop appropriate tactics. Such targets and issues corresponded well with a bargaining tactic, and accordingly, ministers and group leaders negotiated with each other. To pressure ministers, groups also made media appeals. However, affected by the ideological atmosphere that frowned upon particularistic interests, affiliated and unaffiliated groups differed in their use of this tactic. The Manufacturers' Association used the media extensively to engender public discussion and support for its position and became skilled at timing announcements and holding press conferences. The Ihud's ministerial connections reduced its need for publicity. In addition, the Ihud avoided publicity that might evoke an image of it as irresponsible and self-centered. Publicity was employed, however, when necessary to bolster a minister's efforts on the Ihud's behalf and when needed to present the group as unselfish and experiencing a problem of widespread concern.

According to the ideological/strong party paradigm, parties proliferate. Entering the party system is considered the ultimate means for an interest group to obtain its demands. Nevertheless, the groups examined in this study did not turn themselves into political parties. Again, the explanation is found in the ideological/strong party system itself. As the ideological environment was inhospitable to specific, material interest groups and compelled such groups to contour their aims and shape special tactics for surviving, likewise the same milieu was uncongenial for material, interest based parties. Therefore, groups which were able to develop within, and despite, the ideological/strong party system remained as groups, continuing in their special fashion to parlay the party maze. The ideological/strong party system did not preclude groups from forming but conditioned their behavior and constricted their scope. Moreover, as groups and Government found it mutually advantageous to negotiate with one another, the role of groups in the system, separate from parties, became more pronounced. Thus, due to a governing imperative on the party level and the need of parties and groups to overcome ideological obstacles, we find that an ideological/strong party system may coexist with autonomous and strong interest groups and also, as more expected, with party affiliated, though strong, entities.

Toward a Pluralist Pattern

The pragmatic/pluralist paradigm posits that groups are the main actors. "Catch-all" parties, subdued in ideological passion, serve mainly to mobilize for elections, not to mediate group conflicts or make decisions. Parties are but one among several arenas where groups, constituting a separate subsystem, can influence decisionmakers in the Government. According to this model, groups are many and varied in type, autonomous, may have particularistic as well as broader aims, impinge upon several targets, employ several tactics, and ultimately remain as interest groups. Israel's system acquired attributes of this model, in many instances impelled by interest groups, but again, ideological politics imparted a special shape to several aspects of the paradigm.

As Government ministers continued bargaining with groups and balancing their desires, the locus of decision-making became lodged in the Government. An intimate relationship developed between groups and ministers regardless of their party affiliations. The Minister of Agriculture, for example, was expected to negotiate on behalf of the farmers, and indeed, the minister often advised groups on how to present a claim to the Finance Minister. The Minister of Commerce and Industry similarly advised the Manufacturers' Association. This cooperation transformed ministers into interest group representatives, enhanced the status of groups, and diminished the need for parties as intermediaries.

The Government's mode of formulating policy through bargaining meant that, although not openly acknowledged at least in practice, ideology diminished in importance as a basis for decisions. Although the bargaining procedure evolved in order to maintain ideologies intact, the very process of striking a bargain served to mitigate the intensity of the principles themselves and accustomed groups and parties to working together. The fact that a governing party negotiated with a group which was identified with another segment of the political spectrum and reached decisions that were not completely consonant with the party's supposedly cherished beliefs demonstrates how certain principles could be placed in abeyance. Moreover, the experiences of both Left and Right in office reduced the apparent ideological distinctions between them. By the early 1970s, the Labor Government, for example, seriously contemplated economic measures which a Right-led Government might have been expected to propose. And when the Right came to power, it could not concentrate solely on the ideological issue of settlement policy but had to undertake several issue areas and deal with several disparate groups. Nevertheless, ideological considerations never totally lost their relevance, and in fact, accounted for the bargaining procedure that arose. Bargaining and brokering enabled the Government to be flexible; the Government could continue at least paying lip service to its party's ideals while reaching decisions and permitting practices that seemingly contradicted them.

Interest groups seized upon the roles and areas delegated (or abdicated) by the Government, interacted with institutions, and thereby advanced features of pluralism. As the country's first independent interest group, the Manufacturers' Association provided an example for other groups to follow. Countering the ideological climate, the Manufacturers' Association continually attempted to maintain discussion on an unemotional level and thereby introduce a measure of pragmatism into the political culture. Accepting the Government's designation as labor negotiator, the Manufacturers' Association bargained on those issues and proceeded to use the leverage it acquired to bargain on other matters such as credit, prices, tariffs, and taxes. Establishing itself as a Government bargaining partner, the Manufacturers' Association drew attention to the potential role of groups in the governing process and helped inaugurate a pluralist pattern of making decisions where Government arbitrates among interest groups. Seeking to increase its ability to fulfill the role of bargaining partner, the Manufacturers' Association formed the Coordinating Bureau of Economic Organizations in 1965. By broadening and consolidating the interest sector it represented, the Manufacturers' Association advanced yet another feature of the pluralist framework.

From birth, the Ihud was more ideologically oriented than the Manufacturers' Association, but the kibbutz federation placed ideology in abeyance and concentrated on material matters. The Ihud acted as a functional interest group, and by confining itself to the mundane and material world, indirectly or unwittingly, promoted pragmatic tendencies. The Ihud's influence was limited within its party because the Ihud competed with the moshav group. Therefore, to increase its leverage upon decision-makers, the Ihud transcended the party and contacted other similar groups. At first serving as a reluctant spokesman for the other kibbutz federations, the Ihud then pressed for greater coordination and cooperation among them. Even during the ideologically passionate fifties, the Ihud considered kibbutz interests paramount. As competition for power with the moshavim increased, the Ihud urged unification of the kibbutz federations. The Ihud's loss of the Ministry of Agriculture provided the impetus for the kibbutz federations to form an alliance in 1963, a significant step in furthering the pluralist trend. Ironically, the Ihud's party connection and its interaction and reaction to the party system led it to construct a broader interest group apart from parties. Thus, as the Manufacturers' Association and the Ihud pursued their interests, both groups, the former more consciously than the latter, gave the system a pluralist cast, where cohesive interest groups are prominent, pragmatically bargain on particularistic issues, and comprise a distinct subsystem separate from parties.

Though the Ihud was established as a result of a political rift, and by affiliating with Mapai, settled into a strong party pattern, subsequent developments within the party sphere actually impelled the Ihud to exercise some autonomy. As previously explained, still within the strong party frame, the Ihud relegated political activity to separate structures, fearing that passionate politics would interfere with the federation's functioning. As political infighting increased, the Ihud further removed itself from the party realm. Toward the elections of 1961, the Ihud indirectly participated in the campaign, and toward the elections of 1965, banned politicking from Ihud premises. After 1965, the Ihud sought to continue cooperating with other kibbutz groups on agricultural and economic issues and attempted to contain any spillover from the party turbulence. Irony again operated as the party permeated system actually spurred groups to act on a separate plane and unwittingly to create a pluralist model.

Not inhibited by belonging to an ideological party, the Manufacturers' Association went further than the Ihud in intentionally seeking to expand the domain of interest groups. The Ihud generally confined itself to more limited aims, although as its own interests expanded to encompass other than agricultural concerns, it pursued those other issues. The Manufacturers' Association did not confine itself to the narrow issues the Government preferred for it. Even in the early years, the Association raised matters such as the COLA system and tax structure, which challenged prevailing labor oriented policies and involved comprehensive change. Though the group often obtained only contained amendments, it is significant that a group aspired for broader reforms. At first careful to concentrate on issues related to industry, as time progressed, the Manufacturers' Association offered ideas for the whole economy. Especially after 1967, when the country and system appeared more amenable to change, the Manufacturers' Association felt sufficiently confident to propose broader economic reform, including suggestions for promoting the private sector. Raising its sights, the Manufacturers' Association increasingly resembled a group in a pluralist system which unabashedly may present and press ideas on almost any issue.

Not only did the Manufacturers' Association aim for policy revisions but also suggested changes in the decision-making process. Continually pressing for a consultative role with officials, the Manufacturers' Association attempted to push pluralist decision-making in Israel to a level reached in other Western democracies, where officials may discuss and consult with groups on forthcoming policy.

As groups steadily distanced themselves from parties and formed a subsystem of competing, free-floating interest entities, they consequently searched for corresponding tactics and a wider range of targets, although they did not completely relinquish the old methods. In the strong party period, the Ihud's party tie enabled it to establish a network of persons in governing institutions. Ironically, as its party and the system made room for representing another group, moshavim, the Ihud lost its most important link, the Ministry of Agriculture, in 1960. Though the loss proved temporary, it spurred the Ihud to develop other channels. The Ihud first focused on its Kneset contingent and sought to strengthen its authority over its delegates. Then, through those delegates, the group established a Kneset caucus, an alignment of members from several parties, to press agricultural issues. As the Ihud attempted to strengthen the kibbutz movement to compete with moshavim, it favored forums outside of the party where the other kibbutz groups could participate and augment the pressure. Government committees were one such vehicle, and the Ihud promoted their use. These developments further broke down party barriers, whittled away at party discipline, diminished the party's role as decision-maker and group broker, and consequently transformed the strong party model.

Never fettered by a party, the Manufacturers' Association even in the early period pioneered with various tactics. The Association orchestrated media appeals, disseminated informational papers, and undertook studies. However, as the Ihud, it relied heavily upon a powerful personal broker, in its case, Shenkar. After he died in 1959, the group experimented with new tactics and targets. Several tactics were rather bold and therefore unusual for a supposedly staid businessman's organization. The Manufacturers' Association continued and intensified use of the previously mentioned methods but also began to boycott meetings and was somewhat quicker to threaten not to cooperate with the administration. The Manufacturers' Association increasingly lobbied in the Kneset, cultivating committees and cooperating with members across the political spectrum.

In the course of cultivating new channels, groups exerted a centrifugal force upon the system. Their actions thus enhanced the power of arenas besides the central Government, especially the legislature, for setting and influencing policy. Groups not only impinged upon the arenas but in fact, created them. As groups created and impacted upon several arenas and diversified their tactics and targets, groups endowed the system with pluralist qualities.

As both officials and groups favored making decisions in the Government arena, the party apparatus decreased its role in setting policy and concentrated on gathering electoral strength. Parties of both Left and Right became concerned to broaden their bases and augment their electoral potential. Though Left and Right followed different methods and were motivated differently, parties from both segments expanded to resemble a "catch-all" party type. On the Left, Mapai sought to penetrate and attach societal groups which it hoped would conform to the party's creed, whereas parties on the Right groomed themselves for the general electorate without formally appending groups. Parties continued the expansion process by consolidating within their respective camps. Partly due to the influence of ideological politics, these consolidations took on a unique form. Although several mergers occurred, expansion most often was possible through alliances rather than complete unions. In 1965, two such alignments occurred, and that year may be considered a turning point on the party plane toward a pluralist model. On the Right, the Liberal Party allied with Herut to form the Gahal bloc (not party), and on the Left, Mapai and Ahdut ha-'Avodah formed the Alignment, which, as the name implies, was not a complete union. These creative political arrangements allowed ideologically distinct parties to maintain their identities intact and preserve their principles while reaping the electoral benefits of a broader entity. Although there were other reasons for the cautious approach to system change, including the reluctance of individuals and parties to relinquish power and the inertia usually found in bureaucratic organizations, ideological identification was a consideration. Similar in rationale to coalition Governments, the alignment mechanism allowed distinct entities within a bloc to agree to disagree. Thus, Israel's political system acquired pluralist attributes as groups ascended, parties expanded but declined as group arbitrators, and ideology diminished in intensity. However, vestiges of the previous pattern remained. Due to the ever present ideological requirements of Israel's system, the transformation from an ideological/strong party model to a pragmatic/pluralist paradigm was incomplete.

The Israeli example of political development provides new insight into certain assumptions in the political science literature about party-group relationships. Several political scientists argue that strong parties correlate with weak interest groups, weak parties correlate with strong interest groups, and similarly, as parties expand and thereby become weaker, groups become stronger. "Strong" in reference to parties usually means highly organized and ideological or programmatic, and "weak" implies a looser organization with a vaguer ideology or reduced ideological intensity. For groups, "strong" means highly organized, autonomous, and influential, and "weak" carries the opposite definitional characteristics. According to Kirchheimer, a system with broad "catch-all" parties requires strong interest groups to assure electoral support from delimited segments of the electorate and to articulate defined policy alternatives.[1] These are two tasks with which a "catch-all" party, as opposed to a more integrated and ideological party, has difficulty. Similarly, Truman notes that the increasingly diffuse nature of parties stimulates interests to organize, i.e., increase in strength, in order to promote particular policies and exert their claims.[2] To the contrary, Beer argues that merely the structural strength or weakness of parties does not indicate the strength or weakness of interest groups, that strong parties do not necessarily discourage groups, that such parties may be accompanied by strong or weak groups, and weak parties may be accompanied by weak groups.[3] My study demonstrates that, as Beer notes, relationships between parties and groups may be varied. However, my research does not invalidate the observations of Kirchheimer and Truman. Rather, the observations of all are variations that may occur at different stages of political development. Strong and ideological parties may coexist with strong and even autonomous interest groups, with strong and affiliated interest groups, as well as with weak interest groups.

Where these observers have erred is in their explanation of the changes. While the relationships between parties and groups described by Beer, Truman, and Kirchheimer all have occurred, they were not directly or causally related. The changing relationship between parties and groups is more circuitous and complex and encompasses more variables than these observers consider. Groups affect and respond to the changing locus of decision-making, and a party's ability to govern is a major factor in determining its relationship with groups. As was the case in Israel, a strong, ideological party may not be able to carry out its program. Indeed, Kirchheimer remarks that a party of "integration" (strong, ideological party) may find its policy objectives stymied by powerful groups with opposing points of view.[4] Once in power, a party may require the cooperation of strong interest groups in order to govern. Or, the party-in-Government may discover that its program requires modification, and therefore, the party requires group support in order to make those adjustments. Groups become stronger as a result of the interaction between groups and Government, and, in fact, party bodies are bypassed.

Groups may become stronger and independent as parties expand structurally and weaken ideologically, but, as shown by my research, the two sets of changes may occur independently, and the relationship between the two sets is indirect. In fact, in Israel, group efforts to increase their influence often preceded changes in parties and contributed to the differentiation in function of Government and parties.

Groups became stronger in an attempt to circumvent parties which either refused to contemplate ideological reform or, also often for ideological reasons, were not in power. Groups therefore negotiated directly with Government officials, tried to rid themselves of party control, sought to expand and fortify their organizations, and sought to resolve any conflicts in bureaucratic, rather than party, offices. Thus, groups helped remove from parties the responsibility for making decisions and mediating among groups and helped transfer those functions to Government and the bureaucracy.

As groups reoriented themselves, concurrently, the parties and party-Government relations underwent changes. Due to the centralized and hierarchical nature of the parties, decision-making fell to party leaders who sat in the Government. As a result of competition among parties and a growing motivation to control the Government, many parties sought to expand, and, intentionally or not, modified or ignored their ideologies. Parties, therefore, increasingly concentrated on their role as electoral machines to enable their leaders to enter decision-making positions, and they reduced their role as mediators of interest group conflicts. Parties thereby neared the "catch-all" type.

At this point, developments in group and party spheres intertwined. Groups found their opportunities for influencing policy expanded and relocated, mainly in the Government arena. Groups impinged upon the Government ministers, negotiated with them, and in so doing, enhanced their own authority and influence. Thus, "catch-all" parties may be observed to coexist with strong interest groups, but a direct, inverse relationship between parties and groups cannot be inferred. As the role of parties and Government changed, the role of groups simultaneously developed, but the transformation in the party system did not cause nor require the group evolution. The strength or weakness of groups and parties results from the continual interaction of the two together and with other elements of the political system.

Corporatist Trends

The need to govern that produced pluralist features within the political system also generated corporatist traits. Similarly and simultaneously, as groups furthered pluralist features, they also contributed to corporatist arrangements. Corporatism entails the direct delegation of governing authority to groups; groups become surrogate governments. In this pattern, interest groups are concentrated into a limited number of large groups, may or may not be party affiliated, usually have aims related to economic matters, interrelate with other groups but also with ministers and bureaucrats, and primarily negotiate with one another in order to achieve their objectives.

Embryonic corporatist elements were evident very early in Israel's development. They became further pronounced as both Left and Right Governments negotiated directly with groups, and parties as conflict mediators receded further into the background. Thus, there was not a continuum from strong party to pluralist to corporatist phases. Rather, pluralism and corporatism developed parallel to each other and in response to some of the same stimuli. Corporatist characteristics overlapped both the strong party and the pluralist models. Hence, corporatism may be an outgrowth of either pattern.

In its desire to administer programs effectively, Israel's Government aided and abetted corporatist development. Without sufficient bureaucratic manpower for carrying out all necessary governmental functions, Israel's leaders eased the burden on themselves by segmenting the economy and delegating certain responsibilities to groups in each sector. For example, in the early years of independence, the Manufacturers' Association was allowed to import and allocate raw materials to its members, as the Histadrut was permitted to do the same for its members. To secure broad consensus for a Government controlled economy, advisory boards were established within the Prime Minister's Office and within the Ministry of Commerce and Industry. Nevertheless, these efforts were not full-fledged corporatist forms, where groups negotiate with one another and establish policy, but were small steps which augmented the power and purview of groups and thus had corporatist potential.

Government inspired corporatist arrangements developed among groups of the Left and Right, for the Government found it expedient to override ideological and party considerations on both sides of the political spectrum. One of the most clearly defined and earliest cases of corporatism occurred with negotiations between the Histadrut and the Manufacturers' Association. Because a Mapai/Labor Government wanted to evade responsibility for an agreement even slightly disagreeable to workers, it delegated responsibility for this policy area to the interest groups themselves. Even within the sector of collective/cooperative agriculture with which a Left Government sympathized, the Government fostered corporatist forms in order to avert politically charged decisions. The collective/cooperative agricultural interest was fragmented among several parties. In order to forestall accusations of political favoritism toward its affiliated groups, the Mapai/Labor-led Government delegated responsibility to the various groups to resolve distribution dilemmas. Especially when a dispute involved two party affiliated groups, the Mapai/Labor Government deemed it prudent to rely upon a corporatist decision-making process. Thus, in order to circumvent the ideological and party permeated environment and avoid politically difficult decisions, the Government promoted a corporatist mode.

The Mapai/Labor Government advanced several formal corporatist arrangements. It cooperated in the establishment and operation of the Agricultural Center. The Government also supported committee politics, which may be considered a variation of corporatism.

Just as groups contributed to the development of pluralism in Israel by seeking to expand upon powers delegated to them, in a similar dynamic relationship with Government they advanced corporatism. Certain groups actually proposed corporatist arrangements, sought to create conditions for them, and sought to expand the purview of forums that arose. Although the Manufacturers' Association at first reluctantly accepted responsibility for labor negotiations, it then sought to augment its authority as an employers' representative and advance its influence on other issues. So emboldened, the Manufacturers' Association requested from the Government formal designation as the sole representative of private industry. The organization suggested that the Government refuse to deal with, or provide services to, any firm unless that firm was an Association member and transmitted its claims via the organization. This would have institutionalized the role of an interest group, an essential element for corporatist decision-making. Not receiving that authority, the Manufacturers' Association requested at least a consultative role in decision-making. Dissatisfied with the piecemeal policy setting process, where policy resulted from disparate, uncoordinated, and often bilateral, bargains between Government and groups, the Manufacturers' Association called for formulating comprehensive policy, or planning, by mutual agreement among concerned interest groups. It therefore urged establishing an industrial council. The Association partially obtained these aims, and the system acquired some corporatist traits, when an Industrial Council was established in 1958 and an Industrial Forum in 1966.

Though, unlike the Manufacturers' Association, the Ihud did not originate corporatist arrangements, it participated in wide forums that had long existed in the agricultural sector, such as the Agricultural Center and farm production councils under the Ministry of Agriculture. The Ihud thereby furthered the corporatist pattern.

Both the Ihud and the Manufacturers' Association acted, perhaps unwittingly, in ways that prepared the ground for corporatist decision-making. Both groups encouraged convening committees to resolve their respective economic sector's problems. And both expanded their interest group structure – the Ihud by joining the Brit and the Manufacturers' Association by creating the Coordinating Bureau of Economic Organizations. The latter action fulfilled one criterion necessary for corporatism, the existence of comprehensive organizations.

The Israeli case enhances our understanding of conditions under which corporatism may develop and operate. Corporatism has been observed to evolve after interest groups have consolidated their organizations, as well as their control over segments of the economy or essential economic resources. Powerful groups possess the clout to command Government accommodation and their inclusion in decision-making. In Israel, prompted by the Government, corporatist decision-making arrangements occurred first, and these efforts stimulated interest groups to consolidate further.

Experiments in corporatism were limited, however, for several of the same ideological and political reasons that led to their adoption. Though deferring to the Manufacturers' Association on labor negotiations, a Labor-led Government refused to institutionalize the Association. The Government was a labor administration, with an ideology sympathetic to workers. The Government negotiated with the Manufacturers' Association and delegated responsibility to it as a means of postponing the task of modifying its creed and formulating a Government labor program. To have "incorporated" the Manufacturers' Association would have meant that the Government recognized and institutionalized the role of the private sector. A labor administration was not sufficiently pragmatic to overtly take that giant step.

Ideological considerations restricted not only the participants allowed into the corporatist decision-making process but constricted the range of decisions. Attempts to address comprehensive policy that may have required ideological modification usually were averted. For this reason, no Government, neither Labor nor Likud, would even consider including an idea group such as Gush Emunim in a corporatist format. Similarly, a Mapai/Labor Government was reluctant to establish an industrial planning council. More successful attempts with corporatist decision-making forms, therefore, usually occurred among groups within the same broad ideological frame, e.g., the Agricultural Center, and even then, most often on matters concerning distribution and implementation. Corporatist boards usually did not originate legislation or policy and did not create comprehensive plans.

Moreover, an ideological behavioral pattern, labeled the ideological dimension in Chapter 2, influenced the style of corporatist procedures in Israel and affected the role of Government. Workable corporatist arrangements did not always arise from group willingness to sit together and compromise. A changed political culture did not precede corporatism in Israel. Rather, corporatist procedures often were arranged when group or Government decided it was necessary to compel a settlement, similar to self-prescribing bitter, but necessary, medicine. Convening committees for decisions was tantamount to placing disputants in a room and throwing away the key. Government was essential as overseer or gatekeeper to assure that an agreement be reached. When weak Governments existed, such as in 1974, a broad policy board did not succeed. Panels could not substitute for, but only supplement, Government leadership.

Other, less esoteric considerations probably also were involved in constraining the scope of corporatist decision-making. Government leaders were reluctant to completely relinquish control over policy, especially to a group which might become an opposing political force. The Government preferred that the system remain at a pluralist stage where a variety of groups bargained individually and directly with the Government and the Government could orchestrate the outcome.

The Israeli case aids in refining certain assumptions about corporatist development. Corporatism has been observed to occur at a high stage of industrial and capitalist development where labor and business organizations are comprehensive and centralized. And the corporatist decision-making pattern usually is observed on industrial issues, and more often and specifically, on incomes policy. When the Manufacturers' Association sought to consolidate the private sector, it followed a pattern that is assumed to precede corporatist decision-making. The case of the Manufacturers' Association in Israel demonstrates that a high level of organizational development need not be a prerequisite for corporatism and that a corporatist decision-making process may be effective in less developed societies which are not yet organizationally articulated. And the activities of the Agricultural Center illustrate the corporatist process on issues other than industry and wages policy. Therefore, while the most developed form of corporatism may require and entail highly organized groups, corporatist processes may be realizable on certain decisions without highly organized interest entities.

A certain balance of forces among the level of the decision, the role of Government, and the degree of organization of the interest may correspond to a certain level of corporatist decision-making. Some decisions may not require comprehensive interest organizations. To compensate, however, Government may play a more active broker- ing and supervisory role. When interest organizations are more inclu- sive and centralized, the Government may be able to remove itself further and allow the interest groups greater leeway. The expansion of issues and organizations seem to vary together in extending a cor- poratist decision-making process. As was the case in Israel, a main impetus to corporatist patterns is the need to circumvent the party system and to reach decisions acceptable to many groups.

In summary, the Israeli experience enhances our understanding of the development, operation, and limits of corporatist decision-making:

1. Corporatism need not be preceded by comprehensive and centralized interest associations; those organizational structures can develop as part of the corporatist process.

2. The role of Government need not disappear. In fact, the role of Government may be related to the breadth of interest organizations. With many separate organizations representing interests, a more vis- ible Government presence may be necessary to keep all groups gathered together and bargaining with one another.

3. Corporatism need not be confined to incomes policy but may be effective in a variety of issue areas, e.g., agriculture.

4. At any time, on any issue, when Government, party-in- Government, or a group deems it expedient to depoliticize a decision, corporatist arrangements may evolve. By the same token, the Govern- ment or party-in-Government might discourage corporatist arrange- ments on issues with which it has been very closely associated or on matters which might drastically affect a group with which it has been closely affiliated. For example, in Israel a change in COLA policy may have been possible. However, abolishing COLA, which would have directly affronted the Histadrut, closely related to the Labor party-in- Government, would have been too drastic. Corporatist decision- making may have its limits: the apples may be rearranged but not if the applecart will be upset.

As a result of a dynamic between Government and groups, Israel's strong party system acquired both pluralist and corporatist traits. In establishing these decision-making arrangements, affiliated and unaffiliated groups frequently were motivated differently, and there- fore moved at separate paces and prodded the system to different degrees. Assigning a precise time to a pluralist transformation and a corporatist trend, therefore, is difficult. Nevertheless, 1965 continually appears as a year marking institutional developments for parties and groups in both frameworks. For pluralism: as noted, 1965 was a turning point for parties as they formed broad alliances; by that year groups formed and broadened their organizations – the Manufacturers' Association established the Coordinating Bureau in 1965 and the Ihud helped create the Brit two years earlier; groups distanced themselves from parties, demarcating an interest group subsystem; groups widened their aims; groups varied their tactics and cultivated new targets; and groups remained as interest entities. Similarly, for corporatism, by 1965: groups became more comprehensive; groups established and participated in cooperative forums, notably for the Manufacturers' Association, the Industrial Council and Forum (the latter was proposed in 1965) and for the Ihud, the Agricultural Center; and groups negotiated with one another to establish policies and implement programs.

Developments accelerated after 1967, especially toward pluralism. Old groups continued to expand their aims and activities. The Manufacturers' Association, for example, felt the time auspicious for presenting ideas on tax reform as well as ideas on other matters of a broad economic nature. New groups that entered the scene after 1967 continued upon the paths broken by their predecessors. Old and new groups crystallized the transformation of the system.

Groups After 1967:
The Pluralist Crystallization

With the 1967 war victory, both physical and psychological horizons were widened, and the atmosphere was set for a new type of group to emerge. Whereas economic groups emerged when parties were intensely ideological, idea and ideological groups emerged when parties were reducing, or perceived as reducing, their emphasis on such issues. Disillusioned with past concentration on material concerns and the dearth of ideological development, but perceiving the possibility of pressing broader demands and expanded opportunities for operating as a group autonomous of parties, Gush Emunim and other idea and policy oriented groups arose. The fact that groups, rather than parties, formed indicates in itself pluralist development, as pluralism entails a high tendency for groups to organize at the "grass roots" level.

Taking advantage and expanding upon all the precedents and openings in the system pioneered by previous groups, Gush Emunim acted offensively, whereas previous groups had acted defensively. This ideological group promoted policy changes regarding the administered territories by impinging upon all conceivably congenial parties, rather than locking itself into only one. While not wielding its support as a group among parties, Gush Emunim approached party politics more aggressively than previous independent groups by attempting to affect candidate selection via ad hoc committees. Uninhibited by party loyalty and unafraid of appearing narrow, the group learned from the Manufacturers' Association and became adept at dramatizing events for maximum press coverage, organized petition campaigns, and published material to intelligently present its ideas. Group members pressured individual legislators from various parties, thereby abetting a decline in party discipline. They approached ministers perceived as sympathetic to their cause, not only those holding pertinent portfolios. And they dealt with bureaucrats. Gush Emunim did not seek positions in the bureaucracy but sought out any cracks in jurisdiction, exploiting the bureaucracy to its advantage. By creating an ideological interest group, impacting upon parties, and diversifying tactics and targets, Gush Emunim furthered each element of the pluralist frame. Gush Emunim continually exerted a centrifugal force on the system.

In one respect, however, the group seemed to act in a manner expected of groups in a strong party model: the group participated in forming a new party. As groups in the strong party phase in Israel seemed to deviate with respect to party formation, i.e., groups did not become parties, similarly, in the pluralist phase, groups at times deviated with respect to the same factor, in this case forming parties. The explanation is similar for both patterns and derives from the political culture. The ideological political culture discouraged material parties and material interest groups; ideological stagnation generated, or allowed for, ideological groups as well as ideological parties.

In fact, the formation of a party based upon Gush Emunim may be understood within the context of pluralism, where groups expand all possible channels of influence in a system. The proportional representation system in Israel allowed for pressure from small parties, and the group took advantage of that opening as well as exploiting others. Simultaneously, however, it kept its options open by maintaining a parallel group formation. Moreover, establishing a party was a last resort, a move made after careful calculation that the small party would be necessary for the next coalition and would not remain an obscure faction in the legislature.

Some political observers note the continual formation of small parties in Israel and contend that, therefore, the system has not changed, that parties remain the central institution of Israel's political system. Such an observation is too simple and ignores other features and developments in Israel's political system. Groups and parties should not be understood as completely interchangeable entities. The proliferation of parties or groups does not preclude the development of the other. Rather, groups and parties may be conceptualized as forming two parallel planes. The phenomenon of party formation requires a study in itself. New parties may directly enter or arise from the party sphere, following imperatives of the party system; parties may be entirely new organizations or they may be splinters of existing parties. They may form for ideological reasons, for personal power considerations, or for other reasons. Interest groups coexist with parties. They may become parties or remain as groups. A pluralist pattern may overlay or overlap with a strong party model.

The Crystallization Continues:
Groups, the Likud, and Thereafter

The accession of a Likud Government ushered in a change in regime but did not redirect or retard the development of pluralism. Unlike Mapai/Labor, the Likud did not purposely seek to rule by negotiating deals with groups. Nevertheless, the Likud's approach to governing was unintentionally conducive to pluralist development. Reflecting its past emphasis on the individual, the Likud Government viewed society as composed of individuals, "groupings," as well as organized groups. It interpreted Government's job as formulating policy for the whole society while juggling and satisfying as many demands as possible among the various units. Conforming to the Government's ruling model, groups impinged upon the Government to gain consideration for their aims. The Government encountered difficulty in imposing ministerial developed policy, and individual ministers resorted to the "minister-as-arbitrator" model employed by Mapai/Labor. Thus, group-Likud interaction unintentionally solidified the pluralist pattern.

The group subsystem became more coherent, cohesive, and distinct from parties. The Manufacturers' Association sought alliances with Histadrut and Government industrial sectors, hoping they would become members of the Association. With its party in the opposition, the Ihud faced a situation similar to that of the Manufacturers' Association when the Right did not hold office. The Ihud reacted similarly and fended for itself as an independent interest group. The Ihud strengthened ties with other kibbutz federations, uniting with Kibbutz ha-Meuhad to form Takam, drew closer to moshavim, and cooperated more closely with the private sector. Under the first Likud Government, Gush Emunim intensified its activity. It then gave rise to Amanah and Yesha which took places within the interest group configuration as combination material-ideological interest groups.

As independent interest entities, groups concentrated on the Kneset, thereby enhancing that institution's power. The Manufacturers' Association sought to ally with other industrial sectors in the Kneset. Kneset members, becoming more independent, selected pet issues, and the Manufacturers' Association cooperated with and aided their efforts, hoping that industrial interests would benefit. Conforming to, and augmenting the individualist trend among legislators, the Manufacturers' Association attempted to influence MKs of several parties, especially focusing upon new members. With these efforts, the Manufacturers' Association built upon the precedents set by Gush Emunim. The Ihud sought to expand the agricultural caucus in the Kneset, collaborating even with private sector representatives.

While groups under the Likud crystallized a pluralist pattern, they did not call anew for corporatist forms. Neither did this Government appear to contemplate any such experiments.

Combining two parts of the political spectrum and two outlooks on governing, the 1984 National Unity Government was a peculiar phenomenon. Groups related to the ministries and ministers relevant to their concerns and to the ruling style of each office. Government-group interaction thus took on several forms. The unusual nature of the Government, however, makes it difficult to assess if some occurrences were one time only responses to circumstances or if they represent a trend.

The group subsystem not only became more distinct but individual group activity became more pronounced. The tight economy engendered group competition and jealousy. The Ihud/Takam, for example, opposed funding West Bank settlement, regarding such expenditure as diminishing from needed kibbutz aid. Gush Emunim persons, in turn, made disparaging remarks about kibbutzim. Making their case, groups acted aggressively. The period was marked by strikes, production stoppages, and demonstrations, the last notably by the kibbutz group.

Groups also reinforced the pluralist pattern with their by now traditional tactics – targeting ministers, addressing the Kneset, and making media appeals. When the Government, or part of it, established cooperative arrangements for policy-setting, groups such as the Manufacturers' Association participated. The Manufacturers' Association also continually has called upon the Government to adopt structural economic reform, an aim of the July 1985 economic measures not yet achieved. Thus, the Government-group interaction during the national unity term furthered both pluralism and corporatism.

Groups and System Change

Although groups played a prominent role in transforming Israel's political system, systemic change was not always a group aim, and the route to change, therefore, was not always direct. As noted in the introduction and confirmed by the empirical data, demands made by interest groups and their consequences for change may be of several types: particularistic, for or against a policy or portion thereof; more systemic, for alteration of the very system or mechanism by which demands are processed; or they may be particularistic but have consequences, perhaps unintended or unforeseen, for systemic change. Groups of each type existed in Israel. The Manufacturers' Association requested modifications in various economic policies, expressed a desire for comprehensive economic policy change, and pressed for a role in decision-making. As a result of the group's pressure and Government response, different experiments in decision-making procedures were made, and an interest group subsystem developed. The Ihud falls in the last category. The Ihud pressed for material objectives, but as a consequence of its conduct, an interest group coalesced, and the subsystem further developed. Gush Emunim belongs to categories two and three. The group pressed for a comprehensive policy, and its activities spurred institutional developments. Pursuing their aims of these different types, groups interacted with all components of the political system, sometimes attempting to circumvent them, as in the case of group behavior vis-à-vis parties, but always shaping the institutions and being shaped by them until, as the sum of all these activities, the entire system had altered.

Nevertheless, change was not complete. Old features were not obliterated, but rather, new features were overlaid on the old: groups became more prominent, but parties did not disappear; while parties changed their role and consolidated in pluralist fashion, new parties also arose; and groups diversified tactics and targets but also retained their older reliable method of cultivating good personal relationships.

One feature especially resistant to change was the ideological political culture. Ideology and ideological behavioral traits, termed the ideological dimension, marked and limited each transformation. In the early period, when ministers bargained among and balanced interest groups, the system appeared to be moving toward pluralism. However, ideology limited the type of group likely to emerge, precluded issues contravening the prevailing socialist ideology from being addressed, and did not allow for comprehensive policy planning. Peripatetic ministers mediated bargains, but they did so actually to forestall systemic change.

While Israel's institutional arrangement increasingly corresponded to a pluralist pattern, that arrangement was not supported by a pragmatic outlook. Although there were forces promoting change in the ideological political culture, many behavioral traits persisted, and in general, the ideological political culture lagged behind development in other elements. Certain groups, especially the Manufacturers' Association, attempted to alter the ideological behavioral pattern by favoring discussion and negotiation on many issues, comprehensive planning, and unemotional debate of relevant matters. Other groups, however, reinvigorated the ideological culture. The formation and activities of ideological groups furthered institutional and procedural change, but these groups were not pragmatic. They exploited the trappings of a developing pluralist system without contributing to the content. Therefore, parties, Government, and many, but not all, groups negotiated out of necessity, not because they highly esteemed bargaining as an appropriate and optimal means of resolving any difficulties. A superficial version of pluralism developed in Israel, leaving many issues untouched. While the system acquired a certain pluralist façade, the metamorphosis was incomplete.

As pluralist development in Israel was fettered by aspects of the ideological culture, experiments in corporatism similarly were constricted. Attempts to address comprehensive policy that may have required ideological modification were aborted. More successful corporatist experiments occurred when participants occupied the same broad ideological space and decided upon implementation and distribution. In addition, corporatist development has been confined to material interest groups. If residual ideological factors limited bargains that the material groups could reach, certainly ideological groups themselves would have difficulty entering a corporatist forum. Moreover, a party or Government that continued to consider itself the guardian of ideology would have difficulty including such groups in any roundtable.

Prospects for the Future

In Israel by the 1980s, interest groups had emerged from the shadows. In contrast to the earlier picture of parties controlling the political space and setting policy, Israel now projected a picture of clamoring interest groups. Groups surrounded a Government core, and parties had receded into the background, severely curtailed as group mediators. Given this new systemic design, several questions arise: What does this change bode for decision-making and resolving competing group claims? Will the system undergo further transformation, and if so, what pattern is likely to emerge? Will indeed Israel regret – to paraphrase Kirchheimer's concern for European polities – the passing of the strong party era?[5] Several outcomes are conceivable:

1. Projecting the past upon the present, Israel may move further along the pluralist path, as additional groups emerge and become active in several arenas. Several results are possible within the pluralist scenario:

a. Groups might overwhelm the system, and decision-making could completely break down. The public demonstrations from unexpected quarters in recent years do not bode well.

b. As groups interrelate within and impinge upon institutions, procedural changes may occur. One institution may emerge as a main arena for allowing group expression and activity and coordinating their claims. The Kneset is a likely candidate for these functions. Individual legislators have sought the limelight, collaborating with interest groups to establish issue areas for themselves. They may continue this activity and establish procedures in the Kneset for dealing with groups. The Kneset as an institution has increasingly arrogated power to itself and may continue to augment its role. The Kneset has contemplated making membership a full time job and expanding the scope and workload of its committees. It is possible that the Kneset will regularize its hearing process and inaugurate hearings that take testimony from the new idea groups, which until now have been excluded.

2. Corporatist forms may further develop, especially for economic interest groups. While theoretically it is possible to institute corporatist arrangements for idea groups, it is highly unlikely that any Israeli Government would relinquish authority over such areas or that these groups would compromise. Corporatist development is more imaginable for economic groups, and conceivably, either Government or groups might suggest the experiment.

Precedents for group initiatives and cooperation are encouraging. While in the past groups may at times have been reluctant negotiators, they also have expressed their readiness to compromise, conciliate, and contribute to the common good. Indeed, interest group ideas inspired many official programs. The President of the Manufacturers' Association, for example, in 1969, proposed a tripartite agreement for workers, manufacturers, and Government; thus, an interest group initiated Israel's first "package deal." Agricultural group leaders invented a financial aid package and planning system that virtually revolutionized agrarian accounting and ensured the fiscal health of endangered farms. Farm councils designed milk production and other food raising plans. Representatives of agricultural groups proudly relate how they all participated in committees and formulated policies to sustain poorer farmers. In recent years, Labor Prime Minister Peres in the National Unity Government conducted cooperative economic policy-making. The Likud ministers who participated may have learned from the experience. There is nothing in Likud ideology that would preclude the method. Building upon these precedents and expressions of goodwill, the Government and groups may establish a joint economic policy board. Interest groups, with Government supervision, could negotiate with each other to plan programs and policies.

3. Along with any of these outcomes (except for a complete breakdown), the political culture may become more pragmatic. Although until now, procedures evolved in order to maintain ideologies and viewpoints intact, the very process of striking a bargain served to mitigate the intensity of the ideologies themselves and accustomed groups to working together. When groups were allowed to participate in decision-making, they learned to appreciate the dilemmas Government faces. Agricultural groups that were permitted to decide upon a method for allocating conversion funds found themselves debating and considering very classic budgeting problems and became aware that "politics" did not necessarily motivate every

Government decision. Similarly, as idea groups have expanded tactics and forums for pressure while intensely holding an idea, so, too, may those ideas eventually be modified by groups participating in the very arenas they opened. These groups may begin to hear and absorb other points of view. When confronted with the pressures that Government and lawmakers face, they may realize that not all their hoped-for aims are possible or even feasible.

4. However, it is possible that the political culture will become more ideological, and all the accompanying behavioral traits will be reinvigorated. Uncompromising opinion groups may engender other opposing, but equally intransigent, groups to form. Consequently, decision-making may occur in the streets.

5. It also is possible, but improbable, that parties could resurge and regain the function of mediating among groups. If centrifugal forces threaten to overwhelm the system, and no institution or forum emerges to reconcile competing groups, parties and politicians may abandon their power games and instead formulate an ideology or program for the country. Groups themselves may decide to cooperate in forming a party or align with an existing party. An ambitious individual may start a party, hoping to attract a number of groups. Or, one of the existing parties may perceive the necessity of taking charge, formulating policy, and forging agreement among several groups.

Whichever scenario develops, certainly the system will not remain static. Interest groups will be active on the scene, indirectly prodding, if not overtly campaigning, for change. Indeed, whereas groups once existed in obscurity, overshadowed by parties, observers of the current scene in Israel might remark that groups are the predominant feature. A political system that once belittled the significance of groups now must develop procedures to reconcile them. As in the past, groups may propose procedures, and surely groups will be an essential part of any solution.

Notes

Chapter 1

1. Benjamin Akzin, "The Role of Parties in Israeli Democracy," *Journal of Politics,* XVII (November 1955), 509.

2. David B. Truman, *The Governmental Process: Political Interests and Public Opinion* (2nd ed., New York: Alfred A. Knopf, 1971), p. xxi.

3. Samuel H. Beer, "Group Representation in British and American Democracy," *The Annals of the American Academy of Political Science,* LLLXIX (September 1958), 138.

4. For those who follow this method, see: Gabriel A. Almond, "Research Note: A Comparative Study of Interest Groups and the Political Process," *American Political Science Review,* LII (March 1958); Truman, *Governmental Process;* and Graham Wootton, *Interest Groups* (Englewood Cliffs: Prentice-Hall, Inc., 1970), especially p. 47.

5. Samuel H. Beer, *British Politics in the Collectivist Age* (New York: Vintage Books, 1969).

6. For a basic explication of the strong party model, see Samuel P. Huntington, *Political Order in Changing Societies* (New Haven: Yale University Press, 1968).

7. Robert A. Dahl, *Pluralist Democracy in the United States: Conflict and Consent* (Chicago: Rand McNally & Company, 1967), p. 24. For the pluralist model, see *Ibid.;* and also Robert A. Dahl, *Who Governs?* (New Haven: Yale University Press, 1961); and Truman, *Governmental Process.*

8. For theorizations on corporatism, see: Suzanne Berger, ed., *Organizing Interests in Western Europe: Pluralism, Corporatism, and the Transformation of Politics* (Cambridge: Cambridge University Press, 1981); Gerhard Lehmbruch, "Liberal Corporatism and Party Government," *Comparative Political Studies,* X (April 1977), 91–126; Leo Panitch, "The Development of Corporatism in

Liberal Democracies," *Comparative Political Studies*, X (April 1977), 61-89; Leo Panitch, "Recent Theorizations of Corporatism; Reflections on a Growth Industry," *British Journal of Sociology*, XXXI (June 1980), 159-87; Leo Panitch, *Social Democracy and Industrial Militancy: The Labour Party, the Trade Unions and Incomes Policy 1945-1974* (Cambridge: Cambridge University Press, 1976), particularly the conclusion, pp. 235-59; and Leo Panitch, "Trade Unions and the Capitalist State," *New Left Review*, n.v., No. 125 (January-February 1981), 21-44. Not all commentators on corporatism necessarily favor it as a decision-making model.

Chapter 2

1. Leonard Fein, *Israel: Politics and People* (Boston: Little, Brown, and Co., 1968), p. 71.

2. *Ibid.*, p. 93.

3. When I capitalize Government, I am referring to the Cabinet, and throughout this study I use the terms interchangeably.

4. For purposes of this discussion, government includes the local authorities and the Jewish Agency. This description of the government's extensive role relies largely upon Howard Pack, *Structural Change and Economic Policy in Israel* (New Haven: Yale University Press, 1971), pp. 141-68; Nadav Safran, *The United States and Israel* (Cambridge: Harvard University Press, 1963), pp. 168-70; and Safran, *Israel: The Embattled Ally*, pp. 111-14.

5. For a description of the Histadrut's role, see S. N. Eisenstadt, *Israeli Society* (London: Weidenfeld & Nicolson, 1967), pp. 103-4; Fein, *Israel: Politics and People*, pp. 253-57; Foreign Area Studies of the American University, *Area Handbook for Israel* (Washington: U. S. Government Printing Office, 1970), pp. 274-75; and Nadav Safran, *Israel Today: A Profile*, Headline Series, No. 170 (New York: Foreign Policy Association), p. 52.

6. On the shares in the economy of the different sectors, refer to Foreign Area Studies of the American University, *Area Handbook for Israel*, p. 275; "Israel, State of (Economic Affairs)," *Encyclopaedia Judaica*, 1971, IX, col. 821; "Israel, State of (Economic Affairs)," *Encyclopaedia Judaica Decennial Yearbook*, 1973-1982, pp. 372, 376; Manufacturers' Association, *Manufacturers' Association of Israel*, undated pamphlet; and Safran, *The United States and Israel*, p. 168.

Chapter 3

1. For the multi-party view, refer to Akzin, "The Role of Parties in Israeli Democracy;" Fein, *Israel: Politics and People*; and Emanuel E. Gutmann,

"Israel," *International Social Science Journal*, XII, No. 1 (1960), 53–62; Emanuel E. Gutmann, "Israel," *Journal of Politics*, XXV (November 1963), 703–17; and Emanuel E. Gutmann, "Some Observations on Politics and Parties in Israel," *India Quarterly*, XVII (January–March 1961), 3–29.

For those who stress the dominant party view refer to Alan Arian, *The Choosing People* (Cleveland: Press of Case Western Reserve University, 1973) and Peter Y. Medding, *Mapai in Israel: Political Organization and Government in a New Society* (Cambridge: Cambridge University Press, 1972).

Safran in *The United States and Israel* (1963) speculates that Israel's system might gradually evolve into a modified two-party arrangement, but in *Israel: The Embattled Ally* (1978) notes regretfully that this did not develop; David Nachmias in "The Right Wing Opposition in Israel," *Political Studies*, XXIV (September 1976), 268–80 traces the development of larger party blocs.

Gutmann depicts Israel's system as divided into quasi-fiefdoms of parties with each party composed of a core having associated with it a number of interest groups. Refer to "Israel," *International Social Science Journal*, p. 61; "Israel," *Journal of Politics*, pp. 703–17; and "Some Observations," pp. 14–15. Arian in *The Choosing People*, p. 3 relegates pressure groups to the parties, naming Mapai as the main broker and in Asher Arian, *Politics in Israel: The Second Generation* (Chatham, New Jersey: Chatham House Publishers, 1985) again emphasizes the dominant party's controlling place in the relationship.

On the significance and persistence of ideological distinctions, see Alan Arian, *Ideological Change in Israel* (Cleveland: Press of Case Western Reserve University, 1968), and on possible diminishing ideological intensity, see Safran, *Israel: The Embattled Ally*, especially pp. 170–71.

Gutmann implicitly and Safran explicitly (*Israel: The Embattled Ally*, p. 155) refer to a ruling oligarchy composed of party heads. Arian in *The Choosing People* limits the ruling oligarchy to Mapai's leaders, and Myron J. Aronoff in *Power and Ritual in the Israel Labour Party* (Amsterdam/Assen: Van Gorcum, 1977) and in "The Decline of the Israeli Labor Party: Causes and Significance," in *Israel at the Polls: The Knesset Elections of 1977*, ed. by Howard R. Penniman (Washington, D. C.: American Enterprise Institute for Public Policy Research, 1979) explains how an insular elite controlled Mapai.

2. Though Mapai actually was a dominant party during the pre-state period, I am using the term "dominant party period" to distinguish between a coalition with and without the General Zionist Party.

3. Medding, *Mapai in Israel*, pp. 46–47.

4. *Ibid.*, p. 253.

5. The efforts of the Right to consolidate have been brought to light by David Nachmias in "The Right Wing Opposition in Israel," pp. 268–80. His observations call into question the widely accepted assumption that Israel's party system was static.

6. *Ibid.*, p. 274.

7. The significance of this ranking might be subject to debate as Herut received 17 seats to Mapai's 42.

8. Nachmias, "The Right Wing Opposition in Israel," pp. 273, 275, and 276. Again, the significance of this result might be open to interpretation.

9. The Kneset always had this power, but I first noted evidence of its use during this time period.

10. Although Gahal did not oppose the ceasefire provision, it regarded the other elements as a prelude to accepting a broader plan made by United States Secretary of State William Rogers calling for Israel's withdrawal from occupied territory.

11. Safran, *Israel: The Embattled Ally*, p. 194.

12. Yitzhak Rabin, private interview, Tel Aviv, May 2, 1980.

13. Yechiel Kadishai, director of the Prime Minister's Bureau under Begin, private interview, Jerusalem, December 23, 1980.

14. Stanley Maron, "Change and Hope," (Hebrew), *Yahad*, September 7, 1983, p. 2.

Chapter 4

1. Throughout this work I translate the name of the organization as the Israel Manufacturers' Association and use the short term, Manufacturers' Association. In 1921, the organization was titled in Hebrew, "Hitahdut Ba'alei ha-Ta'asiyyah–ve-Notnei 'Avodah be-Tel-Aviv Yafo," translated literally as the "Organization of Owners of Industry–and Employers in Tel Aviv Jaffa." In 1925, the organization was titled, "Hitahdut Ba'alei ha-Ta'asiyyah be-Eretz Yisrael," translated literally as the "Association of Owners of Industry in the Land of Israel." In 1969, the name was changed to "Hitahdut ha-Ta'asiyyanim be-Eretz Yisrael," literally, "The Association of Manufacturers in the Land of Israel," to signify that the Association's purpose was not to represent property interests but to promote industry and that the organization, as stipulated in its constitutional amendments of 1967, was open to managers and heads of any legally designated industrial enterprise, not only to individual private owners.

2. An antecedent of the Herut Party, the Revisionist Party was established in 1925 by Vladimir (Zev) Jabotinsky, a Russian born journalist. The Revisionists advocated immediate mass immigration to Palestine and called for strong retaliatory measures against Arab attacks and action against the British.

3. See description by Eisenstadt, *Israeli Society*, p. 290.

4. Manufacturers' Association, Minutes of Meetings of the Presidium, Meeting of October 28, 1951.

5. *Ibid.*, Meeting of March 12, 1952.

6. *Ibid.*, Meeting of January 19, 1953.

7. *Ibid.*, Meeting of February 25, 1953.

8. *Ibid.*, Meeting of March 14, 1954.

9. *Ibid.*, Meeting of July 4, 1954.

10. Moshe Levi, private interview, Tel Aviv, April 13, 1980.

11. Zalman Suzayev, private interview, Tel Aviv, May 8, 1979.

12. Yehudah Barnatan, private interview, Tel Aviv, June 4, 1980.

13. Manufacturers' Association, Minutes of Meetings of the Presidium, Meeting of November 15, 1956.

14. *Ibid.*, Meeting of June 9, 1957.

15. *Ibid.*

16. Nahum Levin, "Industrial Matters in the Kneset," (Hebrew), *Ha-Ta'asiyyah*, December 1960–January 1961, p. 6; and Dr. A. Rafaeli, "Organizational Problems," (Hebrew), *Ha-Ta'asiyyah*, June–July 1963, p. 9.

17. Yehudah Barnatan, private interview, Tel Aviv, June 4, 1980.

Chapter 5

1. Manufacturers' Association, Minutes of Meetings of the Presidium, Meeting of March 19, 1961.

2. *Ibid.*, Meeting of June 20, 1956.

3. Moshe Levi, private interview, Tel Aviv, April 13, 1980.

4. Manufacturers' Association, Minutes of Meetings of the Presidium, Meeting of April 25, 1961.

5. *Ibid.*

6. *Ibid.*

7. *Ibid.*, Meeting of February 11, 1968.

8. Aryeh Shenkar, "Industry–Its Condition and Its Desires," (Hebrew), *Ha-Ta'asiyyah*, January 1957, p. 4.

9. Manufacturers' Association, Minutes of Meetings of the Presidium, Meeting of September 7, 1958.

10. *Ibid.*

11. *Ibid.*, Meetings of May 28, November 5, and December 3, 1961.

12. Yehudah Barnatan, private interview, Tel Aviv, June 13, 1980.

13. Zalman Suzayev, private interview, Tel Aviv, May 8, 1979.

14. Manufacturers' Association, Minutes of Meetings of the Presidium, Meeting of October 30, 1968.

15. *Ibid.*, Meeting of July 11, 1965.

16. Zalman Suzayev, "The Association and Its Path in the Future," (Hebrew), *Ha-Ta'asiyyah*, April–May 1965.

17. Manufacturers' Association, Minutes of Meetings of the Presidium, Meeting of October 30, 1968.

18. *Ibid.*, Meeting of June 12, 1966.

19. Moshe Levi, private interview, Tel Aviv, April 13, 1980.

20. Yehudah Barnatan, private interview, Tel Aviv, June 4, 1980.

21. Moshe Levi, private interview, Tel Aviv, April 13, 1980.

22. Manufacturers' Association, Minutes of Meetings of the Presidium, Meeting of February 12, 1967.

23. *Ibid.*, Meeting of November 30, 1969.

Chapter 6

1. *Ibid.*, Memorandum to the Prime Minister attached to Minutes of the Meeting of August 6, 1967.

2. *Ibid.*, Meeting of December 30, 1969.

3. *Ibid.*

4. Avraham Shavit, private interview, Tel Aviv, June 25, 1980.

5. *Jerusalem Post*, November 25, 1974, p. 2 and December 10, 1974, p. 1.

6. Manufacturers' Association, Minutes of Meetings of the Presidium, Meeting of June 12, 1977.

7. *Ibid.*, Meeting of July 19, 1977.

8. *Ibid.*, Meeting of November 16, 1977.

9. *Ibid.*, Meeting of November 25, 1977.

10. *Ibid.*, Meeting of December 11, 1977.

11. *Ibid.*, Meeting of December 18, 1977.

12. *Ibid.*

13. *Ibid.*, Meeting of January 15, 1978.

14. *Ibid.*

15. *Igeret Le-Ta'asiyyan,* September 3, 1978 and July 23, 1979.

16. Avraham Shavit, private interview, Tel Aviv, August 3, 1980.

17. Avraham Shavit, private interview, Tel Aviv, June 25, 1980; and Manufacturers' Association, Minutes of Meetings of the Presidium, Meeting of December 11, 1977.

18. Manufacturers' Association, Minutes of Meetings of the Presidium, Meeting of December 11, 1977.

19. *Jerusalem Post,* May 22, 1978, p. 2.

20. Menachem Begin, private interview, Jerusalem, February 6, 1981.

21. Manufacturers' Association, Minutes of Meetings of the Presidium, Meeting of June 12, 1977.

22. In the National Unity Government were Finance Minister, Yitzhak Moda'i, Likud, and then in 1986, Moshe Nissim, Likud; Minister of Industry and Trade, Ariel Sharon, Likud (Today, in English, Israel refers to the Ministry of Commerce and Industry as Industry and Trade.); Minister of Economics and Planning, Gad Ya'aqobi, Labor; Minister of Science and Development, Gideon Patt, Likud.

23. Roy Isacowitz, "8-month package deal surmounts last hurdles," *Jerusalem Post,* January 25, 1985, p. 1.

24. "Meeting of the Presidium 27 Dec. 1987," (Hebrew), *Le-Ta'asiyyan,* February 1988, p. 3.

25. Mark Moshevitz, private interview, Ramat Gan, May 21, 1979.

26. Otto Kirchheimer, *The Transformation of the Western European Party Systems,"* in *Political Parties and Political Development,* ed. by Joseph La Palombara and Myron Weiner (Princeton: Princeton University Press, 1966), p. 193; and Truman, *Governmental Process,* p. 272.

Chapter 7

1. Related by Naftali Ushpiz, private interview, Kibbutz Qiryat 'Anavim, May 17, 1981.

2. Hayyim Gvati, private interview, Tel Aviv, April 29, 1981.

3. Medding, *Mapai in Israel*, pp. 32–33.

4. Gabriel A. Almond and G. Bingham Powell, Jr., *Comparative Politics, A Developmental Approach* (Boston: Little, Brown and Company, 1966), p. 259.

5. Kirchheimer, "The Transformation of the Western European Party Systems," pp. 193–94; and Truman, *Governmental Process*, pp. xxxii–xxxiv, 295–304.

6. Truman, *Governmental Process*, p. xxxii.

7. Ihud, Minutes of Meetings of the Coordinating Committee, Meeting of January 8, 1952.

8. Ihud, Shlomo Kinerti, Minutes of Meetings of the Secretariat, Meeting of July 3, 1955.

9. Ihud, Zev On, Minutes of Meetings of the Coordinating Secretariat, Meeting of August 10, 1955.

10. Ihud, Senta Yoseftal, Minutes of Meetings of the Wider Secretariat, Meeting of September 28, 1955.

11. Ihud, Meir Mandel, Minutes of Meetings of the Coordinating Secretariat, Meeting of October 2, 1955.

12. Ihud, Yosef Yizraeli, Minutes of Meetings of the Coordinating Secretariat, Meeting of August 10, 1955.

13. Ihud, Yosef Gurion, Minutes of Meetings of the Central Committee, Meeting of June 9, 1956, Session 3.

14. Ihud, Senta Yoseftal, Minutes of Meetings of the Central Committee, Meeting of June 8, 1956, Session 1.

15. Ihud, 'Aqiva Goshen, Minutes of Meetings of the Wider Secretariat, Meeting of April 15, 1956.

16. Ihud, David Maltz and Yitzhaq Feniger, Minutes of Meetings of the Central Committee, Meeting of June 9, 1956, Session 3.

17. Ihud, Yitzhaq Feniger, *Ibid.*

18. Ihud, Yitzhaq Feniger and Aryeh Ofir, *Ibid.*

19. Ihud, Senta Yoseftal, Minutes of Meetings of the Central Committee, Meeting of June 8, 1956, Session 1.

20. Arian, *Ideological Change in Israel.*

21. Ihud, Kadish Luz, Minutes of Meetings of the Coordinating Secretariat, Meeting of April 4, 1956.

22. Ihud, Minutes of Meetings of the Wider Secretariat, Meetings of May 11 and 25, 1955.

23. Ihud, Zev Shefer, Minutes of Meetings of the Wider Secretariat, Meeting of May 11, 1955.

24. Ihud, Yosef Efrati, Minutes of Meetings of the Coordinating Secretariat, Meeting of August 10, 1955; and Aryeh Bahir, *Ibid.*, Meeting of February 27, 1956.

25. Ihud, Yosef Gurion, *Ibid.*, Meeting of January 30, 1955.

26. Ihud, Aryeh Bahir, *Ibid.*, Meeting of August 10, 1955.

27. Ihud, Shlomo Kinerti, Minutes of Meetings of the Wider Secretariat, Meeting of April 5, 1956.

28. Kirchheimer, "The Transformation of the Western European Party Systems," pp. 184 and 192.

29. *Ibid.*, p. 193.

30. Beer, *British Politics in the Collectivist Age*, p. 351.

Chapter 8

1. Senta Yoseftal, private interview, Tel Aviv, April 23, 1981.

2. Efrayim Avneri, private interview, Kibbutz Hulda, April–May 1981; and Government of Israel, Ministry of Agriculture and Bank of Israel, *Economy and Agriculture of Israel* (Jerusalem: Government of Israel, 1959).

3. Efrayim Avneri, private interview, Kibbutz Hulda, April–May 1981.

4. Ihud, Minutes of Meetings of the Secretariat, Meeting of January 31, 1954.

5. Senta Yoseftal, private interview, Tel Aviv, April 23, 1981.

6. S. Barnat, "Tightening of Credit and the Kibbutz Economy," (Hebrew), *Ha-Aretz*, March 17, 1954.

7. Ihud, Yosef Efrati, Minutes of Meetings of the Coordinating Secretariat, Meeting of January 30, 1955.

8. Efrayim Avneri, private interview, Kibbutz Hulda, April–May 1981.

9. *Ibid.*

10. Agricultural Center, Minutes of Meetings of the Settlement Committee, Meetings of January 6, 1955; November 10, 1955; and March 29, 1956.

11. "A 'Treasurers' Revolt' of Consolidated Farms Will Be Announced because of Credit Tightening," (Hebrew), *Ha-Aretz*, January 4, 1956.

12. Senta Yoseftal, private interview, Tel Aviv, April 23, 1981.

13. Ihud, Minutes of Meetings of the Coordinating Secretariat, Meeting of March 22, 1956.

14. *Ibid.*

15. Ihud, Minutes of Meetings of the Coordinating Secretariat, Meeting of March 22, 1956.

16. *Ibid.*, Meeting of April 9, 1956.

17. Ihud, Shlomo Kinerti, Minutes of Meetings of the Coordinating Secretariat, Meeting of March 31, 1957.

18. Ihud, Shlomo Kinerti, Minutes of Meetings of the Coordinating Secretariat, Meeting of January 30, 1955.

19. Efrayim Avneri, private interview, Kibbutz Hulda, April–May 1981; and Senta Yoseftal, private interview, Tel Aviv, April 23, 1981.

20. Efrayim Avneri, private interview, Kibbutz Hulda, April–May 1981.

21. Ihud, Minutes of Meetings of the Economic Committee, Meeting of April 24, 1957.

22. Ihud, Efrayim Avneri, Minutes of Meetings of the Economic Committee, Meeting of August 21, 1956.

23. Ihud, Minutes of Meetings of the Secretariat, Meeting of December 28, 1958.

24. *Ibid.*, Meeting of February 15, 1959; Naftali Ushpiz, private interview, Kibbutz Qiryat 'Anavim, May 17, 1981; and Dov Tzamir, private interview, Tel Aviv, May 20, 1981.

25. Ihud, Minutes of Meetings of the Secretariat, Meeting of February 15, 1959.

26. Ihud, Meir Mandel and Moshe Netzer, Minutes of Meetings of the Central Committee, Meeting of August 29, 1959, Session 7.

27. Ihud, Shlomo Kinerti, Minutes of Meetings of the Central Committee, Meeting of August 28, 1959, Session 3.

28. Ihud, Minutes of Meetings of the Secretariat, Meeting of November 8, 1959 and Minutes of Meetings of the Central Committee, Meeting of December 17, 1959, Session 1.

29. Ihud, Meir Mandel, Minutes of Meetings of the Central Committee, Meeting of December 17, 1959, Session 1.

30. This summary of the Lavon Affair relies a great deal upon Medding, *Mapai in Israel*, pp. 261–62.

31. Ihud, Hayyim Gvati, Minutes of Meetings of the Wider Secretariat, Meeting of March 22, 1961.

32. Ihud, Minutes of Meetings of the Wider Secretariat, Meeting of March 22, 1961.

33. *Ibid.*

34. *Ibid.*, Meeting of April 5, 1961.

35. *Ibid.*, Meeting of April 23, 1961.

36. *Ibid.*

37. Ihud, Hayyim Gvati, Minutes of Meetings of the Wider Secretariat, Meeting of August 30, 1961.

38. Ihud, Minutes of Meetings of the Secretariat, Meeting of August 1, 1965.

39. Efrayim Avneri, private interview, Kibbutz Hulda, May 12, 1981.

40. Ihud, Barukh Aznayah, Minutes of Meetings of the Secretariat, Meeting of May 7, 1967.

41. See Truman, *Governmental Process*, pp. 156–87.

42. *Ibid.*, pp. 162–63.

Chapter 9

1. Ihud, Hayyim Gvati, Minutes of Meetings of the Wider Secretariat, Meeting of January 13, 1960.

2. Ihud, Minutes of Meetings of the Wider Secretariat, Meeting of January 13, 1960.

3. Ihud, David Kahanah, Minutes of Meetings of the Active Secretariat, Meeting of December 31, 1961.

4. Ihud, Minutes of Meetings of the Secretariat, Meeting of May 29, 1960.

5. *Ibid.*, Meeting of June 12, 1960.

6. Senta Yoseftal, private interview, Tel Aviv, April 23, 1981.

7. "'Action Committee' for Kibbutz Treasurers," (Hebrew), *Ha-Aretz*, March 24, 1960.

8. As related by Hayyim Gvati, Ihud, Minutes of Meetings of the Secretariat, Meeting of August 7, 1960.

9. Efrayim Avneri, private interview, Kibbutz Hulda, May 12, 1981.

10. Senta Yoseftal, private interview, Tel Aviv, May 20, 1981.

11. Efrayim Avneri, private interview, Kibbutz Hulda, May 12, 1981.

12. *Ibid.*

13. Ihud, David Kahanah, Minutes of Meetings of the Active Secretariat, Meeting of May 17, 1963.

14. *Ibid.*

15. Efrayim Avneri, private interview, Kibbutz Hulda, May 13, 1981.

16. Senta Yoseftal, private interview, Tel Aviv, May 20, 1981.

17. Senta Yoseftal, private interview, Tel Aviv, April 23, 1981.

18. *Ibid.*

19. Efrayim Avneri, private interview, Kibbutz Hulda, May 13, 1981.

20. Ihud, Yosef Perlmutter, Minutes of Meetings of the Economic (Farm) Committee, Meeting of April 13, 1966.

21. Efrayim Avneri, private interview, Kibbutz Hulda, May 13, 1981.

22. *Ibid.*

23. Senta Yoseftal, private interview, Tel Aviv, May 20, 1981.

24. *Ibid.*

25. Ihud, Minutes of Meetings of the Secretariat, Meeting of November 26, 1967.

26. Ihud, Minutes of Meetings of the Economic (Farm) Committee, Meeting of November 13, 1974.

27. *Ibid.*, Meeting of January 4, 1978.

28. *Ibid.*, Meeting of October 5, 1977.

29. *Ibid.*

30. Senta Yoseftal, private interview, Tel Aviv, May 20, 1981.

31. Ariel Sharon, private interview, Jerusalem, March 17, 1981.

32. Senta Yoseftal, private interview, Tel Aviv, May 20, 1981.

33. *Ibid.*

34. *Ibid.*

35. *Ibid.*

36. Ihud, Yehudah Sa'adi, Minutes of Meetings of the Central Committee of the United Kibbutz Movement, Meeting of January 6-7, 1980.

37. Senta Yoseftal, private interview, Tel Aviv, May 20, 1981.

38. *Ibid.*

39. Ihud, Yehudah Sa'adi, Minutes of Meetings of the Central Committee of the United Kibbutz Movement, Meeting of January 6–7, 1980.

40. Senta Yoseftal, private interview, Tel Aviv, April 23, 1981.

41. "From the Mercaz Decisions," (Hebrew), *Yahad*, May 30, 1986, p. 10; "On the Political Way of the Takam, a 'Mibifnim' Interview with Eli Zamir and Yosef Perlmutter – Secretaries of the Movement," (Hebrew), *Mibifnim*, XLIV (October 1982), 213–14; and Senta Yoseftal, personal letter, May 17, 1989.

42. "From Discussions of the Movement's Secretariat," (Hebrew), *Yahad*, August 6, 1982, p. 6; Aharon Yadlin, "We Are a Political Movement," (Hebrew), *Yahad*, July 23, 1982, p. 3; Senta Yoseftal, "The Movement in the Public Maelstrom," (Hebrew), *Yahad*, September 3, 1982, p. 7; and Eli Zamir, "The War in Lebanon and the Palestinian Question," (Hebrew), *Yahad*, August 20, 1982, p. 3.

43. Moshe Kalfon, "After the Election Campaign for the Eleventh Kneset," (Hebrew), *Mibifnim*, XLVI (November 1984), 447–51; and Nahman Raz, "In the Wake of the 1984 Elections," (Hebrew), *Mibifnim*, XLVI (November 1984), 443–46.

44. "On the Political Way of the Takam," p. 217.

45. "Interviews with the Secretaries of Takam," (Hebrew), *Mibifnim*, XLVIII (July 1986), 102.

46. "Takam Requests Government Aid for Recovery of 45 Kibbutzim," (Hebrew), *Yahad*, p. 17.

47. "Another Small Step," (Hebrew), *Kibbutz*, August 19, 1987, p. 8; "Changing Voltage," (Hebrew), *Kibbutz*, August 5, 1987, pp. 1–2; "Labor Settlement Demonstration," (Hebrew), *Kibbutz*, August 5, 1987, p. 2; and Shlomo Leshem, "Still Not Closing," (Hebrew), *Yahad*, November 1, 1985, pp. 3, 7.

48. "Changing Voltage," p. 2.

49. Efrayim Avneri, private interview, Kibbutz Hulda, May 12, 1981.

Chapter 10

1. Hanan Porat, private interview, Kfar 'Etzion, July 24, 1980.

2. Letter in Hebrew from Yosef Burg with attached "specification" dated December 25, 1973, in private collection of Hanan Porat.

3. Flyer in Hebrew titled, "The Group for Settling Shekhem, Report on the Group's Activities," undated, in private collection of Hanan Porat.

4. Notice dated in Hebrew Tevet 5734, found in private collection of Hanan Porat.

5. Yehudah Ben-Meir, private interview, Tel Aviv, May 18, 1980.

6. Zevulun Hammer, private interview, Ramat Gan, April 30, 1981.

7. Gush Emunim newsletter dated "Passover Eve 1974."

8. Hanan Porat, private interview, Kfar 'Etzion, July 24, 1980.

9. *Ibid.*, September 16, 1980.

10. Yitzhak Rabin, private interview, Tel Aviv, May 2, 1980.

11. Uri Elitzur, private interview, Jerusalem, July 31, 1980.

12. The name was derived from the practice on the Jewish holiday of Simhat Torah of circling and dancing with the Torah, called haqafot. In Israel, after the day's religious observance, there are public festivities called Second Haqafot. The demonstration was scheduled to begin that night so persons could gather without arousing suspicion, and hence the name.

13. Uri Elitzur, private interview, Jerusalem, August 13, 1980.

14. *Ibid.*

15. Claus Offe, "The Attribution of Public Status to Interest Groups: Observations on the West German Case," in Berger, *Organizing Interests*, p. 142.

16. Undated brochure in Hebrew titled, "'Ofrah, An Enclosure that Became a Settlement."

17. Hanan Porat, private interview, Kfar 'Etzion, September 16, 1980.

18. Shimon Peres, private interview, Tel Aviv, February 15, 1981.

19. Yitzhak Rabin, private interview, Tel Aviv, May 2, 1980.

20. Yehudah Ben-Meir, private interview, Tel Aviv, July 10, 1980.

21. *Ibid.*

22. Rabbi Yohanan Fried, private interview, Jerusalem, August 28, 1980.

23. Yitzhak Rabin, private interview, Tel Aviv, May 2, 1980.

24. Zevulun Hammer, private interview, Ramat Gan, April 30, 1981.

25. Uri Elitzur, private interview, Jerusalem, July 31, 1980.

26. Rabbi Yohanan Fried, private interview, Jerusalem, August 28, 1980.

27. Yitzhak Rabin, private interview, Tel Aviv, May 2, 1980.

28. *Ibid.*

29. Gershon Shafat, private interview, Tel Aviv, May 1, 1980.

30. Yitzhak Rabin, private interview, Tel Aviv, May 2, 1980.

31. Binyamin Katzover, private interview, Qedumim, March 1, 1981.

32. Yitzhak Rabin, private interview, Tel Aviv, May 2, 1980.

Chapter 11

1. Hanan Porat, private interview, Kfar 'Etzion, September 16, 1980.

2. Truman, *Governmental Process*, p. 296.

3. Uri Elitzur, private interview, Jerusalem, August 13, 1980.

4. Gershon Shafat, private interview, Tel Aviv, May 1, 1980.

5. Beer, *British Politics in the Collectivist Age*, pp. 318–51; and Kirchheimer, "The Transformation of the Western European Party Systems," pp. 177–200.

6. Zevulun Hammer, private interview, Ramat Gan, April 30, 1981.

7. *Ibid.*

8. Menachem Begin, private interview, Jerusalem, February 6, 1981.

9. *Ibid.*

10. Yehudah Ben-Meir, private interview, Savion, November 21, 1980.

11. Zevulun Hammer, private interview, Ramat Gan, April 30, 1981.

12. Yehudah Ben-Meir, private interview, Tel Aviv, July 10, 1980.

Chapter 12

1. In October, the Democratic Movement for Change, a party that did not share Gush Emunim's foreign policy aims, joined the coalition, but the DMC factor does not seem to have affected Government-group relations during the 1977 summer period.

2. Menachem Begin, private interview, Jerusalem, February 6, 1981.

3. *Ibid.*

4. Press accounts attribute statements to Gush Emunim members. Yechiel Kadishai, director of the Prime Minister's Bureau, claims that Gush

Emunim approached the press and not vice versa. Moreover, a Gush Emunim member stated that they never accepted the premise of the September agreement that sites would be considered military areas. When agreeing to the Government plan, they had told officials, "call it what you will, we consider them settlements."

5. Aryeh Naor, Government Secretary, private interview, Jerusalem, December 29, 1980.

6. "Gush Emunim Established 16 Settlements in the West Bank within 6 Months," (Hebrew), *Ha-Aretz*, April 24, 1978.

7. Uri Elitzur, private interview, Jerusalem, August 13, 1980.

8. "Army Stops Reporters From Visiting Gush Emunim Settlement," *Jerusalem Post*, June 8, 1978, p. 2.

9. Yehudah Ben-Meir, private interview, Savion, November 21, 1980.

10. *Ibid.*

11. Gershon Shafat, private interview, Tel Aviv, May 1, 1980.

12. "Hanan Porat: The Settlers of the Territories Will Break Begin," (Hebrew), *Ha-Aretz*, December 29, 1977.

13. Yehudah Ben-Meir, private interview, Savion, November 21, 1980.

14. *Ibid.*

15. Ariel Sharon, private interview, Jerusalem, March 17, 1981.

16. The accords consisted of two framework agreements, providing a working basis for a peace treaty between Egypt and Israel. Relevant to this discussion, Israel agreed to return the Sinai to Egyptian sovereignty and, pending Kneset approval, to withdraw from Sinai settlements. The accords also provided for autonomy to Arabs of the West Bank and Gaza for a five year transitional period at the conclusion of which the final status of the territories would be negotiated. The status of West Bank settlements was not explicitly addressed in the framework agreements. After the Camp David session, a dispute arose about whether Begin had promised to freeze West Bank settlement for three months until a peace treaty with Egypt was concluded or for the duration of any negotiations with other Arab parties.

17. Yehudah Ben-Meir, private interview, Savion, November 21, 1980.

18. Gershon Shafat, private interview, Tel Aviv, May 1, 1980.

19. Binyamin Katzover, private interview, Qedumim, March 1, 1981 and Gershon Shafat, private interview, Tel Aviv, May 1, 1980.

20. Zevulun Hammer, private interview, Ramat Gan, April 30, 1981.

21. Yehudah Ben-Meir, private interview, Savion, November 21, 1980.

22. Gershon Shafat, private interview, Tel Aviv, May 1, 1980.

23. *Ibid.*

24. Yehudah Ben-Meir, private interview, Savion, November 21, 1980.

25. Rabbi Hayyim Druckman, private interview, Tel Aviv, October 12, 1980.

26. Hanan Porat, private interview, Kfar 'Etzion, July 24, 1980.

27. Yehudah Ben-Meir, private interview, Savion, November 21, 1980.

28. Hanan Porat, private interview, Kfar 'Etzion, July 24, 1980.

29. Zvi Slonim, private interview, New York City, October 27, 1988.

30. *Ibid.*

31. Aviva Shabi, "Crisis in the Gush," *Yediot Ahranot* (Hebrew), May 15, 1987, pp. 5, 26.

32. Zvi Slonim, private interview, New York City, October 27, 1988.

33. Zvi Slonim, private interview, New York City, October 27, 1988 and Hanan Porat, private interview, Kfar 'Etzion, July 24, 1980.

Chapter 13

1. Kirchheimer, "The Transformation of the Western European Party Systems," p. 193.

2. Truman, *Governmental Process*, p. 272.

3. Beer, *British Politics in the Collectivist Age*, p. 351, and "Group Representation in British and American Democracy," pp. 130–40.

4. Kirchheimer, "The Transformation of the Western European Party Systems," p. 197.

5. *Ibid.*, p. 200.

Bibliography

Books and Articles

Agricultural Center. *Devarim be-Ve'ida ha-Haqlayit ha-Shtaym-esray.* ("Proceedings of the Twelfth Agricultural Conference.") Tel Aviv: The Agricultural Center, July 1974.

Akzin, Benjamin. "The Role of Parties in Israeli Democracy." *Journal of Politics,* XVII (November 1955), 507–45.

Almond, Gabriel A. "Research Note: A Comparative Study of Interest Groups and the Political Process." *American Political Science Review,* LII (March 1958), 270–82.

_____, and Powell, G. Bingham, Jr. *Comparative Politics: A Developmental Approach.* Boston: Little, Brown, and Company, 1966.

Alpert, Carl. "What Future for General Zionist Kibbutzim?" *New Palestine,* October 27, 1949, p. 10.

Anderson, Charles W. "Political Design and the Representation of Interests." *Comparative Political Studies,* X (April 1977), 127–52.

Arian, Alan. *The Choosing People.* Cleveland: Press of Case Western Reserve University, 1973.

_____, ed. *The Elections in Israel—1969.* Jerusalem: Jerusalem Academic Press, 1972.

_____, ed. *The Elections in Israel—1973.* Jerusalem: Jerusalem Academic Press, 1975.

_____. *Ideological Change in Israel.* Cleveland: The Press of Case Western Reserve University, 1968.

_____, Asher. *Politics in Israel: The Second Generation.* Chatham, New Jersey: Chatham House Publishers, 1985.

273

Aronoff, Myron J. *Power and Ritual in the Israel Labor Party: A Study in Political Anthropology.* Amsterdam/Assen:Van Gorcum, 1977.

Avneri, Efrayim. "Credit Problems in Kibbutz Settlement." (Hebrew), *Niv ha-Kvutzah,* V (January 1956), 40–49.

Bahir, Aryeh. "Our Settlement Aims." (Hebrew), *Niv ha-Kvutzah,* III (December 1953), 30–53.

Balbus, Isaac D. "The Concept of Interest in Pluralist and Marxian Analysis." *Politics and Society,* I (February 1971).

Barkai, Haim. "The Public, Histadrut, and Private Sectors in the Israeli Economy." *Falk Project for Economic Research in Israel, Sixth Report, 1961–1963.* Jerusalem: Falk Project for Economic Research in Israel, April 1964.

Bayne, E. *Four Ways to Politics: Dynamics of Political Parties.* New York: American Universities Field Staff, 1965.

Beer, Samuel H. *British Politics in the Collectivist Age.* New York: Vintage Books, 1969.

———. "Group Representation in British and American Democracy." *The Annals of the American Academy of Political Science,* LLLXIX (September 1958), 130–40.

———. "Pressure Groups and Parties in Britain." *American Political Science Review,* L (March 1956), 1–23.

———. "The Representation of Interests in British Government: Historical Background." *American Political Science Review,* LI (September 1957), 613–50.

Berger, Suzanne, ed. *Organizing Interests in Western Europe: Pluralism, Corporatism and the Transformation of Politics.* Cambridge: Cambridge University Press, 1981.

Bernstein, Marver. *The Politics of Israel: The First Decade of Statehood.* Princeton: Princeton University Press, 1957.

Birnbaum, Ervin. *State and Religion in Israel.* Rutherford: Fairleigh Dickinson University Press, 1970.

Clawson, M. "Israel Agriculture in Recent Years." *Agricultural History,* XXIX (1955), 49–65.

———. "Man and Land in Israel." *Agricultural History,* XXXV (1961), 189–92.

Cohen, Seymour J. "The General Zionist Program in Israel." *New Palestine,* October 29, 1948, p. 6.

———. "General Zionism's Role." *New Palestine,* March 31, 1948, p. 10.

Connolly, William E., ed. *The Bias of Pluralism*. New York: Atherton Press, Inc., 1969.

"Council of Ihud Hakibbutzim Meets." *Israel Labor News*, October 10, 1952, p. 2.

Curtis, Michael and Mordecai S. Chertoff, *Israel: Social Structure and Change*. New Brunswick, New Jersey: Transaction Books, 1973.

Dahl, Robert A. *Modern Political Analysis*. Englewood Cliffs: Prentice Hall, Inc., 1963.

_____. *Pluralist Democracy in the United States: Conflict and Consent*. Chicago: Rand McNally & Company, 1967.

_____. *Who Governs? Democracy and Power in an American City*. New Haven: Yale University Press, 1961.

Dahrendorf, Ralf. *Class and Class Conflict in Industrial Society*. Stanford: Stanford University Press, 1959.

Darin-Drabkin, H. *The Other Society*. London: Gollancz, 1962.

Divine, Donna Robinson. "The Modernization of the Israeli Administration." *International Journal of Middle East Studies*, V (June 1974), 295–313.

Duverger, Maurice. *Party Politics and Pressure Groups: A Comparative Introduction*. Translated by David Wagoner. New York: Thomas Y. Crowell Co., 1972.

Eckstein, Harry. *Pressure Group Politics: The Case of the British Medical Association*. Stanford: Stanford University Press, 1960.

Ehrmann, Henry W., ed. *Interest Groups on Four Continents*. Pittsburgh: University of Pittsburgh Press, 1958.

Eisenstadt, S. N. "Israel." *The Institutions of Advanced Society*. Edited by A. M. Rose. Minneapolis: University of Minnesota Press, 1958.

_____. *Israeli Society*. London: Weidenfeld & Nicolson, 1967.

_____. *Modernization: Protest and Change*. Englewood Cliffs: Prentice-Hall, Inc., 1966.

_____, and Bar-Yosef, Rivkah; and Adler, Chaim, eds. *Integration and Development in Israel*. New York: Frederick A. Praeger, Inc., 1970.

Epstein, E. M. "Zionism: General or Partisan?" *Zionist Review*, April 4, 1947, p. 7.

Epstein, Elias. "New Strength, New Responsibilities for the General Zionists; An Analysis of the Israel Elections." *New Palestine*, December 1950, p. 6.

Epstein, Leon D. *Political Parties in Western Democracies*. New York: Frederick A. Praeger, 1967.

Esping-Andersen, Gosta. "Social Class, Social Democracy, and the State: Party Policy and Party Decomposition in Denmark and Sweden." *Comparative Politics*, XI (October 1978), 42–58.

Etzioni, Amitai. "Agrarianism in Israel's Party System." *Canadian Journal of Economic and Political Science*, XXIII (August 1957), 363–75.

_____. "Alternative Ways to Democracy: The Example of Israel." *Political Science Quarterly*, CXXIV (June 1959), 196–214.

_____. "The Decline of Neo-Feudalism in Israel." *Studies in Social Change.* New York: Holt, Rinehart, & Winston, Inc., 1966.

Etzioni-Halevy, Eva. "Protest Politics in the Israeli Democracy." *Political Science Quarterly*, XC (Fall 1975), 497–520.

_____, and Shapira, Rina. *Political Culture in Israel: Cleavage and Integration Among Israeli Jews.* New York: Frederick A. Praeger, Inc., 1977.

Fein, Leonard J. *Israel: Politics and People.* Boston: Little, Brown, and Co., 1968.

_____. *Politics in Israel.* Boston: Little, Brown, and Company, 1967.

Fingerote, Fred L. "General Zionist Policy." *Herzl Zion Digest*, April 1949, pp. 10–11.

Flink, Salomon J. *Israel: Chaos and Challenge: Politics Vs. Economics.* Ramat Gan: Turtledove Publishing, 1979.

Foreign Area Studies of the American University. *Area Handbook for Israel.* Washington: U.S. Government Printing Office, 1970.

Freudenheim, Yehoshua. *Government in Israel.* Dobbs Ferry: Oceana Publications, Inc., 1967.

Gafny, Arnon. "Trends in Israel's Economy-Lessons and Prospects." Address by the Governor of the Bank of Israel to the Commercial and Industrial Club, Tel Aviv, January 14, 1973. (Mimeo located at Zionist Archives, New York.)

"General Zionist Parties Merge." Jewish Agency Palestine Information Office Digest Press and Events, May 26, 1946, pp. 25–26.

"General Zionists Conference at Tel Aviv." *Ha-'Olam*, November 24, 1949, p. 133.

"General Zionists' Economic Program." *Business Digest*, July 5, 1951, pp. 119–20.

Goldstein, Dr. Israel. "The Need for a Unified Center Party; the General Zionist Victory." *New Palestine*, December 1950, p. 6.

Gutmann, Emanuel. "Israel." *International Social Science Journal*, XII, No. 1 (1960), 53–62.

_____. "Israel." *Journal of Politics*, XXV (November 1963), 703–17.

_____. "Some Observations on Politics and Parties in Israel." *India Quarterly,* XVII (January–March 1961), 3–29.

Gvati, Hayyim. "Ways for Developing Agriculture." (Hebrew), *Niv ha-Kvutzah,* IX (March 1960), 11–21.

_____. Manuscript in Hebrew for a book not yet published on the history of agriculture in Israel.

Halevi, Nadav and Klinov-Malul, Ruth. *The Economic Development of Israel.* New York: Frederick A. Praeger, 1968.

Halpern, Ben. "The Politically Divided Communes." *Jewish Frontier,* September 1951, pp. 17–19.

Hancock, M. Donald. "Productivity, Welfare, and Participation in Sweden and West Germany: A Comparison of Social Democratic Reform Prospects." *Comparative Politics,* XI (October 1978), 4–23.

Horowitz, David. *The Economics of Israel.* Oxford: Pergamon Press, 1967.

_____. *The Enigma of Economic Growth: A Case Study of Israel.* New York: Frederick A. Praeger, 1972.

Huntington, Samuel P. "The Change to Change: Modernization, Development, and Politics." *Comparative Politics,* III (April 1971), 283–322.

_____. *Political Order in Changing Societies.* New Haven: Yale University Press, 1968.

Hurewitz, J. C. *Middle East Politics: The Military Dimension.* New York: Frederick A. Praeger, 1967.

_____. *The Struggle for Palestine.* New York: W. W. Norton & Company, Inc., 1950.

"Interviews with the Secretaries of Takam." (Hebrew), *Mibifnim,* XLVIII (July 1986), 99–115.

Isaac, Rael Jean. *Israel Divided: Ideological Politics in the Jewish State.* Baltimore: The Johns Hopkins University Press, 1976.

"Israel, State of (Economic Affairs)." *Encyclopaedia Judaica.* 1971. Vol. IX.

"Israel, State of (Economic Affairs)." *Encyclopaedia Judaica Decennial Yearbook 1973–1982.*

Israel, Government of. Ministry of Agriculture and Bank of Israel. *The Economy and Agriculture of Israel.* Jerusalem: Jerusalem Post Press, 1959.

Israel, State of. Ministry of Commerce and Industry. Center for Industrial Planning. *Plan for the Development of Industry in 1971–1976–1981.* May 1973.

Israel, State of. Prime Minister's Office. Economic Planning Authority. *Israel Economic Development: Past Progress and Plan for the Future.* Jerusalem: March 1968.

Kalfon, Moshe. "After the Election Campaign for the Eleventh Kneset." (Hebrew), *Mibifnim*, XLVI (November 1984), 447–52.

Kanovsky, Eliyahu. *The Economy of the Israeli Kibbutz.* Cambridge: Harvard University Press, 1966.

Kariel, Henry. *The Decline of American Pluralism.* Stanford: Stanford University Press, 1961.

Kesselman, Mark. "The Conflictual Evolution of American Political Science: From Apologetic Pluralism to Trilateralism and Marxism." *Public Values and Private Power in American Politics.* Edited by J. David Greenstone. Chicago: University of Chicago Press, 1982.

Key, V. O., Jr. *Politics, Parties, and Pressure Groups.* New York: Thomas Y. Crowell Co., 1964.

Kirchheimer, Otto. "The Transformation of Western European Party Systems." *Political Parties and Political Development.* Edited by Joseph LaPalombara and Myron Weiner. Princeton: Princeton University Press, 1966.

Kornhauser, William. *The Politics of Mass Society.* Glencoe, Ill.: The Free Press, 1959.

Lazar, David. "Israel's Political Structure and Social Issues." *Jewish Journal of Sociology*, XV (June 1973), 23–44.

Lehmbruch, Gerhard. "Liberal Corporatism and Party Government." *Comparative Political Studies*, X (April 1977), 91–126.

Lerner, Abba and Ben-Shahar, Haim. *The Economics of Efficiency and Growth: Lessons from Israel and the West Bank.* Cambridge, Mass.: Ballinger Publishing Company, 1975.

Lijphart, Arendt. *Democracy in Plural Societies.* New Haven: Yale University Press, 1977.

Likhovski, Eliahu. S. *Israel's Parliament: The Law of the Knesset.* Oxford: Clarendon Press, 1971.

Lissak, Moshe. "Patterns of Change in Ideology and Class Structure in Israel." *Jewish Journal of Sociology*, VII (February 1965), 46–62.

_____, and Gutmann, Emanuel, eds. *Political Institutions and Processes.* Jerusalem: The Hebrew University, 1971.

Lustick, Ian S. *For the Land and the Lord, Jewish Fundamentalism in Israel.* New York: Council on Foreign Relations, Inc., 1988.

Luz, Kadish. "The Movement in Its Trials." (Hebrew), *Niv ha-Kvutzah*, IV (September 1955), 654–61.

McConnell, Grant. *Private Power and American Democracy.* New York: Vintage Books, 1970.

Mahler, Gregory S. *The Knesset.* Rutherford: Fairleigh Dickinson University Press, 1981.

Mandel, Meir. "In These Days and Beyond Them." (Hebrew), *Niv ha-Kvutzah*, V (April 1956), 232–42.

Mandelbaum, Paulette Ann. "Pollution and the Making of Public Policy: Israel, 1965–1975." Unpublished Ph.D. dissertation, Columbia University, 1977.

Maor, Yitzhaq. "The Kibbutz and the Party." (Hebrew), *Niv ha-Kvutzah*, IV (September 1955), 670–76.

Margalit, Ya'aqov. "To Wake Up the Party." (Hebrew), *Niv ha-Kvutzah*, V (July 1956), 425–34.

Medding, Peter Y. *Mapai in Israel: Political Organization and Government in a New Society.* Cambridge: Cambridge University Press, 1972.

Merhav, Peretz. *The Israeli Left: History, Problems, Documents.* San Diego: A. S. Barnes & Company, Inc., 1980.

Nachmias, David. "A Note on Coalition Payoffs in a Dominant Party System: Israel." *Political Studies*, XXI (Summer 1973), 301–5.

_____. "Right Wing Opposition in Israel." *Political Studies*, XXIV (September 1976), 268–79.

_____. "Status Inconsistency and Political Opposition: A Case Study of an Israeli Minority Group." *Middle East Journal*, XXVII (Autumn 1973), 456–70.

"The New Alignment in the Kibbutz Movement." *Il Hamekasher*, August 1951, pp. 6–12.

"New Kibbutz Union Formed: Ichud Hakibbutzim Vehakvutzot." *Israel Youth Horizon*, November–December 1951, pp. 13–14.

Newmann, Dr. Emanuel. "Israel's Peaceful Revolution, the Victory of the General Zionists and Its Implications; Emergence of a Liberal Center." *New Palestine*, December 1950, p. 5.

Ofir, Aryeh. "Convening the Eighth Convention." (Hebrew), *Niv ha-Kvutzah*, V (July 1956), 416–25.

_____. "The Eighth Convention and Its Lessons." (Hebrew), *Niv ha-Kvutzah*, V (October 1956), 606–13.

"Our Program, General Zionist Organization – Centre Party." *Business Digest*, July 5, 1951, p. 121.

Pack, Howard. *Structural Change and Economic Policy in Israel*. New Haven: Yale University Press, 1971.

Panitch, Leo. "The Development of Corporatism in Liberal Democracies." *Comparative Political Studies*, X (April 1977), 61–89.

_____. "Recent Theorizations of Corporatism: Reflections on a Growth Industry." *British Journal of Sociology*, XXXI (June 1980), 159–87.

_____. *Social Democracy and Industrial Militancy: The Labour Party, the Trade Unions and Incomes Policy 1945–1974*. Cambridge: Cambridge University Press, 1976.

_____. "Trade Unions and the Capitalist State." *New Left Review*, n.v., No. 125 (January–February 1981), 21–44.

Patinkin, Don. "The Israel Economy: the First Decade." *Falk Project for Economic Research in Israel, Fourth Report, 1957 and 1958*. Jerusalem: Falk Project for Economic Research in Israel, November 1959.

Penniman, Howard R., ed. *Israel at the Polls: The Knesset Elections of 1977*. Washington, D. C.: American Enterprise Institute for Public Policy Research, 1979.

Plamenatz, John. "Interest." *Political Studies*, II (February 1954), 1–8.

Plasner, Yakir and Efrat, Yisrael. *Shitat ha-Ashrai Merukaz ve-Trumatah le-Ma'amado ha-Kalkali shel ha-Mesheq ha-Kibbutzi*. ("The Method of Concentrated Credit and Its Contribution to the Economic Position of the Kibbutz Economy.") Rehovot: The Research Center for Agricultural Economics, 1971.

"On the Political Way of the Takam, a 'Mibifnim' Interview with Eli Zamir and Yosef Permutter – Secretaries of the Movement." (Hebrew), *Mibifnim*, XLIV (October 1982), 211–21.

Raz, Nahman. "In the Wake of the 1984 Elections." (Hebrew), *Mibifnim*, XLVI (November 1984), 441–52.

"Report of the Ihud Convention." *Furrows*, December 1953, pp. 14–15, 18.

Ross, Philip E. "Israeli Economic Dependence." Unpublished paper, Middle East Institute, Columbia University, May 1980. (Located at Zionist Archives, New York.)

Rubner, Alex. *The Economy of Israel: A Critical Account of the First Ten Years*. London: Frank Cass, 1960.

Safran, Nadav. *Israel: The Embattled Ally*. Cambridge: Harvard University Press, 1978.

_____. *Israel Today: A Profile.* New York: Foreign Policy Association, 1965.

_____. *The United States and Israel.* Cambridge: Harvard University Press, 1963.

Sanbar, Moshe. "The Political Economy of Israel, 1948–1980." *Jerusalem Letter,* No. 36. Jerusalem: The Jerusalem Center, December 8, 1980.

Sasson, Yechiel. "The Birth of a New Kibbutz Movement." *Furrows,* December 1952, pp. 9–13.

Schiff, Gary. *Tradition and Politics: The Religious Parties of Israel.* Detroit: Wayne State University Press, 1977.

Schnall, David J. *Radical Dissent in Contemporary Israeli Politics: Cracks in the Wall.* New York: Frederick A. Praeger, Inc., 1979.

Schwartzbart, Dr. I. "Decisive Moment for General Zionism." *New Palestine,* December 13, 1949, p. 14.

"The Second Convention of the Ihud ha-Kvutzot Ve-ha-Kibbutzim." (Hebrew), *Niv ha-Kvutzah,* III (December 1953), 5–10.

Seligman, Lester G. *Leadership in a New Nation: Political Development in Israel.* New York: Atherton Press, 1964.

Shapiro, Yonathan. *Ha-Demoqratiyah be-Yisrael.* ("Democracy in Israel.") Ramat Gan: Masada, 1977.

_____. *The Formative Years of the Israeli Labour Party: The Organization of Power 1919–1930.* London and Beverly Hills: Sage Publications Ltd., 1976.

Sherman, Neal. "From Government to Opposition: The Rural Settlement Movements of the Israel Labor Party in the Wake of the Election of 1977." *International Journal of Middle East Studies,* XIV (February 1982), 53–69.

Shoshani, Eliezer. "The Ihud as a Result of Changes." (Hebrew), *Niv ha-Kvutzah,* V (July 1956), 407–15.

Skidell, A. "Kibbutz Convention in Kinerret." *Habonim,* January 1952, p. 18.

Torczyner, J. "Future of General Zionism." *Jewish Standard* (London), August 12, 1949, p. 3.

Toshav, A. "The Struggle for Control." (Hebrew), *Ha-Doar,* November 11, 1949, pp. 27–30.

Truman, David B. *The Governmental Process: Political Interests and Public Opinion.* New York: Alfred A. Knopf, 1971.

"Union of Kvutzot and Kibbutzim." *Israel Life and Letters.* January–April 1952, p. 108.

U. S. Department of Labor. Bureau of International Labor Affairs. *Country Labor Profile: Israel*, by Les Finnegan and Margaret L. Plunket, 1979.

Vaidler, Yehoshua. "The Economy in the State and in the Agricultural Sector." (Hebrew), *Niv ha-Kvutzah*, V (April 1956), 224–31.

Willner, Dorothy. "Politics and Change in Israel: The Case of Land Settlement." *Human Organization*, XXIV (Spring 1965), 65–72.

Wootton, Graham. *Interest Groups*. Englewood Cliffs: Prentice-Hall, Inc., 1970.

Yishai, Yael. "Interest Groups in Israel." *Jerusalem Quarterly* (Spring 1979), pp. 128–44.

Yoseftal, Senta. "The Kibbutz Economy at Its Foundation." (Hebrew), *Niv ha-Kvutzah*, V (January 1956), 50–54.

Zidon, Asher. *Knesset: The Parliament of Israel*. Translated by Aryeh Rubinstein and Gertrude Hirschler. New York: Herzl Press, 1967.

Unpublished Material and Group Papers

Agricultural Center. Minutes of Meetings of the Settlement Committee, 1955–1957.

_____. Minutes of Meetings of the Economics Committee, 1956–1959.

Avneri, Efrayim. Private interviews. Kibbutz Hulda, April–May 1981.

Barnatan, Yehudah. Private interviews. Tel Aviv, June 4, 13, 1980.

Baron, Uri. Private interview. Tel Aviv, August 28, 1980.

Begin, Menachem. Private interview. Jerusalem, February 6, 1981.

Ben-Meir, Yehudah. Private interviews. Tel Aviv and Savion, May 18, July 10, November 21, 1980.

Ben Ya'aqov, Eliezer. Private interview. Tel Aviv, April 28, 1981.

Biton, Charlie. Private interview. Jerusalem, May 3, 1981.

Council of Jewish Settlements in Judea and Samaria, Gaza District, and the Jordan Valley. List of representatives, Gush Emunim Jerusalem office files, November 2, 1978.

_____. Platform of a Council of Jewish Settlements in Judea and Samaria, Gaza, and the Jordan Valley, Gush Emunim Jerusalem office files, n.d. (Typed sheet.)

Crystal, A. Z. Private interviews. Tel Aviv, May 6, June 17, and telephone, October 23, 1980.

Druckman, Hayyim. Private interview. October 12 and telephone, October 20, 1980.

Elitzur, Uri. Private interviews. July 31, August 13, 1980.

Epstein, Gershon. Private interview. Queens, New York, November 8, 1988.

Fried, Yohanan. Private interview. Jerusalem, August 28, 1980.

Gali, Ya'aqov. Private interview. New York, October 25, 1988.

General Zionist Party. List of party committees, March 4, 1956, located in minutes of meetings of the Executive Committee.

_____. Membership list of directorate, July 22, 1954, located in minutes of meetings of the Executive Committee.

_____. Minutes of Meetings of the Executive Committee. Meetings of December 15, 1952; September 8, 1955; and September 14, 1955.

Group for Settling Shekhem. Draft of letter to Golda Meir from Binyamin Katzover in the name of the group that wants to settle at Shekhem, files at Qedumim, 21 Iyar 5733. [May 23, 1973.]

_____. Draft of letter to Yigal Allon from Binyamin Katzover in the name of the group that wants to settle at Shekhem, files at Qedumim, 21 Iyar 5733. [May 23, 1973.]

_____. Draft of letter to Minister of Communication Shimon Peres from the Group for Settling Shekhem, files at Qedumim, 11 Sivan 5733. [June 11, 1973.]

_____. Letter to Prime Minister Golda Meir from the committee of the group, files at Qedumim, 5 Elul 5733. [September 2, 1973.]

_____. Secretariat. Internal memo, files at Qedumim, 9 Elul 5733. [September 6, 1973.]

_____. Letter to Minister Zerah Varhaftig from the Group for Settling Shekhem, files at Qedumim, dated Sabbath Vayishlah, probably November 1973.

_____. Letter to Menachem Begin from Yo'ezer Ariel and Yosef Porat on stationery of the Group for Settling Shekhem, files at Qedumim, Sabbath Eve Vayishlah, probably November 1973.

_____. Letter to MK Zevulun Hammer from Yo'ezer Ariel and Yosef Porat in the name of the Group for Settling Shekhem, files at Qedumim, Sabbath Eve Vayishlah, probably November 1973.

_____. Letter to Yosef Porat of the Group for Settling Shekhem from Menachem Begin, files at Qedumim, 26 Kislev 5734. [December 21, 1973.]

_____. Letter to Beni Katzover from Zevulun Hammer, Deputy Minister for Education and Culture, files at Qedumim,∖ 20 Kislev 5734. [December 25, 1973.]

_____. Report on Activities of the Group, flyer, personal files of Hanan Porat, n.d., probably late 1973 or early 1974.

_____. Flyer to members, personal files of Hanan Porat, n.d., probably end of 1973.

_____. Letter to Hanan Porat from a leader of the Group for Settling Shekhem about starting to publicize their existence and pressure the NRP, personal files of Hanan Porat, 9 Tevet 5734. [January 3, 1974.]

_____. Letter to Minister of Defense Moshe Dayan from the Group for Settling Shekhem, files at Qedumim, 8 Tevet 5734. [January 2, 1974.]

_____. Letter to MK Menachem Begin from the Group for Settling Shekhem, files at Qedumim, 8 Tevet 5734. [January 2, 1974.]

_____. Letter to Minister of Interior Yosef Burg from the Group for Settling Shekhem, files at Qedumim, 12 Tevet 5734. [January 6, 1974.]

_____. Report on activities, files at Qedumim, n.d., probably early 1974. (Typed.)

_____. Notes on a meeting of three women settlers with the Prime Minister, files at Qedumim, n.d., probably late 1973 or early 1974.

_____. Letter to MK Shlomo Gross from the Group for Settling Shekhem, files at Qedumim, 22 Tevet 5734. [January 16, 1974.]

_____. Letter to Menachem Begin from the Group for Settling Shekhem, files at Qedumim, 22 Tevet 5734. [January 16, 1974.]

_____. Letter to Minister Yosef Burg from the Group for Settling Shekhem, files at Qedumim, 26 Tevet 5734. [January 20, 1974.]

_____. Letter to MK Yigal Hurvitz from the Group for Settling Shekhem, files at Qedumim, 1 Shvat 5734. [January 24, 1974.]

_____. Letter to MK Ariel Sharon from the Group for Settling Shekhem, files at Qedumim, start of month Shvat 5734. [January 24, 1974.]

_____. Letter to MK Shmuel Tamir from the Group for Settling Shekhem, files at Qedumim, 1 Shvat 5734. [January 24, 1974.]

_____. Form letters for sending to officials from the Group for Settling Shekhem, files at Qedumim, 4 Shvat 5734. [January 27, 1974.]

_____. Letter to Yosef Porat and Yo'ezer Ariel from the Director of the Prime Minister's Bureau, files at Qedumim, 4 Shvat 5734. [January 28, 1974.]

————. Letter to Mafdal representatives in the committee negotiating on the coalition, files at Qedumim, 6 Shvat 5734. [January 29, 1974.]

————. Letter to the Group for Settling Shekhem from Zevulun Hammer, Deputy Minister of Education and Culture, files at Qedumim, 7 Shvat 5734. [January 30, 1974.]

————. Letter to Minister of Interior Yosef Burg from the Group for Settling Shekhem, files at Qedumim, 8 Shvat 5734. [January 31, 1974.]

————. Letter to MK Yehudah Ben-Meir from the Group for Settling Shekhem, files at Qedumim, 8 Shvat 5734. [January 31, 1974.]

————. Letter to Minister of Defense Moshe Dayan from the Group for Settling Shekhem, files at Qedumim, 8 Shvat 5734. [January 31, 1974.]

————. Letter to Minister Yosef Burg, files at Qedumim, 11 Shvat 5734. [February 3, 1974.]

————. Press Release, files at Qedumim, February 5, 1974.

————. Letter to the Group for Settling Shekhem from Dr. A. Rimalt, chairman of the Liberal Party, files at Qedumim, 14 Shvat 5734. [February 6, 1974.]

————. Draft of letter to Yosef Burg from Beni Katzover in the name of the group, files at Qedumim, 24 Adar 5734. [March 18, 1974.]

————. Draft of letter to Minister of Defense Moshe Dayan from Binyamin Katzover for the Group for Settling Shekhem, files at Qedumim, 24 Adar 5734. [March 18, 1974.]

————. Letter to Beni Katzover from Moshe Dayan, files at Qedumim, March 26, 1974.

————. Minutes of Meeting, files at Qedumim, n.d., probably spring, 1974. (Handwritten.)

————. Draft of letter to Minister Galili, files at Qedumim, 9 Sivan 5734. [May 30, 1974.]

————. Draft of letter to Prime Minister Rabin from Beni Katzover in the name of the group, files at Qedumim, 9 Sivan 5734. [May 30, 1974.]

————. Letter to Prime Minister Rabin from Beni Katzover in the name of the group, files at Qedumim, 9 Sivan 5734. [May 30, 1974.]

————. Draft of letter to Minister of Defense Shimon Peres, files at Qedumim, 9 Sivan 5734. [May 30, 1974.]

————. Draft of letter to Minister Gad Ya'aqobi from Beni Katzover for the Group for Settling Shekhem, files at Qedumim, 9 Sivan 5734. [May 30, 1974.]

_____. Draft of letter to members of Kneset from Beni Katzover in the name of the group, files at Qedumim, 9 Sivan 5734. [May 30, 1974.]

_____. Draft of letter to Kneset members Hammer, Ben-Meir, Sharon, and Geula Cohen thanking them for help in the attempt to go to Shekhem, files at Qedumim, 17 Sivan 5734. [June 7, 1974.]

_____. Draft of letter to Prime Minister Rabin from Beni Katzover in the name of the group, files at Qedumim, 19 Sivan 5734. [June 9, 1974.]

_____. Letter to Kneset members from Binyamin Katzover for the Group for Settling Shekhem, files at Qedumim, 26 Sivan 5734. [June 16, 1974.]

_____. Draft of press release, files at Qedumim, 25 Tamuz 5734. [July 15, 1974.]

_____. Minutes of Meeting of the "Elon Moreh Nucleus," files at Qedumim, 11 Av 5734. [July 1974.]

Gush Emunim. Minutes of Meetings.
Summary of meeting of the Political Committee, personal files of Yohanan Fried, 18 Heshvan 5735. [November 3, 1974.]

Summary of meeting of the Secretariat and Political Committee, personal files of Yohanan Fried, 23 Heshvan 5735. [November 8, 1974.]

Decisions from Secretariat meeting of January 13, 1975, personal files of Yohanan Fried, memo of 1 Shvat 5735. [January 14, 1975.]

Summary of January 15, 1975 Secretariat meeting, personal files of Yohanan Fried, memo of 7 Shvat 5735. [January 19, 1975.]

Report of Meeting of the Publicity Committee, personal files of Yohanan Fried, 29 Shvat 5735. [February 10, 1975.]

Meeting to discuss settlements and planning settlements, Jerusalem office files, March 23, 1975. (Handwritten.)

Meeting of the Secretariat, personal files of Yohanan Fried, 20 Adar, no year, probably 1975.

Summary of Meeting of the Settlement Committee, personal files of Hanan Porat, Heshvan 5737. [October–November 1976.]

Meeting of the Secretariat, Jerusalem office files, n.d., probably 1977 before elections. (Handwritten.)

Meeting of the Secretariat, points for discussion at a Council meeting about establishing a fund, Jerusalem office files, n.d., (Typed sheet.)

Notes of a meeting of treasurers of Gush Emunim settlements with Mr. Moskowitz in the Interior Ministry, Jerusalem office files, August 7, 1978.

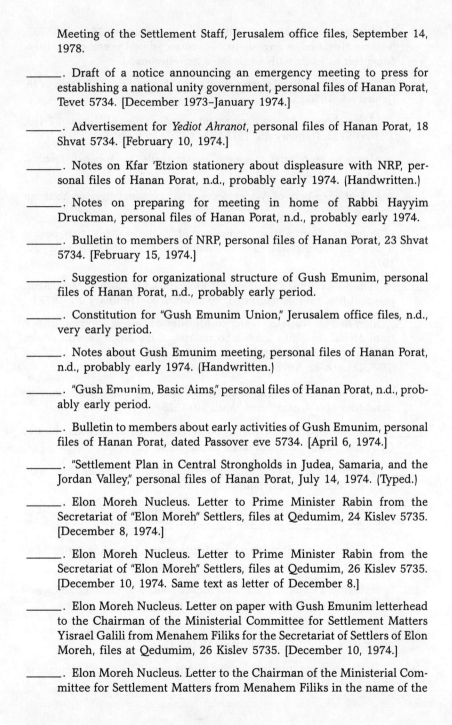

Meeting of the Settlement Staff, Jerusalem office files, September 14, 1978.

_____. Draft of a notice announcing an emergency meeting to press for establishing a national unity government, personal files of Hanan Porat, Tevet 5734. [December 1973–January 1974.]

_____. Advertisement for *Yediot Ahranot*, personal files of Hanan Porat, 18 Shvat 5734. [February 10, 1974.]

_____. Notes on Kfar 'Etzion stationery about displeasure with NRP, personal files of Hanan Porat, n.d., probably early 1974. (Handwritten.)

_____. Notes on preparing for meeting in home of Rabbi Hayyim Druckman, personal files of Hanan Porat, n.d., probably early 1974.

_____. Bulletin to members of NRP, personal files of Hanan Porat, 23 Shvat 5734. [February 15, 1974.]

_____. Suggestion for organizational structure of Gush Emunim, personal files of Hanan Porat, n.d., probably early period.

_____. Constitution for "Gush Emunim Union," Jerusalem office files, n.d., very early period.

_____. Notes about Gush Emunim meeting, personal files of Hanan Porat, n.d., probably early 1974. (Handwritten.)

_____. "Gush Emunim, Basic Aims," personal files of Hanan Porat, n.d., probably early period.

_____. Bulletin to members about early activities of Gush Emunim, personal files of Hanan Porat, dated Passover eve 5734. [April 6, 1974.]

_____. "Settlement Plan in Central Strongholds in Judea, Samaria, and the Jordan Valley," personal files of Hanan Porat, July 14, 1974. (Typed.)

_____. Elon Moreh Nucleus. Letter to Prime Minister Rabin from the Secretariat of "Elon Moreh" Settlers, files at Qedumim, 24 Kislev 5735. [December 8, 1974.]

_____. Elon Moreh Nucleus. Letter to Prime Minister Rabin from the Secretariat of "Elon Moreh" Settlers, files at Qedumim, 26 Kislev 5735. [December 10, 1974. Same text as letter of December 8.]

_____. Elon Moreh Nucleus. Letter on paper with Gush Emunim letterhead to the Chairman of the Ministerial Committee for Settlement Matters Yisrael Galili from Menahem Filiks for the Secretariat of Settlers of Elon Moreh, files at Qedumim, 26 Kislev 5735. [December 10, 1974.]

_____. Elon Moreh Nucleus. Letter to the Chairman of the Ministerial Committee for Settlement Matters from Menahem Filiks in the name of the

Secretariat of "Elon Moreh" Settlers, files at Qedumim, 26 Kislev 5735. [incorrectly dated in English 10.2.75, correct date December 10, 1974. Same text as letter with Gush Emunim letterhead.]

_____. "Informational Page," personal files of Yohanan Fried, 25 Tevet 5735. [January 8, 1975.]

_____. Memo about publicity department, personal files of Yohanan Fried, 3 Shvat 5735. [January 15, 1975.]

_____. Memo to Secretariat members, personal files of Yohanan Fried, 5 Shvat 5735. [January 17, 1975.]

_____. List of members of Wider Secretariat, personal files of Yohanan Fried, 8 Shvat 5735. [January 20, 1975.]

_____. Publicity Committee, summary of activities for the period Kislev–Shvat, personal files of Yohanan Fried, 8 Shvat 5735. [January 20, 1975.]

_____. Memo describing informational program with Moshav Movement, personal files of Yohanan Fried, 29 Shvat 5735. [February 10, 1975.]

_____. Elon Moreh Nucleus. Letter to Minister of Justice Hayyim Tzadok from Menahem Filiks for the Secretariat of the Nucleus with return address of Gush Emunim Jerusalem office, files at Qedumim, 11 Nisan 5735. [March 23, 1975.]

_____. Letter to the Secretariat from Naftali Ofir suggesting activities, personal files of Yohanan Fried, April 10, 1975.

_____. Elon Moreh Nucleus. Memo on recent events at Sebastia, files at Qedumim, dated sixth Hanukah candle 5736. [December 4, 1975.]

_____. Secretariat decision on Sebastia, personal files of Yohanan Fried, n.d., probably end of 1975. (Handwritten.)

_____. Notes about telegram to the Presidents' Conference, personal files of Yohanan Fried, n.d., probably December 1975. (Handwritten.)

_____. "Internal Information Pages for Settlements," Jerusalem office files, n.d., after 1977.

_____. "Settlement Council, guidelines for the council of Gush Emunim settlements," Shvat 5738. [January–February 1978.]

_____. Flyer announcing dedication of a synagogue in Jericho, Jerusalem office files, Adar 5738. [February–March 1978.]

_____. Draft of a constitution for the Settlement Movement, Jerusalem office files, August 20, 1978.

_____. Bulletin to members, Jerusalem office files, Elul 5738. [September 1978.]

_____. Memo reviewing developments in settlement, signed Uri Ariel, Jerusalem office files, January 1979.

_____. "Gush Emunim – Publicity Department," memo on operation of publicity committee, personal files of Yohanan Fried, n.d.

_____. Report of the "Campaign" Staff: Summary of the March in Samaria, personal files of Yohanan Fried, n.d.

_____. Memo outlining matters for discussion concerning publicity, personal files of Yohanan Fried, n.d.

_____. Draft constitution for Dotan settlement, Jerusalem office files, n.d.

_____. Draft of aims of Gush Emunim, personal files of Yohanan Fried, n.d.

_____. Settlement Plan in Strongholds in Judea and Samaria, Jerusalem office files, n.d.

_____. Notice to group leaders cautioning against violence toward soldiers, Jerusalem office files, n.d.

Gvati, Hayyim. Private interviews. Tel Aviv, April 29, May 6, 1981.

Hammer, Zevulun. Private interview. Ramat Gan, April 30, 1981.

Ihud ha-Kvutzot ve-ha-Kibbutzim. Minutes of Meetings of the Active Secretariat, 1961–1963. (Handwritten.)

_____. Minutes of Meetings of the Appointments Committee, October 16, 1951.

_____. Minutes of the Assembly of Farm and Building Coordinators, September 2, 1974.

_____. Minutes of Meetings of the Central Committee, June 8–9, 1956; August 27–29, 1959; December 17–18, 1959; May 12–13, 1960; September 30, 1961; November 30, 1960–December 1, 1961; April 4–7, 1962; September 12–14, 1963; July 10–11, 1977.

_____. Minutes of Meetings of the Central Committee of the United Kibbutz Movement, January 6–7, 1980.

_____. Minutes of Meetings of the Coordinating Committee, 1951–1952.

_____. Minutes of Meetings of the Coordinating Secretariat, 1953–1957. (Handwritten.)

_____. Minutes and Summaries of Meetings of the Department of Economics (Mahlaqah le-Kalkalah.), December 1, 1970; November 12, 1972, November 26, 1972.

_____. Minutes of Meetings of the Department of Economics and the Farm (Ha-Mahlaqah le-Kalkalah ve-Mesheq.), January 13, 1965; March 3, 5, 10, 1965; July 4, 1965.

_____. Minutes of Meetings of the Economic Committee (Va'adah ha-Kalkalit.), August 21, 1956; with the Coordinating Secretariat, November 18, 1956; with the Economic (Farm) Committee, April 24, 1957.

_____. Minutes of Meetings of the Economic (Farm) Committee (Va'adat ha-Mesheq.), 1951–1958, 1965–1975, 1977–1980.

_____. Minutes of Meetings of the Joint Committee, October 9, 1951.

_____. Minutes of Meetings of the Secretariat, 1951–1955, 1957–1960, 1964–1978. (Handwritten until approximately 1974.)

_____. Minutes of Meetings of the Wider Secretariat, 1955–1957, 1959–1961.

_____. Letter from Senta Yoseftal to David Kalderon, Jewish Agency Settlement Department, March 26, 1965. (Located in material of the Economic (Farm) Committee.)

_____. Letter to Finance Minister Pinhas Sapir from Efrayim Raizner on housing, August 1, 1966. (Located with material of the Economic (Farm) Committee.)

_____. Memo from Dov Tzamir and Eliezer Ben-Ya'aqov to member kibbutzim on progress in the housing situation, August 11, 1966. (Located with material of the Economic (Farm) Committee.)

_____. Letter from Eliezer Ben-Ya'aqov to Efrayim Raizner on the housing situation, August 13, 1967. (Located with material of the Economic (Farm) Committee.)

_____. Speech prepared for the Agricultural Center representative on water issues, September 24, 1969. (Located with material of the Economic (Farm) Committee.)

_____. Letter to the head of the subcommittee of the Asher Committee studying the tax base, prepared by the Kibbutz Movement Alliance, November 29, 1971. (Located with material of the Ihud Economic (Farm) Committee.)

_____. Summary of Meeting with the Agricultural Center on the topic: Conclusions of the Ya'aqobi Committee and Water Prices, December 27, 1971. (Located with material of the Ihud Economic (Farm) Committee.)

Israel. Ministry of Agriculture, Tel Aviv. Files. "Suggestions for Improving the Financial Situation in Agricultural Settlements," memo, n.d., probably 1965.

————. Letter from the Minister of Agriculture to the Finance Minister about improving the financial situation in agricultural settlements, October 22, 1965.

————. Letter from the Finance Minister to the Minister of Agriculture, November 7, 1965 in response to the Minister of Agriculture's letter of October 22.

————. Letter from the Bank of Agriculture to the General Accountant's Office of the Ministry of Agriculture, n.d., probably 1965.

————. Report of the Committee for Examining the Problem of Financing Investments in Agricultural Settlement, n.d., probably 1965.

————. Material on the 90 million lira fund, 1965.

————. Material on the committee for covering the gap, 1967.

————. Material on the financial gap, 1971–1973.

————. Letter from the Ihud Secretariat to the Kibbutz Movement Alliance suggesting allocations and a formula for calculating the financial gap, February 3, 1971.

————. Memo of a meeting of the concentrated credit department in the office of the director-general, March 3, 1971.

————. List of Allocations for 71/72, n.d., after May 1971.

————. Material on the special action program, 1972.

Kadishai, Yechiel. Private interview. Jerusalem, December 23, 1980.

Katzover, Binyamin. Private interview. Qedumim, March 1, 1981.

Klapka, Chezy. Private interview. Tel Aviv, May 18, 1981.

Levi, Moshe. Private interview. Tel Aviv, April 13, 1980.

Levinger, Moshe. Private interview. Hebron, June 29, 1980.

Manufacturers' Association of Israel. Membership lists of the executive bodies, 1967–1981. (Typewritten sheets.)

————. Minutes of Meetings of the Presidium, 1951–1978.

Moshevitz, Mark. Private interview. Ramat Gan, May 21, 1979.

Naor, Aryeh. Private interview. Jerusalem, December 29, 1980.

National Religious Party, Qiryat Arba' branch. Flyer transmitting letter from Yosef Burg on the party's commitments toward settlement, personal files of Hanan Porat, December 25, 1973.

Olshansky, Yehudah. Private interview. New York, October 17, 1988.

Peres, Shimon. Private interview. Tel Aviv, February 15, 1981.

Porat, Hanan. Private interviews. Kfar 'Etzion, July 24, 31, 1980.

Rabin, Yitzhak. Private interview. Tel Aviv, May 2, 1980.

Sarig, Mordekhai. Private interview. Tel Aviv, March 12, 1980.

Shafat, Gershon. Private interviews. Tel Aviv, April 14, May 1, 1980.

Sharon, Ariel. Private interview. Jerusalem, March 17, 1981.

Shavit, Avraham. Private interviews. Tel Aviv, June 25, August 3, 1980.

Slonim, Zvi. Private interviews. Qedumim, March 1, 1981, and New York City, October 27, 1988.

Suzayev, Zalman. Private interviews. Tel Aviv, May 8, 11, 1979.

Tzamir, Dov. Private interview. Tel Aviv, May 20, 1981.

Ushpiz, Naftali. Private interview. Kibbutz Qiryat 'Anavim, May 17, 1981.

Ya'aqobovitz, Dov. Private interview. Tel Aviv, June 12, 1980.

Yoseftal, Senta. Private interviews. Tel Aviv, April 23, May 20, 1981.

_____. Personal letter. May 17, 1989.

Newspapers and Periodicals

Ha-Aretz, 1948–1979.

Ha-Boqer, July 27, 1951.

Igeret Le-Ta'asiyyan, newsletter of the Manufacturers' Association, January 23, March 10, August 26, October 26, November 10, December 1, 1977; February 6, 12, May 28, August, September 3, 25, December 25, 1978; February 11, March 11, May 11, June 20, July 3, 23, September 7, November 15, 1979.

Israel Economic Bulletin, May 1953.

Israel Export Journal, April 1953.

Jerusalem Post, 1951–1979, 1984–1985.

Kibbutz (Hebrew), weekly newspaper of the United Kibbutz Movement, 1986–1987.

Ma'ariv, January 31, 1974.

Mibifnim, journal of the United Kibbutz Movement, October 1982; December 1983; November 1984; May, September 1985; February, July 1986; January 1987.

Niv ha-Kvutzah, monthly journal of Ihud ha-Kvutzot ve-ha-Kibbutzim, January, 1952; December, 1953; September, 1955; January, 1956; July, 1956; February, 1958; March, 1960; July, 1964; August, 1969.

Ha-Ta'asiyyah, monthly magazine of the Manufacturers' Association, 1946–1974.

Le-Ta'asiyyan, monthly magazine of the Manufacturers' Association, December 1987; January, February, April, 1988.

Takamon, publication of the United Kibbutz Movement, October–November 1986; January–February 1987.

Yahad, biweekly magazine of the United Kibbutz Movement, 1982–1986.

Yediot Ahranot, May 15, 1987.

Pamphlets, Booklets, and Brochures

Akzin, Benjamin. *The Structure and Platform of the Likud.* May, 1977. (Typed sheets.)

Council of Jewish Settlements in Judea, Samaria, Gaza, Jordan Valley, Settlements of Benjamin, Settlements of the Judean Desert, Gush 'Etzion, Qiryat Arba', Gaza. Untitled booklet in Hebrew about autonomy, Gush Emunim Jerusalem office files, n.d.

General Zionism as an Ideological Current: A Review of the Basic Lines in the Development of the Liberal Party in Israel. Jerusalem: Einsfeld Fund and the Institute for Economic Research in the Name of Yosef Sapir, 1979. (Booklet in Hebrew arranged by Tamar Henkin and distributed by the Liberal Party, Tel Aviv.)

Gush Emunim. *Elon Moreh, Hidush ha-Yishuv ha-Yehudi be-Shomron.* ("Elon Moreh: Renewal of Jewish Settlement in Samaria.") Jerusalem office files, n.d., probably 1976.

————. *'Alon Emunim.* ("Emunim Leaflet.") Jerusalem office files, Av 5735 [July 1975.]

————. *Degel be-Rosh ha-Har.* ("A Flag at the Top of the Mountain.") Jerusalem office files, n.d., probably late 1978 or early 1979. (about attempts to settle Elon Moreh.)

_____. *Gush Emunim.* ("Gush Emunim.") Jerusalem office files, n.d., probably 1976.

_____. *Gush Emunim.* ("Gush Emunim.") Jerusalem office files, n.d., before 1977 elections.

_____. *Gush Emunim, Daf Kesher.* ("Gush Emunim, a Communication Page.") Jerusalem office files, n.d., probably spring 1976.

_____. *Gush Emunim: Movement for the Renewed Fulfillment of the Zionist Ideal.* Jerusalem office files, n.d., probably 1976.

_____. *'Gush Emunim': Tenuah le-Hidush ha-Hagshamah ha-Tzionit.* ("'Gush Emunim': A Movement for Renewed Fulfillment of Zionism.") Jerusalem office files, n.d., probably 1974. (Printed pages explaining background and purposes of Gush Emunim.)

_____. *Gush Emunim, ha-Yishuvim ha-Hadashim be-Yehudah ve-Shomron.* ("Gush Emunim, The New Settlements in Judea and Samaria.") Jerusalem office files, Spring, 1978. (Mimeo with cover map.)

_____. *'Ofrah, Geder Shehikimah Yishuv.* (" 'Ofrah: An Enclosure that Became a Settlement.") Jerusalem office files, n.d.

_____. *Tohnit Av le-Hityashvut be-Yehudah ve-Shomron.* ("Master Plan for Settling Judea and Samaria.") Jerusalem office files, n.d., probably 1978.

_____. *Al Yishuv ha-Aretz Anu Neevakim.* ("On Settling the Land We Will Struggle.") Jerusalem office files, n.d., probably early 1974.

_____. Department of Information. *Gush Emunim.* Jerusalem office files, n.d., probably late 1978. (Mimeo expressing disappointment with policies of Begin Government.)

Israel, Government of. Ministry of Foreign Affairs Information Department. *Highlights of the Programme of the Democratic Movement for Change in the Elections to the Ninth Knesset.* Jerusalem, June 12, 1977. (Typed sheets, cover page in Hebrew.)

_____. *Likud Platform for the Ninth Knesset, Main Points.* Jerusalem, May 29, 1977. (Typed sheets, cover page in Hebrew.)

Kohn, Moshe. *Who's Afraid of Gush Emunim. Jerusalem Post,* reprint, n.d.

The Liberal Party in Israel – Central Committee. *Din ve-Heshbon le-Ve'idah ha-Artzit ha-Shniyah.* ("Report to the Second National Conference.") July 2–4, 1968.

The Liberal Party of Israel Information Department. *The Liberal Party of Israel.* Tel Aviv, n.d.

Manufacturers' Association of Israel. *Ha-Hitadut be-Shirut ha-Ta'asiyyah.* ("The Association in the Service of Industry.") n.d.

_____. *Hitahdut ha-Ta'asiyyanim be-Yisrael, Doh le-Shnat 1979–1980.* ("The Manufacturers' Association in Israel, Report for 1979–1980.")

_____. *Manufacturers Association of Israel.* n.d.

Soloveitchik, Rabbi Aharon. *Law of Conquered Areas Related to the Commandments Regarding the Land.* Jerusalem: Institute of Harav Kook, 1974. (Hebrew.)

Weitz, Raanan. *Which Way Are We Aiming: a Framework Plan for Economic, Social and Organizational Development Suitable to Possible Policy Solutions. Jerusalem, July 1976.* (Hebrew, Gush Emunim Jerusalem office files.)

Reference Works

Cohen, Erik. *Bibliography of the Kibbutz.* Givat Haviva: Social Research Center on the Kibbutz, 1964.

Divrei ha-Kneset, July, 1977.

Israel Government Yearbook, 1950–1972.

The Middle East. London: Europa Publications, Ltd., 1955 and 1959.

Middle East Contemporary Survey. Tel Aviv: The Shiloah Institute, 1983–1984.

Middle East Journal. "Chronology," 1974–1988.

Shnaton ha-Memshalah. ("Israel Government Yearbook."), 1950–1979.

Shur, Shimon. *Kibbutz Bibliography.* Tel Aviv: Higher Education and Research Authority of Kibbutz Movements, 1972.

Index

Agricultural Center: conduct of Ihud members in, 151; example of corporatist decision-making board, 242, 243, 245; as forum for interest groups, 32, 122–23, 125, 128, 129, 145, 162, 163; Ihud use of Mapai faction in, 112; and loan conversion, 121–125, 128; and Mapai/Labor Government, 241; structure and role of, 104–5, 111, 141; and water allocation issue, 143
Agriculture, 26, 28, 62
Agriculture, Minister of, 50, 143, 153, 156, 159; and interest group relations, 157, 233; mentioned, 18. *See also* Dayan, Moshe; Gvati, Hayyim; Luz, Kadish; Naftali, Peretz; Sharon, Ariel
Agriculture, Ministry of, 129, 141, 142, 162, 234, 236; and agricultural interest groups, 121, 125, 150–51, 163; and committee politics, 127, 151, 241; composition of, 105–6, 112, 131; and Ihud, 126–27, 155; jurisdiction and responsibilities of, 104–5, 120; and kibbutzim, 149–50, 155; and loan conversion, 121–25, 127; and moshavim, 150, 155; as target of agricultural groups, 121, 122; as target of Ihud, 31, 110, 112, 115–16, 121, 139, 154; and water allocation, 143
Ahdut ha-'Avodah, 21; and Alignment of 1965, 33, 136, 147, 237; in coalition, 1955, 113; and formation of Labor Party, 36; and kibbutz federation, 104; and Ministry of Agriculture, 112

Alignment (est. 1965), 33, 147, 237
Alignment (est. 1969): in elections, 37, 38, 40, 41; formation of, 36; and Gush Emunim, 184; and settlement policy, 188
Alliance of the Kibbutz Movements. *See* Brit ha-Tnu'at ha-Kibbutzit
Allon, Yigal, 147, 206
Almogi, Yosef, 135, 143
Almond, Gabriel A., 109
Amanah, 212, 219, 248
Armoni, Yitzhak, 221
Avneri, Efrayim, 122, 151, 162
Aznayah, Barukh, 137

Bahir, Aryeh, 115
Bank of Israel, Governor of, 87, 122
Bank Leumi, 54, 126–27
Banks, Organization of, 73
Barnatan, Yehudah, 70, 76
Basic Laws, 22
Basic Principles, 23–24
Beer, Samuel H., 117, 238; *British Politics in the Collectivist Age*, 3
Begin, Menachem: and autonomy plan and peace ideas, 205, 208, 214, 216; Government of, 76, 211; and Gush Emunim, 178, 201–4, 212, 213–14; and Kneset members, 214–15; on Likud and Gush Emunim, 195–96; and Manufacturers' Association, 87; Prime Minister, 40, 201–5, 208, 210–15, 217; retirement of, 41; and settlement

297

119, 121, 122, 124, 125, 129, 141, 150,
153; and identification as interest
group, 103, 108, 112–18, 160–62, 234;
ideology of, 117, 148–49, 229, 234;
and Jewish Agency, 112, 129, 155; and
Kibbutz ha-Meuhad, 155, 157, 248;
and Kneset, 110, 114–15, 129–31, 151,
155, 163, 238; and Lavon and Lavon
Affair, 132–35, 136–38; and Likud
Government, 152–57, 164; and loan
conversion, 120–25, 128, 144–45, 147;
and Luz, 112, 124–25; and
Mapai/Labor Government, 152, 153,
154, 155, 160–62, 165; and
Mapai/Labor Party, 103–6, 108–18,
119, 121, 123–25, 129–39, 143–44,
144–48, 151, 152, 153, 154, 155,
160–65, 234; and milk ceilings, 150;
and Minister of Agriculture, 153; and
Minister of Finance, 121, 122, 124–25,
162; and ministries, 31; and Ministry
of Agriculture, 105–6, 110, 112,
115–16, 121, 126, 127, 129, 131, 139,
141, 155, 162, 163, 234, 236, 241; and
Ministry of Finance, 126; and
moshavim, 111–12, 113, 124, 131, 143,
155–56, 161, 162, 163, 164, 234, 236,
248; and National Unity Government
(est. 1984), 41; and other kibbutz
federations, 112, 120–27, 131, 142,
143, 145, 155, 162, 234–36, 248; and
party and political relations, 103–4,
106, 108, 109–10, 111–12, 118, 120–21,
124, 126, 129–39, 146–47, 165,
228–30, 231, 234–35; and personal
politics of, 119–25, 161–62; and Rafi,
132, 135–39, 147, 165; Secretariat of,
106, 107, 109, 111, 112, 114–15, 116,
117, 121, 124, 130, 133–37, 141, 144,
153; structure of, 107–8; and system
change, 132, 249; tactics of, 120–25,
141, 143–44, 147, 148–49, 151,
153–55, 161–62, 164, 232, 236; targets
of, 114–15, 119–25, 129–31, 147, 148,
150–52, 154, 155, 162–64; type of
interest group, 226; view on
settlement of West Bank, 248; and
water allocation issue, 142–43. *See also*
Agriculture; Efrati, Yosef; Gvati,
Hayyim; Kibbutz(im); Kibbutz ha-Artzi;

Kibbutz ha-Meuhad; Moshav(im);
Personal politics; Takam
Independent Liberal Party, 34, 75, 76
Industry, 26–28, 62
Industrial Council, 68–71, 241
Industrial Forum, 72, 241
Industry and Trade, Minister of: 90, 91.
See also Commerce and Industry,
Minister of; Sharon, Ariel: Minister of
Industry and Trade
Industry and Trade, Ministry of, 92,
261n.22. *See also* Commerce and
Industry, Ministry of
Interest groups: and change, 4; and
change in Israel, 43, 198, 225–26, 228,
244–45, 249–51; and characteristics of
subsystem, 9; in corporatist model, 6–7,
9–10, 239–40; defined, 2; demands of,
4, 94, 161, 249; demands of, in Israel,
35, 37–38; and development of
corporatism in Israel, 239, 241, 245,
248, 252; and development of
pluralism in Israel, 233–36, 241,
245–49; and development of
subsystem in Israel, 35–36, 118, 128,
148, 155, 232, 235, 245, 247, 248; and
Government in Israel, 23, 37, 82,
128–29, 148, 231, 232, 238–39, 251; in
Israel's ideological political culture, 19,
229, 250; and Kneset, 25, 220; levels
of analysis of, 3–4; and Likud
Government, 247; and Mapai, 32,
34–36, 229–31; and ministers in Israel,
31, 41, 79–80, 230–31; and the
ministries in Israel, 31; and National
Unity Government (est. 1984), 248;
after 1973 war in Israel, 39; and
parties, 10, 72, 99, 108–9, 132, 137–39;
and parties in Israel, 1–2, 35–37, 148,
230–32, 238–39; in pluralist model,
5–6, 7, 9, 110, 232; in political science
theory, 2–3; and representation in
agricultural institutions in Israel,
105–7; and the Right in Israel, 41; in
strong party model, 4, 8, 9, 109–10,
226–27; and strong party model in
Israel, 226–32; and systems, 3–4;
tactics of, in Israel, 30–31, 34–37, 216,
·231, 248–49, 250; targets of, in Israel,
30–31, 34–38, 250; types and